Praise for

Child-Centered Practices for the Courtroom

"I read *Child-Centered Practices* through the eyes of a (former) judge, heartened and enthused by the path it defines for courts and beyond courts: evidence-based, yet creative, constructive, collaborative initiatives. It's an inspiring read, amply buttressed by the references, tools, and models needed to improve the lives of young children in foster care, their families, and communities."

—**Judith S. Kaye**
Chief Judge of the State of New York (ret.)

"This is a bold and important book. Imagine 'child-centered' courtrooms…courts engaged in helping families 'heal'…progress toward goals requires more than attendance at programs….These and other vitally important ideas are unfortunately too rarely appreciated in many juvenile and family courts. This is 'must' reading for all of those legal, child welfare, and mental health professionals involved with maltreated children and their families."

—**Charles H. Zeanah, M.D.**
Sellars-Polchow Professor of Psychiatry,
Tulane University School of Medicine

"A powerful, practical guide to changing the child welfare system so that it actually works for children. The authors, deeply knowledgeable about the frustrating realities of the current system, urge rejection of traditional approaches in favor of evidence-based programs that actually work to protect children and help them recover from the trauma of child maltreatment."

—**Elizabeth Bartholet, J.D.**
Morris Wasserstein Professor of Law,
and Faculty Director, Child Advocacy Program,
Harvard Law School

"These are more than useful guidelines. The authors provide excellent and readable reviews of current research from the sciences of early child development, mental health, and evidence-based programs for helping children and parents who have been immersed in child maltreatment and trauma. Practical advice and compelling examples of effective interventions are provided from service providers, judges, and others that will be welcomed by many including parents, policy makers, and professionals. The extensive appendices—with sample documents, tools, and links to other resources—provide additional value."

—**Robert N. Emde, M.D.**
Emeritus Professor of Psychiatry,
University of Colorado School of Medicine;
Former President of the Society for Research in Child Development;
Honorary President of the World Association of Infant Mental Health

"Documents an innovative judicial system—infant/early childhood mental health collaboration that holds great promise for safeguarding maltreated young children and helping parents learn to nurture their children's healthy development. Each of the authors is an authority in her field, and their partnership has opened up exciting new vistas for models of interdisciplinary collaboration that have a national impact and can lead to lasting positive change for beleaguered children and their families."

—**Alicia F. Lieberman, Ph.D.**
Irving B. Harris Endowed Chair in Infant Mental Health Professor,
and Vice Chair for Academic Affairs, Department of Psychiatry,
University of California, San Francisco;
Director, Child Trauma Research Project,
San Francisco General Hospital

"Simply a beautiful book—informative, practical, and comprehensive...If you are a professional working with families in child welfare, this book is the best comprehensive resource that you will want to have. If you are not a professional working with families in child welfare, after reading this book, you'll want to be. Katz, Lederman, and Osofsky clearly display their high level of competence and why they are respected and admired by their peers."

—**Stephen J. Bavolek, Ph.D.**
President, Family Development Resources, Inc.;
Executive Director, Family Nurturing Centers International

"Fills a critical void—translating what is known about the effects of trauma and maltreatment on early child development into practical guidance for those who must meet the needs of children and families within the child welfare system. Building from strengths, the authors carefully document how they have sought to transform the fragmented decision-making processes of family court and child welfare systems into cohesive and collaborative services that support positive outcomes for vulnerable children and their families."

—**Rosemary Chalk**
Director, Board on Children, Youth, and Families, Institute of Medicine,
National Research Council, Washington, D.C.

Child-Centered Practices
for the Courtroom and Community

Child-Centered Practices for the Courtroom and Community

A Guide to Working Effectively with Young Children and Their Families in the Child Welfare System

Lynne F. Katz, Ed.D.
Judge Cindy S. Lederman
Joy D. Osofsky, Ph.D.

with Candice Maze, J.D.

·P A U L·H·
BROOKES
PUBLISHING CO.®

Baltimore • London • Sydney

Paul H. Brookes Publishing Co.
Post Office Box 10624
Baltimore, Maryland 21285-0624
USA

www.brookespublishing.com

"Paul H. Brookes Publishing Co." is a registered trademark of
Paul H. Brookes Publishing Co., Inc.

Typeset by Broad Books, Baltimore, Maryland.
Manufactured in the United States of America by
Sheridan Books, Inc., Chelsea, Michigan.

Library of Congress Cataloging-in-Publication Data

Katz, Lynne F.
   Child-centered practices for the courtroom and community : a guide to working effectively with young children and their families in the child welfare system / by Lynne F. Katz, Cindy S. Lederman, and Joy D. Osofsky, with Candice Maze.
      p.   cm.
   Includes index.
   ISBN-13: 978-1-59857-073-1 (pbk.)
   ISBN-10: 1-59857-073-0
   1. Child welfare—United States.   2. Children—Legal status, laws, etc. —United States.   3. Child abuse—United States.   4. Child development—United States.   5. Family policy—United States.   I. Lederman, Cindy S.   II. Osofsky, Joy D.   III. Title.

HV741.K363   2011
362.70973–dc22
                                                                                    2010033394

British Library Cataloguing in Publication data are available from the British Library.

2015   2014   2013   2012   2011
10   9   8   7   6   5   4   3   2   1

Contents

About the Authors vii
Preface xi
Acknowledgments xv
Introduction xvii

1 Profile of Infants, Toddlers, and Parents Involved
  in the Child Welfare System 1

2 Use of Evidence-Based Parenting Programs for Parents
  of At-Risk Young Children 17

3 Healing the Infant–Parent Relationship 37

4 Supporting the Development of Very Young Children 53

5 Early Care and Education Settings
  that Support Child Development 63

6 Developing a Coordinated System of Care 73

7 Demystifying the Court Process: How to Be an
  Effective Advocate in Juvenile and Family Court 91

8 Understanding and Preventing Vicarious Traumatization
  and Compassion Fatigue 99

  Conclusion 107

Appendixes

A Questions Every Judge and Lawyer Should Ask
  About Infants and Toddlers in the Child Welfare System 113

B Sample Court Reports 123
  Dependency Parenting Provider Initiative Court Reports:
    Completion and Submission Guidelines 124
    Initial Report 127
    Status Report 132
    Final Report 137
    Notice of Termination of Services 143
  Early Head Start Sample Court Report 148
  Infant Mental Health Therapist Report 151

C Sample Memorandum of Understanding for Cross-Agency
  (Child Welfare/University) Collaboration 161

D Sample Court Orders 165
   Miami Juvenile Court Order for Early Intervention Services
   Evaluation Through Part C of the Individuals with
   Disabilities Education Act (IDEA) 166
   Miami Juvenile Court Order of Referral to Healthy Start 168

E Sample Protocol for Identifying an Accredited Early Care
   and Education Program Placement for Children Involved
   with the Dependency Court 171

F Individualized Family Support Plan (IFSP) for Early
   Intervention Services and Evaluation Report (Florida) 173

G Infant Mental Health–Related Documents and Tools
   Sample Referral Eligibility Checklist 186
   Early Childhood Relationship Observation
   Coding Scales (EC-ROCS) 188
   Examples of Developmentally Appropriate Toys 193
   Sample Child–Caregiver Relationship Assessment .195

Index 197

About the Authors

Lynne F. Katz, Ed.D., Research Assistant Professor, University of Miami Department of Psychology with a secondary appointment in Pediatrics; Director, Linda Ray Intervention Center, University of Miami, 750 N.W. 15th Street, Miami, Florida 33136

Dr. Katz is Director of the University of Miami's Linda Ray Intervention Center and a research assistant professor in the department of Psychology. Since 1993, she has been Director of the early intervention service and research project at the Center for children at risk due to prenatal cocaine exposure. In her leadership role as an early intervention specialist, she has worked to create linkages with community stakeholders serving high-risk young children in the child welfare system. She has served as Principal Investigator of the Miami Safe Start Promising Approaches site, providing early intervention clinical services for children exposed to violence and maltreatment at community domestic violence and homeless shelters where young children and their families reside. Dr. Katz has coordinated the Strengthening Families and Ages and Stages programs for the Juvenile Court's Dependency Drug Court Initiatives. She was Director of the Miami site of the Florida Infant and Young Children's Mental Health Project, funded by the state legislature through the Florida Department of Children and Families. She was an active collaborative partner in the development of the Miami Juvenile Dependency Court Parenting Initiative. Dr. Katz has served as Co-Chair of the Community-Based Care Alliance of Miami-Dade and Monroe Counties. She is a recipient of the Wall of Honor Award presented by the Miami Juvenile Court for her contributions to the development of quality programs for young children in foster care. She has also received awards at both the State of Florida and regional Dependency Court summits for her service to children and families in her community.

Judge Cindy S. Lederman, Circuit Court Judge, Eleventh Judicial Circuit, State of Florida; Juvenile Justice Center, 3300 N.W. 27th Avenue, Miami, Florida 33142

Judge Lederman has served in the Miami-Dade Juvenile Court since 1994, including 10 years as the Court's Presiding Judge. Elected to the Miami-Dade County Court in 1988, before her elevation to Circuit Court in 1994, she was a leader of the team that created the Dade County Domestic Violence Court and served as that Court's first Presiding Judge.

Judge Lederman's interest in bringing science and research into the courtroom results from her 10-year involvement with the National Research Council (NRC) and Institute of Medicine (IOM) at the National Academy of Sciences. Judge Lederman was a member of the NRC's Committee on the Assessment of Family Violence Interventions and panel on Juvenile Crime, Treatment, and Control and served from 1996 to 2004 on the Board on Children, Youth, and Families of the NRC and IOM. In 1999, Judge Lederman was awarded a fellowship from ZERO TO THREE: The National Center for Infants, Toddlers, and Families in their Leaders of the 21st Century program. She served as the former president of the National Association of Women Judges, faculty member of The National Judicial College, and former member of the American Bar Association House of Delegates. In addition, Judge Lederman was a 6-year member of the Board of Trustees of the National Council of Juvenile and Family Court Judges.

Judge Lederman graduated with high honors from the University of Florida in 1976 and with departmental honors in Political Science, and received her Juris Doctor degree from the University of Miami School of Law in 1979. She is licensed to practice law in the states of Florida and New York.

Joy D. Osofsky, Ph.D., Barbara Lemann Professor, Departments of Pediatrics and Psychiatry, Louisiana State University Health Sciences Center, 1542 Tulane Avenue, Second Floor, New Orleans, Louisiana 70112

Dr. Osofsky is a psychologist and psychoanalyst and Professor of Pediatrics and Psychiatry at Louisiana State University Health Sciences Center (LSUHSC). She is Head of the Division of Pediatric Mental Health. She is also an adjunct professor of Psychology at the University of New Orleans. Dr. Osofsky is Co-Director of the Louisiana Rural Trauma Services Center, a center in the National Child Traumatic Stress Network, and Director of the Harris Center for Infant Mental Health at LSUHSC. After Hurricane Katrina, she was asked to be Director for Child and Adolescent Initiatives for Louisiana Spirit, the state crisis counseling program. She is editor of *Children in a Violent Society* (Guilford Press, 1997), two editions of the *Handbook of Infant Development* (Wiley, 1979, 1987), and co-editor of the four-volume *WAIMH Handbook of Infant Mental Health,* which received the Association of American Publishers/Professional and Scholarly Publishing PROSE Award as the best multivolume reference/science book in 2000. Dr. Osofsky's edited book, *Young Children and Trauma: Intervention and Treatment* (2004), includes contributions related to mental health, child welfare, the judiciary, and law enforcement. Dr. Osofsky was editor of the *Infant Mental Health Journal* from 1998 to 2009.

Dr. Osofsky is Past President of ZERO TO THREE: National Center for Infants, Toddlers, and Families and Past President of the World Association for Infant Mental Health. She served on the Pew Commission for Children in Foster Care. Dr. Osofsky has conducted research, intervention, and clinical work with high psychosocial risk infants, children, and families exposed to maltreatment and community and domestic violence. For the past 18 years, she has been consulting and collaborating with juvenile courts around the country, including the 11th Circuit Juvenile Court in Miami/Dade County, related to the development and evaluation of programs to benefit high-risk young children and families in court. In 2002, she published jointly with two judges and two lawyers a technical assistance brief, *Questions Every Judge and Lawyer Should Ask About Infants and Toddlers in the Child Welfare System* (see Appendix

A). In 1998, Dr. Osofsky was awarded the Badge of Honor by the New Orleans Police and Justice Foundation for her work with children and families exposed to violence. In 2002, she was awarded the Medal of Honor by the Mayor of New Orleans for her work with the police and the community and the Nicholas Hobbs Award for contributions to public policy by Division 37 of the American Psychological Association. In 2006, she was presented with the Child's Heart Award by the Juvenile Court Judges of the 11th Judicial Circuit in recognition of her contributions to enhancing the health and well-being of children. Following Hurricane Katrina in August 2005, Dr. Osofsky was asked to serve as Clinical Director for Child and Adolescent Initiatives for Louisiana Spirit for the U.S. Department of Health and Human Services, Office of Mental Health, and the Department of Education. On August 29, 2006, she was honored with a proclamation from the New Orleans City Council recognizing her work helping children and families in the aftermath of Hurricane Katrina. In November 2007, she received the Sarah M. Haley Memorial Award for Clinical Excellence from the International Society for Traumatic Stress Studies for her work with trauma. In September 2008, she received an award from LSUHSC for extraordinary effort and commitment during Hurricane Gustav. In June 2009, for their work in schools following Hurricane Katrina, the LSUHSC team from the Department of Psychiatry was awarded a 2009 Distinguished Partners in Education Award by the Board of Elementary and Secondary Education of the State Department of Education. In 2010, Dr. Osofsky was honored with a Presidential Commendation from the American Psychiatric Association for leadership in mental health recovery following Hurricane Katrina and was awarded the distinction of Honorary President of the World Association for Infant Mental Health.

old vines choking sprouts
skilled hands clear a fertile path
letting flowers bloom

Senior Judge William E. Gladstone

Preface

Our individual work with maltreated infants and toddlers began in different ways and at different times. Our professional paths crossed at just the right moment, leading to a decade of collaboration and a wide range of combined efforts, locally and nationally, directed at improving outcomes for abused and neglected babies. Here, we briefly share our personal and collective journey. We are a judge, a psychologist, and an early interventionist/education expert who are privileged to work in the child welfare field and privileged to work together.

Honorable Cindy S. Lederman

In 1994, I received a telephone call that would change my life. Rosemary Chalk, a study director at the National Research Council (NRC) and Institute of Medicine (IOM) at the National Academy of Sciences, invited me to join an NRC study committee focusing on family violence. When I received the call I did not know what the NRC was. I later learned that the NRC was the largest operating arm of the National Academy of Sciences, an organization created by the U.S. Congress during Abraham Lincoln's presidency to advise the government on scientific matters. I accepted the invitation and I arrived in Washington, D.C., for the first meeting confident that all the programs and services I sent families to every day actually helped them. I was quickly and firmly disabused of this notion by the researchers and academics that comprised the study committee. I was introduced to a fascinating new world: a world of research and evaluation and science. My professional life changed forever.

I continued to work with the NRC and IOM for 10 years, and, as a result, I have come to understand the absolute necessity of integrating research as well as evidence-based programs, policies, and practices in juvenile court and the child welfare system. Research-based practice is imperative if we are truly to help children and families.

In 1997, Miami's Juvenile Court was awarded a substantial federal grant from the Office of Violence Against Women, Office of Justice Programs, U.S. Department of Justice. The grant was to allow us to study, for the first time in a court setting, the relationship between family violence and child maltreatment. We were funded to plan and implement a national demonstration project to learn more about the nexus of child maltreatment and family violence, to develop strategies to keep children safe without removing the children from their battered mothers, and to study the impact and extent of family violence on children in the child welfare system. This national demonstration project, called the Dependency Court Intervention Program for Family Violence (DCIPFV), a precursor to the "Greenbook" initiative,[1] provided the

---

[1]The Greenbook initiative is shorthand for a set of recommendations from the National Council of Juvenile and Family Court Judges Family Violence Department captured in *Effective Intervention in Domestic Violence and Child Maltreatment Cases: Guidelines for Policy and Practice* (1998).

field with published research, an implementation handbook, experience, and direction from this innovative intervention (Lederman et al., 2000; Maze et al., 2005). Several colleagues from the NRC Committee on Family Violence Interventions were invited to join this new demonstration project. From the inception of DCIPFV, Susan Schechter, Cathy Spatz Widom, and Joy D. Osofsky were intimately involved. Dr. Osofsky was the project's expert on childhood and trauma.

When I first was assigned to dependency court in 1994, the State of Florida was not routinely evaluating any children when they came into care. Children were rarely in court, and young children were invisible. Eventually, around 2002, with great fanfare the Secretary of the Florida Department of Children and Families implemented psychosocial assessments on all children in care age 5 and older. Consistent with our Florida policy, we in Miami began to look at the impact and extent of family and community violence on our children older than age 5 in the child welfare system. The results were startling—so disturbing that we began to wonder if young children were equally affected.

I was skeptical about working with babies and toddlers. I was not sure how productive it would be in terms of learning about the impact and extent of violence on such young children. Then, once we learned, what could we do? I was ignorant of the science of early childhood development. Dr. Osofsky assured me that we needed to embark on this endeavor and taught me about her clinical work with babies and toddlers. And we began. Several years later I was awarded a fellowship from ZERO TO THREE, which furthered my education and enabled me to join a national network of early childhood experts and ZERO TO THREE fellows that continues to enhance my learning.

The more I learned about the needs of maltreated young children, the more I realized that systems integration reform was needed. Helping one child, case by case, would never be good enough. That was the next challenge. Thankfully, I began to work in Miami with Dr. Lynne Katz.

Dr. Lynne F. Katz

Being asked to "approach the bench" by a judge is not something most providers have any experience doing. There are visions of what we typically see on television or in the movies about the interactions between judges and witnesses, and these visions are intimidating and anxiety producing. When I was asked to approach the bench, I thought the worst. It was the very first case in which I appeared in court in front of Judge Lederman, completely unaware of the protocols for such an appearance or what information the judge would want. As a University provider of early intervention services for babies and toddlers in the child welfare system, I knew that in our discipline we spoke another "language," our own jargon, that of early childhood special education. We were not familiar with the terminology used in court by the judge and other court staff. However, when it was my time to approach the judge and speak, I forged ahead and outlined what we knew about the child's progress and what we had observed during our home visits to the family. I gave details about the areas of compliance or noncompliance by the parents that we had observed directly and reported that adults were living in the home who had not been authorized to do so. Specifically, I told the court that a father against whom the mother had obtained a restraining order had brought the child out for the morning van pickup for school after he had spent the night there. I also prepared a report for the judge that included the developmental assessments of the child and a quantitative progress report summarizing how the early intervention program was meeting the child's needs.

When I finished my report, Judge Lederman called for "a sidebar" and asked if we could meet to discuss a possible collaboration to improve the quality of parenting and children's services. I stepped back, excited at the opportunity and challenge. Shortly thereafter, we convened a work group that brought together provider representatives, the child welfare agency policy makers, and the judge. Our group determined that we wanted to respond to the court's need for evidence-based parenting programs for families in the child welfare system. Over the course of a year, we reviewed dozens of programs that had outcome data. We determined what components would be crucial for our community participants to get the parenting programs they needed and began to identify a few programs from which the providers could choose. There was ongoing debate and discussion about how retooling could ever work, and the process was frustrating at times.

Eventually, the Dependency Parenting Provider Initiative was born. Today, nearly 5 years later, it is embedded in the system of care and is a standard practice for all parents needing a parenting program to complete their case plans. Keeping the providers engaged at the core of the decision-making process without offering additional funding required extensive consensus building. It was challenging as well for the providers to retool their ways of delivering parenting programs in order to be part of the "approved" parenting provider list. However, even with that system finally in place, our work group, and Judge Lederman, came to the realization that not all parents could successfully complete a group parenting skills class—even an evidence-based program. There was a real need for another "track" for these parents and their young children, a clinical, one-on-one, relationship-based intervention. For that we turned to our clinical partner, Dr. Joy Osofsky, to help our community begin to build and implement that aspect of the system of care.

Dr. Joy D. Osofsky

As a developmental and clinical psychologist and mental health professional, I have worked during most of my professional career with infants, young children, and families at high social and emotional (psychosocial) risk. Early in my career, I became interested in prevention in infancy and early development, a field now known as infant mental health. I believed that if you intervene as early as possible when risk is identified, even prenatally or during the perinatal period, the effect will be much greater than if you wait until the problems become more severe and are not identified until the child enters school. However, few systems that interface with young children were initially designed for prevention and early intervention.

Years ago, several of my colleagues and I, concerned about the effects of violence exposure on young children, identified this issue as a serious public health problem. Yet, few listened to our concerns. Indeed, for infants, toddlers, and preschoolers, the erroneous assumption historically has been that they are too young to be affected by exposure to violence or witnessing domestic violence. In 1994, Judge Cindy Lederman and I were asked to serve on a National Academy of Sciences research panel on the evaluation of family violence interventions. It was during this assignment that we first met. During the course of the committee deliberations, it became increasingly evident that the crucial needs of very young children exposed to domestic violence would only be heard if there were strong advocates from a variety of disciplines. A child advocacy lawyer, Judge Lederman, and I became those strong voices on the committee.

As Judge Lederman explained previously, during the time we served on the National Academy of Sciences committee, she was initiating the federally funded Dependency Court Intervention Project for Family Violence (DCIPFV), focusing on the co-occurrence of child maltreatment and domestic violence. She asked me to con-sult with her on the project to emphasize and articulate the needs of young children and their parents. Although evaluations were routinely available for older children, they were not for those younger than 5 years of age.

Judge Lederman's courtroom was not unique at that time—in most dependency courts the needs of young maltreated children were not being met. Who would inform the judge about the developmental needs of the young child? How could the judge succeed at stopping intergenerational abuse and neglect without more serious and comprehensive interventions and services than those that were available in most juvenile courts? Where would the services be found? Unfortunately, most mental health providers were not trained to provide services for infants and toddlers. The false assumption was that little could be done for very young children. The generally held misperception was that the young child displaying concerning behaviors would "grow out of it" or, if the behaviors persisted as the child grew older, these issues would be addressed at that point. Indeed, until the past decade, few people under-stood how to evaluate and treat infants and young children younger than 5 years old.

As the wise pediatrician and psychoanalyst Donald Winnicott said many years ago, "There is no such thing as a baby"—meaning a baby only exists in a relationship (Winnicott, 1965). Observing babies in their relationships is the way we learn about their development. As Judge Lederman and I talked further about the issues involved with evaluating children less than 5 years old, another dilemma presented itself. Clinicians can only really understand and help young children in the context of a relationship; however, their primary relationships are often interrupted. Judge Lederman and I sat in her chambers for 2 hours looking at tapes of how we conduct evaluations and provide treatment services to infants and young children with their parents and caregivers. These discussions led to my contributions to the program that included training for the important clinical components of relationship-based evaluations, Child–Parent Psychotherapy services, and consultation with Dr. Katz and her colleagues at the Linda Ray Intervention Center about meaningful ways to present the information in court to judges and lawyers who do not come from a men-tal health or child development background.

Relationships are the cornerstone of the healthy development of very young children. The parents, infants, and toddlers in the juvenile dependency court have multiple issues that need to be addressed in the context of healing the relationship. Our cross-disciplinary relationship became the template for our ongoing effort to cre-ate healing communities for infants, toddlers, and their parents. We have been priv-ileged to serve these families and we share the story of our collaboration to encour-age you and to provide the tools for your work in your community on behalf of these most vulnerable children.

REFERENCES

Lederman, C., Malik, N., & Aaron, S. (2000). The nexus between child maltreatment and domestic violence: A view from the court. *Journal of the Center for Families, Children and the Court, 2,* 129–135.

Maze, C., Aaron, S., & Lederman, C. (2005). *Domestic violence advocacy in dependency court.* Reno, NV: National Council of Juvenile and Family Court Judges.

Schechter, S., & Edleson, J.L. (1998). *Effective intervention in domestic violence and child maltreat-ment cases: Guidelines for policy and practice.* Reno, NV: National Council of Juvenile and Family Court Judges.

Winnicott, D.W. (1965). *The maturational processes and the facilitating environment: Studies in the theory of emotional development.* London: Hogarth Press and Institute of Psycho-Analysis.

Acknowledgments

Lynne F. Katz, Ed.D.

Over the last 19 years, I have had the opportunity to work in the supportive environment of the University of Miami, where creativity, research, and community outreach are valued and encouraged for faculty. I have had the privilege of being mentored by Dr. Keith Scott throughout my career, and I thank him for giving me the initial go-ahead to see where our early intervention court work activities would lead. That was more than 10 years ago. Today, the lessons learned from this work and the associated research have had an impact on local, state, and national policy. The staff of the Linda Ray Intervention Center works as well, every day, on behalf of children, and their experiences have served as the basis for many of the early intervention stories in this book. Every day, I am amazed and blessed by the commitment of the teachers and classroom assistants, research team, infant mental health clinicians, parenting coordinator, social workers, information technology support staff, and facility staff of the Center. I equally appreciate being able to depend on my Associate Director, Mary Grace Yale-Kaiser, who helps keep all the balls in the air. Without you all, I could not do the community outreach work on behalf of babies and toddlers with very special needs. It is a privilege, as well, to work every day with the children and their families at the Center, who trust that we will respect and help them. The overwhelming support of the Miami judiciary, child welfare community leaders, and our funders, who have come to value what the Linda Ray Intervention Center provides for the community, has given impetus to our work.

To my family in Miami, Atlanta, Dallas, Philadelphia, and Washington, D.C., I thank you all for your patience and for understanding my lifelong commitment to Miami's most vulnerable young children. Thank you all, and especially Ed, for giving me the time and the space needed to work on the development of this book with Judge Lederman, Dr. Osofsky, and Candice Maze, my truly valued colleagues and friends.

Judge Cindy S. Lederman

I am blessed with a patient, gentle husband, Robert, who always makes my dreams his dreams. Our daughter, Clare, came to us straight from heaven. During the writing of this book, she reached her 20th birthday and is no longer a teenager. We are all celebrating.

There is no more important work that any judge can do than serve in our nation's juvenile courts. I deeply appreciate the friendship and support of my fellow jurists in the Miami-Dade Juvenile Court, especially the brilliant Judge Jeri Beth Cohen. My mentor, Judge William E. Gladstone, taught us all by his exceptional work what a juvenile judge should be. I continue to aspire to be half the judge he is.

I am grateful to Rosemary Chalk for making that call over a decade ago inviting me into to the world of science and research at the National Research Council and Institute of Medicine at the National Academy of Sciences. I listened and learned from my colleagues there who were so generous with their knowledge and who inspired me to wonder.

I am privileged to work in the child welfare system with the most compassionate and dedicated professionals in the court system. Every day, we work together to try to improve the lives of children and families. I am proud of my Division 02 team, with whom I have had the honor of working for 15 years.

Finally, I have learned so much from the wonderful children in the child welfare system who touch my heart and who inspire my work.

Joy D. Osofsky, Ph.D.

I am very appreciative of the faculty of the Louisiana State University Health Sciences Center (LSUHSC) Department of Psychiatry Trauma Team, the support of the Department of Pediatrics, and the LSUHSC Harris Center for Infant Mental Health in their creative work on behalf of young traumatized infants, young children, and their families. The important infant mental health work in New Orleans has played a key role in the development of the training, consultation, and supervision work that has helped to build and support the Miami Juvenile Court Program. Specifically, I want to acknowledge the work of Dr. Amy Dickson, as Director of the Orleans Parish Infant Team for more than a decade, for her leadership in supporting the development of relationship-based work for Orleans Parish Juvenile Court and for the LSUHSC Harris Center for Infant Mental Health. She has played an important role in developing and modifying the relationship-based assessments and services for the court, which have influenced the training and work we provide in Miami. Dr. Mindy Kronenberg has worked closely with me in training, consultation, and providing support for the evaluation of relationship-based assessments that have been important in order to determine the effectiveness of the mental health interventions. The Child–Parent Psychotherapy training that I was able to provide for clinicians in Miami was based on the training model developed by my close colleagues, Drs. Alicia Lieberman and Patricia Van Horn. Thanks also to Silvia Alvarez McBride, LMHC, from the Linda Ray Intervention Center, who has contributed important ideas for ways to engage and support families in treatment and to present information on parent–child relationships to judges in court. Finally, I want to thank my supportive and patient husband, Howard, who has always provided a vital secure base for me and our three wonderful, now young adult, children as I pursue work with very high-risk children and families. Partial support for the preparation of this book was provided by a grant from the A.L. Mailman Family Foundation.

Introduction

Throughout this book, the reader will follow Pam and her two young sons through their experiences in the child welfare system. Their story is one of intergenerational abuse and neglect, of recovery from early childhood trauma, and of a mother struggling to learn how to care for and nurture her young children. Pam and her babies were guided, supported, and taught by professionals from a variety of disciplines who worked collaboratively within an integrated, coordinated system of care to heal old wounds, to reverse the children's developmental delays, to repair the family relationships, and to build Pam's maternal capacity to make difficult, child-centered decisions about her children's lives.

Pam first entered the child welfare system when she was 3 years old. The oldest of three siblings, Pam was removed from her mother because medical professionals identified a severe healing burn to her left medial calf, an acute bruise on her cheek, and an area of hyperpigmentation to her left forearm from a healed burn. No medical care had been sought for Pam for either of the burns.

Prior to entering the system, Pam lived with her grandmother until her mother demanded that Pam be returned to her when Pam was 3 years old. Her grandmother became increasingly concerned every time she saw Pam. Pam had lost weight and had unexplained cuts and bruises. The grandmother would insist that Pam spend a few days with her in order to heal. One day, when Pam came to her grandmother's home for a visit she said she was afraid to go for her bath because she had scars all over her back. Her grandmother comforted her and asked what had happened. Pam admitted that her mother's boyfriend had blindfolded her and tied her hands behind her back and bound her feet. When Pam's grandmother confronted her daughter's boyfriend the next day, he threatened her with a gun and forbade her from having any further contact with Pam. At this point the grandmother could not keep the family secret any longer and she called an abuse hotline to report the violence and injury to her granddaughter.

The court formally placed Pam in the custody of her grandmother under the protection of the Department of Children and Families. This allowed Pam to remain in her grandmother's home with the requirement that her mother participate in and satisfactorily complete a number of prescribed services, including a traditional lecture format (didactic) weekly parenting class where she would learn about child development, appropriate behavior guidance, and other strategies for positive parenting. Furniture was purchased for the family home. After Pam's mother completed the class she was reunified with her daughter and the court and child welfare agency closed the case.

Seven years later, Pam's mother had a second child and the family again came to the attention of the child welfare system because Pam and her younger sister had begun running away from home. Pam's mother called the police. Pam and her sister were found and Pam was taken to a temporary mental health crisis placement where she was diagnosed with depressive disorder. Medication was prescribed and Pam was scheduled for individual therapy; however, Pam's mother refused to accept services for her children, taking no responsibility for their acting-out behaviors and blaming the children for the situation the family was in. There was no court intervention and voluntary services were offered. Pam and her siblings were allowed to remain in the custody of their mother.

Just a few months later, Pam's mother, high on the drug ecstasy, threatened to kill her children. Her boyfriend had been incarcerated for sexually abusing Pam and her sibling. The children were again removed from their mother's custody and placed in a foster home. There had been 13 reports to the child welfare agency about this family over the course of 8 years.

At 14 years old, Pam was now in the 9th grade for the second time, and was failing all of her classes. She was hostile and depressed and 4 months pregnant. Pam had received no prenatal care. The psychologist who conducted a comprehensive assessment of the family did not recommend reunification in this case.

Five months later, Pam gave birth to a baby boy named Victor. They lived together in Pam's foster home. The foster parent became very concerned that Pam would take Victor out all day and return after 11 p.m. She noted that Pam was not affectionate with Victor and did not understand basic parenting responsibilities.

Ever since childhood, Pam had endured trauma and loss. Victor's father was murdered when Victor was only a few months old. This tragic event—one of the many Pam had endured in her short life—had never been dealt with therapeutically and contributed to her spiraling into depression. She began using drugs and neglecting Victor. The foster mother had no choice but to report her actions. Pam and Victor were moved out of the foster home and both were placed in the custody of a paternal aunt. However, her aunt soon saw that Pam was not meeting the physical, emotional, or medical needs of Victor. She continued to place him in unsafe situations and was arrested for shoplifting with Victor in tow.

At 17 years old, Pam became pregnant again. She announced that she was moving in with her new boyfriend and informed her aunt that she was leaving Victor with her. Despite the fact that Pam had received no therapy to deal with her depression, and that she was noncompliant with medication that had been prescribed by the mental health crisis placement doctor, she was still allowed unsupervised visitation with Victor. Clearly, the system was failing Pam and Victor. However, she quickly became overwhelmed by the stresses in her life and was inconsistent in visiting Victor. She became less and less involved with him. When admonished by the court about her failure to at least speak on the telephone with Victor every day, she explained that by the time she remembered to call, it often was too late. Pam continued to reiterate that she loved her son and wished to be reunified with him, yet her own enduring problems caused her to be inconsistent and noncompliant.

Victor, too, was being negatively affected by the unpredictable and unstable relationship with his mother. The longer the periods between visits, the more negative his responses to her became. He would strike out at her when she tried to embrace him and would seek comfort in his growing relationship with his aunt, who provided the nurturing, comforting caregiving he needed; he was building attachment to her as she cared for him over time. When he threw tantrums with Pam and rejected her, it only caused more conflict between them. Pam would threaten, "Do you want me to hit you back?" driving him further away emotionally. It was a relationship gone sour in every respect at this point.

Pam gave birth to her second son, Jason, when Victor was 2 and a half years old. Pam was now 18 years old and no longer a "child" in the eyes of the child welfare system. An anonymous report was called into the statewide abuse hotline by the child care program where Jason was enrolled, expressing concern for baby Jason, who was coming to school unkempt and hungry and appeared to be losing weight. Even in light of Pam's poor track record with Victor and her observed inability to care for Victor, the protective investigator assigned to investigate the call to the abuse hotline found no reason to remove Jason or even take the matter to court to request a petition seeking court supervision. It was not hard to imagine what Jason's future developmental trajectory could look like. Nothing about Pam had changed and in fact, over time, she once again had been unable to meet her child's needs in the most basic sense and did not possess even the minimal skills to be a "good enough" parent (Winnicott, 1960).

What does it mean to be a *good enough* parent (Winnicott, 1960, 1965)? There is an assumption that, with every birth, parents have a new and wonderful priority accompanied by a strong desire to meet their child's needs and nurture their child. Unfortunately, for a large number of parents and infants, this is not the case. In this tenuous time for families, greater stress and challenges have placed our children at more risk and disadvantage now than ever before (Heckman, 2007).

This book is a practitioner's guide for those studying about, or already working in, a profession seeking to improve outcomes for abused and neglected infants and young children and their families. Drawing on decades of personal expertise, experience, and familiarity with intervention research, this book explains why and how to harness the science of early childhood development, provides definitions of and strategies to build and access established *evidence-based* interventions and services, and offers frontline providers information relevant to the collaborative potential of the child welfare system and the court and community partners. The goal is to provide field-initiated real-life strategies that communities can use to help heal their most vulnerable families and to potentially change the course of their lives for generations to come.

FOCUSING ON MALTREATED INFANTS AND TODDLERS: UNIQUE CHALLENGES AND OPPORTUNITIES

Young children are the fastest growing population in the child welfare system. Every year, approximately 1 million cases of child abuse and neglect are substantiated in the United States. The rate of victimization is the highest among children younger than 3 years old (U.S. Department of Health and Human Services, 1997–2010). Of the almost 600,000 children in foster care in 2002 in the United States, one in five of them entered care for the first time during his or her first year of life. Young children are also more vulnerable than older children in that they remain in care longer and are at greater risk of abuse while in care (Wulczyn & Hislop, 2002).

Many parents of very young children in the child welfare system want to be good parents, but in reality they often have no personal experience or frame of reference to draw upon. Across America, many of the parents who appear before juvenile and family court judges have no knowledge of developmental milestones and appropriate expectations for a very young child. They believe that picking a baby up and comforting her when she cries is spoiling the baby and will only promote more crying. These parents must be taught to smile at, praise, and play with their babies in a reciprocal, nonintrusive way. They need to be encouraged to talk to their babies, even when they do not yet talk back, as that is how their baby will learn language. They need to understand why their toddler is throwing a temper tantrum and develop the strategies needed to effectively handle this normal behavior.

Difficult and challenging as it may be, the most profound duty of professionals who work in and with the child welfare system is to cultivate and sustain the parents' relationship with their baby and to provide skills and support to develop their ability to parent. It is the responsibility of everyone working with the family—from the judge to the clinician to the early intervention specialist to the social worker—to focus on what they can do to help the parents develop a loving, nurturing relationship with their young child and to help them to keep their child on a healthy developmental trajectory. This sets the stage for all that follows throughout that child's development process.

Chapter 1 provides a comprehensive overview of the research and science about early child development and the critical importance of attachment relationships. Because healthy relationships are essential, this chapter discusses the impact of parental neglect and violence, substance abuse, and mental illness on the parent–child relationship. Community violence and other traumas are explained here as well.

THE NEED FOR EFFECTIVE PRACTICES, INTERVENTIONS, AND PROGRAMS

How can communities across the country best intervene to teach a young mother, who was never nurtured by *her* parents, to provide a safe, stable, loving environment for her child? How best should the system support a mother who is being battered by her partner to escape the violence and keep her children safe? What type of motivation can be inspired in an often-absent father who is cocaine addicted so that he will stop abusing drugs and become a healthy, constant presence in the life of his child? How can the system help a child who has been traumatized to recover—developmentally and emotionally—after being abused and neglected by the very people from whom she should have received unconditional support and security? The healing process—for children, parents, and professionals—is slow, enormously challenging, frustrating, and multifaceted. However, working together, teaching, mentoring, and supporting parents of very young children can be extremely rewarding, even in the course of the most frustrating day. Nothing is more rewarding than watching a parent and child smile with joy in response to each other for the very first time in their relationship.

It is essential that high-quality, effective, meaningful, culturally attuned interventions and practices are implemented and used in the work that is done with families. This will mean that new, first-time parents, and those with a family already who never experienced "good enough" parenting as children, will need to learn and practice new skills and be able to exhibit greater understanding of their child's needs. They cannot do this alone. They need supportive, helping professionals to help raise their self-esteem and self-confidence and to support them in generalizing the solutions that will improve their parenting ability into daily interactions with their children.

Nearly every parent whose children are in the dependency system due to abuse or neglect of their child is ordered to attend parenting classes. Usually, parents are sent to the same kind of class, regardless of what actions brought them into the child welfare system or the age of their children. Traditionally, the classes have been group based, with the same teacher–student lecture format that has failed the parents previously in traditional school settings and will likely fail them again. In too many communities, there are no evidence-based parenting programs for families in the child welfare system. Most parenting programs provide little monitoring of the skills acquired by the parents, no ability to determine what parents have learned, and inconsistent training of staff in adult learning processes. Many programs have no interactive component for the parent to practice skills with her child together with the parenting teacher who can model appropriate parenting. Chapter 2 explains the concept of *evidence-based programs* and specifically discusses evidence-based parenting programs. Drawing on the authors' experiences developing a comprehensive multiprogram network of evidence-based parenting programs using group formats in Miami, Florida, Chapter 2 offers guidance and information about selecting, implementing, and integrating an evidence-based parenting program system with community-based providers.

HEALING THE PARENT–CHILD RELATIONSHIP: INFANT MENTAL HEALTH AND CHILD–PARENT PSYCHOTHERAPY

Chapter 3 explains the growing field of infant mental health that focuses on the needs of very young children across their developmental cycle, and it provides an overview of one example of an evidence-based intervention, Child–Parent Psychotherapy (CPP), that is used effectively with very young children within the context of their meaningful relationships (Lieberman & Van Horn, 2004). For some parents, the nature of their past and present experiences will necessitate their being served individually rather than in a group parenting program. For these families, the CPP model will be more effective. Chapter 3 also discusses the authors' view of the process for implementing CPP as a treatment option in Miami and offers useful suggestions for clinicians and professionals working to engage at-risk parents with very young children in similar relationship-building parent–child clinical interventions.

SUPPORTING THE HEALTHY DEVELOPMENT OF INFANTS AND TODDLERS: GETTING ON TRACK

Young children in the child welfare system have a significantly greater potential for having developmental delays than children in the general population (Leslie et al., 2004). They represent a group that has more need for intervention services to help ameliorate or reduce delays when they are identified. Research indicates that identifying needs early and working with families in culturally and linguistically appropriate ways is the best path to support children's development in the face of the risk factors in their lives. A number of collaborative partners need to work together through this process of assistance and intervention, running the gamut from early educational intervention to child care centers to clinical providers.

The Effect of Maltreatment on the Well-Being of Very Young Children

In addition to the risks encountered in the living environments of infants and toddlers in the National Survey of Child and Adolescent Well-Being (NSCAW),[1] the results of the study indicate that many of these children have developmental and behavioral difficulties. These findings are described in detail here.

Cognitive Development and Behavioral Problems

Assessments were made of the children's cognitive skills and neurological and developmental functioning, while caregivers reported on the children's behavior. These sources indicate that cognitive and behavioral problems are pervasive in this age group:

- Nearly one third of children ages 3 and younger are falling significantly behind in their cognitive and language skills.

---

[1]Administration for Children and Families through the Personal Responsibility and Work Reconciliation Act of 1996, § 429A, National Random Sample Study of Child Welfare (PL 104-193).

- More than half of the children under age 2 are classified as having a high risk for developmental delays or neurological impairment. Between one quarter and one half are at risk cognitively.
- 27% of children ages 2–3 are reported by caregivers as having clinical/borderline behavior problems, compared with 17% of children the same age in the general population.

Physical Development

Certain segments of infants and toddlers in the NSCAW fall below the average height for children their age. Specifically, children who remain at home and are receiving child welfare services and children living in foster care are below average in height. In addition, 1-year-olds in the NSCAW are below average height compared with the general population, with those in kinship foster care falling the most behind in their height.

In addition, there is wide variability in children's body mass index (an indicator of weight for height). Many children are either at risk for being or are underweight or overweight at the time of the baseline assessment. This is important, because having a low body mass index may place children at risk for delays in physical development and may indicate that their nutritional needs are not being met (Administration for Children and Families. [1997–2010]. *National Survey of Child and Adolescent Well Being*, Research Brief No. 4: Infant and toddlers in the child welfare system. Retrieved July 15, 2010, from http://www.acf.hhs.gov/programs/opre/abuse_neglect/nscaw/reports/infants_todd/infants_todd.pdf).

Chapter 4 discusses the value of early intervention systems and services in helping infants and toddlers with delays to get back on a healthy developmental trajectory. This chapter addresses Part C of the Individuals with Disabilities Education Improvement Act of 2004 (IDEA; PL 108-446) and the variety of interventions available to very young children and their parents, kin, and alternative caregivers. Chapter 4 also explains how the authors worked with their communities and developed and designed a system for ensuring that all infants and toddlers were screened for eligibility for early intervention services and how those children referred for services are tracked and monitored.

Many infants and young children in the child welfare system spend a large portion of their day in community child care centers, family day care homes, or programs such as Early Head Start (EHS) or Head Start. This reality creates the potential for both positive and negative outcomes on child development and, ultimately, school readiness. Chapter 5 discusses the definitions and importance of high-quality early care and education settings, and how communities can come together to provide opportunities for very young children and families that support their development. The authors describe their experience in Miami designing a comprehensive system to address child care placement issues and the implementation of a federally funded collaboration among EHS, the community child welfare providers, and the court.

CREATING A SYSTEM OF CARE FOR MALTREATED INFANTS: A SYSTEMS INTEGRATION APPROACH

Developing evidence-based or research-informed programs in a community that can be effective for the multirisk and complex families with which the child welfare system works is the first essential step in creating a coordinated approach to helping and healing maltreated infants and their parents. However, this is only the first step. To truly advance the goal of reducing intergenerational abuse and neglect, a comprehensive system of care must be developed. Infants, young children, and their parents must receive the services they need with professionals who are planning, coordinating, and communicating across systems, services, and interventions. In this book—to be used as a practitioner's guide—the reader will hear three distinct voices. The perspective of the judge, the clinician, and the early intervention specialist will be presented throughout the book with the goal of providing a multidisciplinary roadmap for building healing communities for young children and their parents in the child welfare system.

Creating an integrated system of care that uses evidence-based programs and practices is an enormous task. However, the ability to truly affect outcomes for infants and parents will depend heavily on the ability of professionals to engage families in those programs and to maintain consistent, meaningful involvement. The process is labor intensive, but the payoff for effective engagement and intervention with families, resulting in safe and healthy children, is worth the effort.

Chapter 6 offers guidance and nuts-and-bolts information on designing, building, and implementing an integrated system of care for very young children and their parents in the child welfare system. A description of the creation and operation of the Miami model is provided as an illustration of how such a feat can be undertaken and how other communities can also build on their own strengths to develop a system of care that meets the needs of their young children and families.

THE JUVENILE AND FAMILY COURT AND CHILD WELFARE SYSTEM—WHERE HEALING CAN BEGIN

Nowhere is the problem of meeting the needs of young children and their families more evident than in our country's child welfare system and juvenile courts. These institutions are designed to act as protectors of children. However, they are also steeped in human suffering and are the last resort for families that have been failed by their communities, the social service and educational systems, and society at large. Impoverishment and deprivation are paired with hope and guidance in one of the most challenging social institutions in our nation. Parents are expected to accept responsibility for the harm they have caused their children, commit to learning new skills and parenting practices, and modify their behavior. This is a monumental task when system failures, burned-out professionals, and judicial inexperience can be barriers to the access and the support parents and their children need to successfully heal their family.

Yet, this is a time when the courts are often expected to be a panacea for every societal ill (Hora & Stalcup, 2008). The juvenile dependency court, more than any other court, must identify, address, and resolve issues of domestic violence, substance abuse, child abuse, child neglect, and other problems that require significant investment of time, energy, and resources to properly address, if not solve. Problem-solving courts have emerged on the scene as an alternative to traditional courts (where the judge is expected to make decisions about the facts as presented and interpret established law). Nontraditional, problem-solving courts grew out of the efforts of practical, creative, and intuitive judges and court personnel grappling to find an alternative to the revolving door of justice (Flango, 2004). It is within this problem-solving context of the juvenile court that the focus by judges on healing and promotion of individual well-being has emerged as the benchmark for effectively handling child maltreatment cases

(Ronner, 2008). Guided by the principle of *therapeutic jurisprudence,* the juvenile court has thus emerged as an institution that can offer children and parents support, guidance, and motivation to help break intergenerational cycles of abuse and provide the opportunity to begin healing the family. This problem-solving, healing environment offers both the court and professionals the unique opportunity to have a significant impact on the health and well-being of children now and for generations to come.

The authors of this book would like to introduce a new metaphor for the role of the judge in our juvenile and family courts today. This new conceptualization was created by Cecilia Casanueva, Ph.D., Research Psychologist, Children and Families Program, RTI International, and Jenifer Goldman Frasier, Ph.D., MPH, Senior Research Psychologist, Children and Families Program, RTI International, while observing in court during their time working in Miami. After sitting in dependency court for hours observing child welfare cases, they described the role of the judge as equivalent to that of an orchestra conductor. The judge is actively involved in overseeing and coordinating all of the professionals working together in the courtroom, each performing distinct roles in distinct ways but working in concert, with the same ultimate goal of bringing their expertise, information, and knowledge to the judge, who puts it all together and makes an informed decision that is aimed at helping children and their families.

All of the professional voices work together, coordinated by the judge, to create an integrated chorus with one message: Heal the family and the children and, hopefully, reunify them. Just as a conductor oversees the orchestra with all the musicians reading from the same music, having studied their own distinct parts and roles within the whole, each musician plays his or her own instrument in his own interpretative way at the appropriate time in the score to create a symphony. A judge in juvenile and family court can lead the court process in an analogous way.

However, the juvenile dependency court and the judge cannot do this work alone, especially when the needs of the public and the role of the court are changing. On its own, the court does not have the resources or expertise needed to palliate or remedy the problem. Historically, the judge was an impartial, detached arbiter who listened to the testimony and made rulings based on his or her interpretation of the facts and the law. Today, there are a growing number of judges who believe—as Judge Judith Kaye, former Chief Judge of the State of New York, does—that the court should do more than just process cases (Kaye, 2004).

The work is a collaboration in which the judge, community stakeholders and service providers, funders, researchers, clinicians, early intervention professionals, child care providers, and parenting programs come together for the common shared purpose of creating a healing process for the young child and the family. Once the judge reaches out to these constituencies they will each have a key role to play in making sure that the community and systems respond to the needs of young children and their families. Whether the stakeholder provides direct services, provides or reallocates funding to programs that have been shown to be effective, offers meaningful training to sustain a high-quality work force across disciplines, or develops accountability and data collection protocols, collaboration and cooperation will be essential to ensuring an integrated and informed systems change. This process requires courage, community support, and a collective commitment to achieve the desired goals.

Chapter 7 discusses the changing role of the courts in American society and the role of the judge in a child welfare case. Chapter 7 also demystifies the child welfare (dependency) court process for nonlawyers and the cadre of collaborative partners of the court, providing concrete information and guidance about preparing for and appearing in court and interacting with the community partners and the judge in meaningful ways.

TAKING CARE OF ONESELF

Working with young traumatized children and their parents is inherently difficult and even, at times, traumatizing for the professionals who do the work. Clinicians, case managers, social workers, lawyers, and judges engage in challenging and frustrating work under incredibly adverse circumstances. At every turn, these professionals and practitioners bear witness to human suffering, deprivation, and emotional impoverishment. Many who enter this field do so because they are passionate about protecting children and healing families. There is now empirical evidence that practitioners integrate and take on some of this suffering as their own, potentially causing their own physical and mental health to be at risk. Chapter 8 provides an overview of this phenomenon, known as *vicarious traumatization* or *compassion fatigue,* and offers tools to practitioners for reducing the personal impact of working in the child welfare system while maintaining the courage and commitment needed to be effective and caring.

SUMMARY

The early and lifetime experiences of all parents shape and mold their beliefs about parenting. Thus, for those parents who were not nurtured or properly parented, there is no healthy frame of reference to draw from that can inform and guide their own parenting. The more that is learned about families that enter the child welfare system, the more the system and its professionals are able to thoughtfully and scientifically approach the task of teaching parents the fundamentals of providing a safe and stable and nurturing home for their children.

It is a daunting and exhausting task for judges, child welfare professionals, community providers, and clinicians to help families acquire new skills and learn to modify their behavior. This is especially true with parents who find these basic skills to be incomprehensible. However, it is the mandate of all who work in this field to do what it takes to help heal infants and young children and help their parents to be mothers and fathers who are "good enough." There is no more important or rewarding work.

REFERENCES

Flango, V. (2004). *DWI courts: The newest problem-solving courts. National Center for State Courts.* Retrieved on February 23, 2009, from http://www.ncsconline.org/WC/Publications/KIS_ProSol_Trends04-DWI.pdf

Heckman, J.D. (2007, May). *Investing in disadvantaged young children is good economics and good public policy* (keynote address). National Summit on America's Children, Congressional Caucus, Washington, DC.

Hora, P.F., & Stalcup, T. (2008). Drug treatment courts in the twenty-first century: The evolution of the revolution in problem-solving courts. *Georgia Law Review, 42,* 717.

Individuals with Disabilities Education Improvement Act (IDEA) of 2004, PL 108-446, 20 U.S.C. §§ 1400 *et seq.*

Kaye, J. (2004). Delivering justice today: A problem solving approach. *Yale Law and Policy Review, 22,* 125.

Leslie, L.K., Hurlburt, M.S., Landsverk, J., Barth, R., & Slymen, D.J. (2004). Outpatient mental health services for children in foster care: A national perspective. *Child Abuse and Neglect, 28,* 699–714.

Lieberman, A.F., & Van Horn, P. (2004). *Don't hit my mommy! A manual for child–parent psychotherapy with young witnesses of family violence.* Washington, DC: Zero to Three.

Ronner, A. (2008). The learned-helpless lawyer: Clinical legal education and therapeutic jurisprudence as antidotes to Bartleby syndrome. *Touro Law Review, 24,* 604–624.

U.S. Department of Health and Human Services. (1997–2010). *National Survey of Child and Adolescent Well-Being No. 4: Infants and toddlers in the child welfare system.* Washington DC: Administration for Children and Families.

Winnicott, D.W. (1960). The theory of the parent–infant relationship. *International Journal of Psychoanalysis, 41,* 585–595.

Winnicott, D.W. (1965). *The maturational processes and the facilitating environment.* Madison, CT: International Universities Press.

Wulczyn, F., & Hislop, K. (2002). Babies in foster care: The numbers call for attention. *Zero to Three Journal, 22*(4), 14–15.

1

Profile of Infants, Toddlers, and Parents Involved in the Child Welfare System

Pam, like so many mothers in the child welfare system, did not know that her infant Victor, like all infants, learns through play. She was observed to ignore Victor, playing with his toys herself. Pam did not know how to participate or interact with Victor in a nurturing way. She grew up in an emotionally impoverished and abusive family, spent her teenage years in the child welfare system, and had likely never been played with as a child. She had minimal parenting skills and did not know how important it is to talk to and be affectionate with Victor and to attend carefully and responsibly to his needs. When Pam did relate to Victor, she tended to be intrusive and rough with him and frequently teased him.

As is common with parents trying to cope with the many stresses that accompany their lives, Pam was depressed, showing little emotion. It is not uncommon for parents who have to deal with so much stress themselves to find little in their lives that is fun—taking care of their child often is looked at as one more burden. They do not feel the joy of playing with their infant and, consequently, the infant often will not smile, laugh, or respond to give back to the parent. In addition, Pam talked very little to Victor. Many young mothers feel foolish talking to infants who are unable to talk back. Pam assumed that Victor did not understand her because he was just "too little." Like so many young mothers, Pam did not know how important it is to talk to her infant to help him learn language. For example, research tells us that by age 3, children of educated mothers have been exposed to a vocabulary of 30 million words, whereas children of the same age living with mothers with low education levels and low income have been exposed to closer to 10 million words (Hart & Risley, 1995). The gap is startling. And how would Pam, who did not experience "good-enough" parenting herself, know the importance of language for her young infant? Based on Pam's history, parenting impairments, and young age, Victor and his brother Jason were already at high risk for developmental delays in the areas of language, social, and emotional development. Victor's early experiences of neglect, separation, and loss compounded this risk. Pam's history of abuse as a child and substance abuse and depression as a teenager affected her ability to parent and made her emotionally unavailable to her children. Moreover, the emotional deprivation and abuse that Pam experienced during her childhood left her struggling to envision or express her hopes and dreams for herself and her children.

THE NEGATIVE EFFECTS OF MALTREATMENT AND TRAUMA ON EARLY DEVELOPMENT

Young children who are abused and neglected experience many risk factors that can affect their development. They enter the child welfare system already at risk. Both developmental delays and behavior problems are common among these children, occurring at a much higher rate than in the population of children who do not experience abuse (Leslie et al., 2005). In addition, abuse and neglect account for 79% of child fatalities for children younger than age 4 years and 44% of fatalities for infants younger than age 1 year (U.S. Department of Health and Human Services, Administration on Children, Youth, and Families, 2005). The youngest children are the most vulnerable. (See Appendix A, Questions Every Judge and Lawyer Should Ask About Infants and Toddlers in the Child Welfare System.)

The problems experienced by young abused and neglected children only increase as they grow older; many of these children experience school and behavior problems, truancy, delinquency, and, as adolescents, risk-taking behaviors including substance abuse. Related to the earlier traumas they experienced, they tend to choose friends who also have problems and enter relationships that may continue the violence (Putnam, 2006). Another risk factor for children in the child welfare system is the trauma of exposure to domestic violence, which can even negatively affect the child's IQ score (Koenen et al., 2003). A comparison of groups of children of the same socioeconomic status who experienced the same level of abuse indicated that those who witnessed domestic violence showed significantly poorer verbal abilities than those who did not, which affected their ability to communicate and learn in school.

The science of early childhood development, including brain development research, has unequivocally debunked the myth that infants are too young to be affected by exposure to violence (National Scientific Council on the Developing Child, 2007; Osofsky, 2003). Indeed, young children are more vulnerable than older children; they remember violent events and are negatively affected (Huth-Bocks, Levendosky, & Semel, 2001). When young children are exposed to domestic violence, the predictability and consistency that is so important for their lives is disrupted (Baker, Jaffe, & Ashbourne, 2002). A violent environment negatively affects a child's need to feel safe. From the beginning, there is a critical need for early intervention to protect children against even more risks as they grow older (Dicker, 2009; Harden, 2007; Osofsky, 2004). It is important for practitioners working with infants and young children to have sound knowledge about early child development.

Facts and Myths about the Effects of Trauma and Maltreatment on Early Child Development

MYTH: Many people believe that young children are not affected by trauma. If they show behavior problems and emotional difficulties, it is believed they will grow out of it.

FACT: Young children *are* affected by exposure to traumatic events. Negative effects can show up as a variety of symptoms including numbing (showing few emotions), unresponsiveness, new fears, and anxious behaviors.

MYTH: Many people believe that removing a child from a harmful caregiving environment will undo the negative effects of stress and trauma (Fox, 2009).

FACT: Negative early childhood experiences alter the development of the body's systems that regulate stress response and can enhance the effects of stress on a young child. These young children need protection, consistency, and nurturing care.

MYTH: Many people believe that young children do not show depression or anxiety.

FACT: Young children can show the effects of abuse and neglect in their emotions and behavior.

(Fox, 2009)

INFANT MENTAL HEALTH: THE IMPORTANCE OF SUPPORTING EARLY RELATIONSHIPS

The experiences of Pam and Victor unfortunately are played out almost every day in dependency court. A parent who was subjected to abuse and neglect as a child appears before the judge unable to parent his or her own child, who has now been taken into state custody as a result of abuse and neglect. Parents repeat what they know.

Despite considerable scientific and research evidence (Shonkoff & Phillips, 2000), discussions on children's mental health have consistently excluded infants and toddlers, focusing instead on school-age children and adolescents. The public mental health system rarely acknowledges that services are needed and can be provided for children under the age of 6 years. The field of infant mental health has helped to raise awareness and educate multidisciplinary professionals and parents about the many ways that infants and toddlers communicate before they are able to use language. Infants' and toddlers' emotions, in addition to their behaviors, can be recognized and understood through careful observations that assess their developmental, social, and emotional needs. Indeed, in the infant mental health field, many say that "play is the language of young children." Play is very important for children to learn and also a way for adults to understand their needs. However, there is still a long way to go before the perception of the public about the developmental and psychological needs of young children is aligned with the research in this area.

The Effects of Early Adversity on Child Development

1. **Early experiences influence the developing brain.** From the prenatal period through the first years of life, the brain undergoes its most rapid development; and early experiences determine whether the brain's architecture is sturdy or fragile. During early sensitive periods of development, the brain's circuitry is most open to the influence of external experience, for better or worse. During these sensitive periods, healthy emotional and cognitive development is shaped by responsive, dependable interaction with adults. Chronic or extreme adversity can interrupt typical brain development.

2. **Chronic stress can be toxic to developing brains.** Learning how to cope with stress is an important part of healthy development. When strong, frequent, or prolonged adverse experiences, such as extreme poverty or repeated abuse, are experienced without adult support, the stress becomes toxic...to developing brain circuits.

3. **Significant early adversity can lead to lifelong problems.** Toxic stress experienced early in life and common precipitants of toxic stress—such as poverty, abuse and neglect, parental substance abuse or mental illness, and exposure to violence—can have a cumulative effect on an individual's physical and mental health. The likelihood of developmental delays in children increases, and as the child grows into an adult, there is an increased likelihood of alcoholism, depression, heart disease, and diabetes.

4. **Early intervention can prevent the consequences of early adversity.** Intervening as early as possible increases the likelihood of success.

5. **Stable, caring relationships are essential for healthy development.** Research supports the conclusion that providing supportive, responsive relationships as early in life as possible can prevent or reverse the damaging effects of toxic stress.

From The Center on the Developing Child at Harvard University. (2009). *In brief: The impact of early adversity on children's development*, www.developingchild.harvard.edu; reprinted by permission.

The keystone of positive development for a young child is a healthy, nurturing relationship. This is especially true for infants. In fact, the development of the attachment relationship is one of the most critical developmental tasks of infancy (Bowlby, 1969; Cassidy & Shaver, 2008). Attachment theory, proposed by Bowlby, states that an infant has a tendency to seek closeness to another person and feel secure when that person is present. The science of early childhood development demonstrates that early relationships and attachments to a primary caregiver are the most consistent and enduring influence on social and emotional development for young children and that early relationships form the basis for all later relationships (Bowlby, 1988; Emde & Robinson, 2000; Shonkoff & Phillips, 2000).

Emotionally available, reliable, and consistent caregivers support the development of secure attachments for infants and help them develop the capacity to self-regulate—be able to control—both their behaviors and emotions. Infants and young children with secure attachments are more positive in their interactions with adults and peers than children who lack secure attachments (Cassidy & Shaver, 2008; Thompson, 2008). When the attachment relationship is secure, the infant experiences relatively short periods of distress and can be comforted easily. These infants and young children also may develop a more positive self-concept, more advanced memory processes, and a better understanding of emotions. Alternatively, unresponsive, frightening, or chaotic caregiving is associated with insecure and disorganized attachments, leaving the infant vulnerable with less ability to self-regulate emotions, distress, and behaviors. This inability to regulate behaviors and emotions was seen in Pam's son Victor. As she visited less and less, his responses became more negative toward her, which contributed to the inconsistency in the relationship. Indeed, he was so confused about what to expect from his mother that he would strike out at her when she tried to embrace him.

Infants who do not have an opportunity to form a reliable attachment with a trusted adult (e.g., infants and toddlers who experience multiple placements) may suffer grave consequences (see Harden, 2007; Dicker, 2009). Unlike adults, infants and toddlers have fairly limited ways of responding to stress and trauma. They may respond by inconsolable crying and withdrawal from daily activities. They also may experience difficulty sleeping, nightmares, lack of appetite due to depression, anxiety, and traumatic stress reactions. A common response to stress in infants and toddlers is difficulty managing emotions, which is exhibited most often as anger and aggression or withdrawn behavior, sometimes resulting in difficulties adjusting to child care settings. When toddlers are not exposed to sensitive caregiving, they sometimes try to gain attention through more negative behaviors (Cicchetti & Toth, 1997; DeBellis & Van Dillen, 2005; Osofsky, 2004). If the underlying causes of the stress are not addressed, they can develop over time into serious mental health problems, including depression, attachment disorders, and posttraumatic stress disorder.

Unfortunately, despite the potentially severe consequences, especially for young children in the child welfare system, these disorders are rarely identified. Neither parents nor most providers know enough about how to recognize the early warning signs to make effective referrals. A child whose medical home is the hospital emergency room is not receiving any preventive pediatric care. Furthermore, for those who want to refer children for mental health services, there is very limited availability of evidence-based treatments for infants and preschoolers in most communities. The intergenerational cycle of abuse and neglect continues by parents such as Pam, who did not learn through their own experiences when they were growing up how to parent in a positive way.

Pam, and now her son Victor, and so many other children in the child welfare system, suffer from cumulative disadvantage—that is, exposure to multiple traumas including abuse and neglect. The numerous problems these families face without intervention can have an unfortunate impact on later development. Even establishing a schedule and routine for their infant may be too much for these parents. Feeding their infant at regular intervals; helping him or her to regulate behaviors and emotions; ensuring he or she receives adequate sleep; and, as he or she gets older, creating a routine that allows the infant to arrive at day care or preschool on time are simply beyond the skill set of these parents. To make the situation even more difficult, parents with children in the child welfare system frequently have undiagnosed mental illness, depression, anxiety, and other mental health problems including borderline personality disorder. Many attempt to cope with their life stressors and mental health issues by using and then abusing drugs and alcohol. When these parents are young, they often engage in risky behaviors such as running away, skipping school, and using drugs, often with their infants in tow.

Young Parents

- Children of teen mothers are more likely to be born prematurely and at low birthweight.
- Children of teen mothers are more likely to live in poverty.
- Children of teen parents suffer higher rates of abuse and neglect.
- Daughters of teen mothers are more likely to become teen mothers themselves.
- Teen mothers are more likely to drop out of school.
- Children of teen mothers are at greater risk for social, emotional, and behavior problems.

(Brooks-Gunn & Chase-Lansdale, 1995)

HIGH-RISK PARENTS: MENTAL ILLNESS AND THE INTERGENERATIONAL CYCLE OF ABUSE

Infants do not exist in isolation. Risk conditions in the parents, including mental illness and substance abuse, affect the young child; therefore, conditions that can disrupt parenting, such as maternal depression and anxiety disorders, must be understood to help heal the parent–child relationship. Although parents with mental illness and/or who abuse substances may be there physically, they are not emotionally available to their infant and/or young child. They also may be unable to set limits and administer healthy discipline. This will often result in the children lacking social skills as well. The children often seem out of control. Early adverse experiences from the parents' early life, sometimes described as "ghosts in the nursery," affect the parents' ability to be consistent, responsive, and nurturing with their own children (Fraiberg, Adelson, & Shapiro, 1975).

THE EFFECTS OF PARENTAL SUBSTANCE ABUSE ON INFANTS

Parental substance abuse affects infants in several different ways. First, the fetus in utero can be affected by a parent using substances during pregnancy that can have negative developmental consequences. Second, parenting behaviors—for example, consistency, nurturance and emotional availability—are likely to be significantly affected by a parent's use of substances, leading to both abuse and neglect. Third, there is a strong relationship between parental substance abuse and other risk conditions that influence the social environment of the infant (Boris, 2009). Research has revealed that environmental risk factors associated with prenatal substance exposure (i.e., exposure to violence, neglect, lack of medical care, poor parenting) pose a greater risk for developmental delays than the possible effects that drugs or other substances have on the developing fetus. Although children exposed to substance-abusing parents are at risk for developmental delays, there is good evidence that they are likely to benefit from intervention and prevention services (Bono et al., 2005).

Exposure in Utero

As a group, substance-abusing women are at least twice as likely as non–substance-abusing women to lose custody of their children. This is a result of recurrences of substance abuse resulting in an increased risk for maladaptive parenting and child neglect (U.S. Department of Health and Human Services [DHHS], 1999). About 4%—or almost 173,000 newborns—are exposed to illicit drugs in utero. Ten percent of these infants are also exposed to alcohol in utero (DHHS, 2004). With this degree of exposure, parental substance abuse is a serious public health problem as well as a complex risk factor for both the infant and the parent (Boris, 2009).

The best studies suggest that caseworkers and investigators report substance abuse in about 11%–14% of investigated cases and in 18%–24% of cases with substantiated maltreatment (Testa & Smith, 2009). The prevalence of substance abuse, however, is higher for children taken into foster care, with estimates ranging from 50% to 79% among young children removed from parental custody.

Each year, more than 5,000 infants are born with fetal alcohol syndrome (FAS) and nearly 50,000 infants are born with some variation of fetal alcohol spectrum disorder (FASD). The term *FASD* refers to a spectrum of conditions that include FAS, fetal alcohol effects (FAE), alcohol-related neurodevelopmental disorder (ARND), and alcohol-related birth defects (ARBD). *Fetal alcohol spectrum disorder* is an overall term that describes the range of effects that can occur in an individual whose mother drank alcohol during pregnancy. These effects may include physical, mental, behavioral, and/or learning disabilities, with possible lifelong implications. The latest estimate for FAS in the United States is a rate of 19.5 per 10,000 live births, about 12,000 infants a year. The rate may actually be much higher because physicians may miss the diagnosis and mothers may fail to report alcohol use during pregnancy (The Florida Center for Child and Family Development, 2007).

The best longitudinal data available related to exposure in utero focuses on the effects of alcohol abuse during pregnancy. Research shows that prenatal alcohol exposure affects verbal and nonverbal intelligence (Kodituwakku, 2007) and causes changes in social behavior, including difficulties in behavioral and emotional regulation and difficulty reading social cues (Kelly, Day, & Streissguth, 2000). Children who have been exposed to alcohol in utero often have significant difficulties with adaptive functioning; that is, they are challenged to deal with day-to-day events.

It is also known now that cocaine use during pregnancy can result in negative birth outcomes such as preterm delivery, low birth weight, and some neurobehavior problems (Zeanah, 2009). Although early pregnancy is a particularly vulnerable time, damage to the fetus can occur throughout pregnancy as a result of continued cocaine exposure as organ systems grow to maturity.

Social Risk

In addition to the developmental implications of substance abuse, social risk for infants and very young children, such as lack of parental emotional availability and neglect, is significant due to substance use and its negative effects on parenting. Links have been found between early impulsive behaviors (e.g., aggression and acting out) and later substance abuse in children of substance-abusing parents (Kendler, Myers, & Prescott, 2007). The risk for children who have been maltreated may be even greater. One longitudinal study found a strong link between child maltreatment and early alcohol use (Kaufman et al., 2007). The severity of maltreatment, existence of early psychopathology, and poor mother–child relationships also predicted early alcohol use (Kaufman et al., 2007).

Substance-abusing parents consistently have been found to have difficulty accurately perceiving and sensitively responding to their children's emotional signals (Mayes, 1995). There is clear evidence that such impulsive caregiving and unpredictability negatively affects the parent–child relationship and ultimately may lead to behavior problems. Beyond aggressive, impulsive, and acting-out behaviors, studies also show that a child's early social behaviors can be independent predictors of language ability in first grade (Acra, Bono, Mundy, & Scott, 2009).

Often, due to their own issues, substance-abusing parents have a limited understanding of basic child development and ambivalent feelings about having and caring for children. They often have little knowledge of appropriate discipline, tending to use harsh discipline and coercive control. Due to the numbing effects of using substances, these parents, like parents with depression, are often absent as well as emotionally unavailable to their children even when they are with them (Keller, Cummings, & Davies, 2005; Pears, Capaldi, & Owen, 2007; Smyth, Miller, Mudar, & Skiba, 2003). Because women with substance use disorders often experienced emotional neglect as children, it is generally thought that for parenting interventions to be effective, they must first focus on emotional impairments in the mother–child relationship to improve parenting interactions and foster optimal child development (Suchman, Mayes, Conti, Slade, & Rounsaville, 2004).

Interventions with substance-abusing parents are critical, both for them and their children. Treatment programs that focus on addiction and clinical interventions that center on the association with trauma for the parent can help with the rehabilitative process. However, engaging substance-abusing parents in treatment for the length of time needed to sustain sobriety is a critical challenge for providers. This poor record for drug treatment enrollment and retention among mothers in particular has led to the creation of interventions aimed at reversing this trend. (See Text Box for research related to *The Engaging Moms Program*.)

The Engaging Moms Program

In response to the need for effective drug court interventions, the effectiveness of the Engaging Moms Program (EMP) versus intensive case management services (ICMS) on multiple outcomes for mothers enrolled in family drug court was investigated. In this intent-to-treat study, mothers ($N = 62$) were randomly assigned to either usual drug court care or the Engaging Moms drug court program. Mothers were assessed at intake, and 3, 6, 12, and 18 months following intake. Results indicated that at 18 months post drug court enrollment, 77% of mothers assigned to EMP versus 55% of mothers assigned to ICMS had positive child welfare dispositions. There were statistically significant time effects for both intervention groups on multiple outcomes including substance abuse, mental health, parenting practices, and family functioning. EMP showed equal or better improvement than ICMS on all outcomes. The results suggest that EMP in family drug court is a viable and promising intervention approach to reduce maternal addiction and child maltreatment.

(Dakof et al., 2010)

Substance abuse represents a particular dilemma related to parenting because parents may use substances as a way to self-medicate to contain painful or difficult emotions (Khantzian, 1997). These parents have difficulty regulating their own emotions and as a result are less able to deal with their young child's emotions, even those that are developmentally appropriate.

PARENTAL DEPRESSION AND OTHER MENTAL HEALTH DISORDERS THAT AFFECT PARENTING

Depression is common in parents with young children in the child welfare system. Parental depression significantly affects both the parent's emotional availability to a child and also the child's emotions and mood. Both research and clinical work has shown a significant relationship between parental depression and hostile, negative, and disengaged parenting (England & Sim, 2009).[1] Depressed parents tend to be less consistent and nurturing with their infants and young children, often not having the emotional energy to take care of them. Because young infants are so dependent on their parents, they are especially sensitive to their moods (Osofsky, 2004). Although less is known about parenting in depressed fathers, the research indicates similar patterns as those found with depressed mothers.

The Impact of Parental Depression on Very Young Children

- Depressed parents have more difficulty being emotionally available to their children.
- Depressed parents tend to be more irritable, angry, and intrusive.
- Depressed parents have more difficulty listening to their children.
- Depressed parents are less responsive to their infant's cues and signals.
- Children of depressed parents are at high risk for neglect.
- Children of depressed mothers are more likely to have behavior problems, anxiety, or depression.
- Children of depressed parents experience more stress.
- Children of depressed mothers often must become "caregivers" for their parents.

(*Source:* England & Sim, 2009)

The negative outcomes for children of depressed parents include more difficult temperaments, less secure attachments, more dysregulated behaviors (e.g., increased aggression, withdrawal, and unstable moods; fewer positive emotions; more difficulties in school), and generally higher risk behaviors. Children raised by depressed parents are themselves at higher risk for depression with earlier age of onset, longer duration, greater functional impairment, and higher likelihood of recurrence. They are also at risk for higher rates of anxiety and other mental health disorders.

---

[1]The research findings in this area are primarily related to mothers.

THE IMPACT OF SCHIZOPHRENIA AND BIPOLAR PERSONALITY DISORDER ON PARENTING

Schizophrenia and bipolar disorder are diagnoses seen among parents in dependency court as well. Rates of custody loss are high in mothers diagnosed with schizophrenia, higher than for mothers with depression and bipolar disorder (Singh et al., 2007). Parents facing mental illness are among the most sad and challenging cases. The mentally ill parent states that she loves her child and that being a parent gives her life meaning; however, her illness often may create significant risks for the child. The law requires that extensive efforts be made to reunify the mentally ill parent with her child, taking into consideration the obstacles involved.

Although few studies have examined the psychopathological profiles of children of bipolar parents, some research has been done. One such study concluded that children of bipolar parents had an elevated risk for developing bipolar and other psychiatric disorders (Singh et al., 2007). A study comparing mothers with bipolar disorder to mothers without mental illness found that mothers with bipolar disorder were less engaged and less affectionate with their children and more prone to show negative and downcast emotions when playing with them (Ostler, 2008).

VIEW FROM THE BENCH
Infants in Court

I have to admit that when I first noticed the signs outside every courtroom in Miami-Dade that said "No cell phones, food, or infants allowed" I thought the sign was entirely appropriate. I did not really want those ringing telephones and crying infants disrupting my calendar. Two years ago when the decrepit signs were being replaced with beautiful new ones, we literally drove the installer and the sign out of our juvenile court building. Everyone was appalled at the thought of not allowing infants into court. Infants and toddlers are every bit as entitled to be there as anyone else. They are a welcome and necessary part of the juvenile and family court process.

EARLY TRAUMA: CHILDREN'S EXPOSURE TO VIOLENCE

Some children are exposed to multiple types of violence and/or maltreatment over their lifetimes. In 2008, the Office of Juvenile Justice and Delinquency Prevention supported by the Centers for Disease Control and Prevention sponsored the first national comprehensive survey to measure children's exposure to violence in their homes, schools, and communities across all age groups, from birth to age 17, and the cumulative effects of violence over a child's lifetime (Finkelhor et al., 2009). The report illustrated that every child reacts to exposure to violence differently. Some children show remarkable resilience; however, all too often, children exposed to violence undergo lasting physical, mental and emotional harm. They experience difficulties with attachment, regressive behavior, anxiety, depression, aggression, and conduct problems as they grow older. They may be more prone to future dating violence, delinquency, further victimization, and involvement with the child welfare system and/or juvenile justice. Research has found that early identification, early intervention, and continued follow-up are valuable strategies to prevent or decrease the effects on children of exposure to violence (Finkelhor et al., 2009).

CO-OCCURRING PARENTAL CONDITIONS: COMPOUNDING THE RISK FOR INFANTS

In the case study at the beginning of the chapter, Pam suffered abuse and neglect, bringing to parenting the "ghosts" from her past. She also struggled with depression and abused substances, compounding the risk for Victor. Too often, these co-occurring mental health and substance abuse issues are unrecognized in parents. If the depression is not addressed, a parent may abuse substances as a way to "self-medicate" and deal with stress. This just compounds the problems for both the parent and the child. For Pam, a therapeutic program that could help her examine her history of exposure to violence and other risk factors supported the healing process she needed to work on to be a better parent to Victor and prepare her to start off on the right foot with her new baby, Jason.

Co-Occurring Mental Health Disorders and Substance Abuse

The co-occurrence of mental health problems and substance abuse represents a serious concern for parenting issues. Alarmingly, few people with co-occurring disorders receive treatment for either problem (Wu et al., 2003). Compounding the concern, a significant proportion of adults with co-occurring mental health and substance abuse conditions are parents of infants and young children. Given that there are limited treatment providers with knowledge about the effects of substance abuse on children, these infants and young children are at high risk unless services can meet their needs. The presence of psychiatric and personality disorders appears to exacerbate the parenting problems of many substance-abusing mothers and contributes to the likelihood that the biological child may be permanently placed out of the home (DHHS, 1999; Suchman et al., 2008).

Co-Occurring Domestic Violence and Substance Abuse

Although substance abuse does not cause domestic violence, there is a statistical relationship between these two serious problems. Studies of domestic violence frequently indicate high rates of alcohol and other drug use by perpetrators before and during abuse. The issues of domestic violence and substance abuse can interact with and exacerbate each other and should be treated simultaneously. A report from the U.S. Department of Justice showed that 61% of domestic violence offenders also have substance abuse problems. The report also found that 36% of victims in domestic violence programs also had substance abuse problems. An additional report from the National Coalition Against Domestic Violence (NCADV) found that 69% of women in treatment for substance abuse say they were sexually abused as children (NCADV Public Policy Office, 2007).

THE IMPORTANCE OF RESILIENCE: ORDINARY MAGIC

Even in the face of the many risks—for both parents and their infants—there is still reason to hope. Intervening early and effectively can reverse or halt the potentially destructive consequences of early trauma and neglect. Although it is known that traumatic exposure can disrupt and derail a young child's typical developmental trajectory, more positive and resilient behaviors and responses also are possible (Masten 2001; Masten & Obradović, 2006; Osofsky, 2004). It is possible for a child to achieve better than expected outcomes after being exposed to adverse experiences including child maltreatment and other traumas, usually because of their own strengths and the support of a caring person.

Individual resilience is the capacity for an individual to show positive adaptation during or following exposure to negative, adverse, or traumatic experiences. When a child shows unusual competence and positive functioning even under adverse circumstances, they usually also have protective factors working for them. These include reasonable intelligence, easier temperament (enabling them to reach out to adults), and a supportive person in their environment. Resilience also can be observed in children as they regain typical functioning following exposure to traumatic experiences or adversity. This response can be observed when a young child is placed in a positive foster care environment or adopted after being in an abusive and neglectful environment. At times, a child may show extraordinary accelerated catch-up growth when rearing conditions improve. Ann Masten (2001) referred to resilience as "ordinary magic." She and others have observed that the healing of traumatized and maltreated children often comes solely from the support provided by a positive, loving relationship.

Even in the highest risk situations, strength and resilience can grow out of positive relationships (Lieberman, Padron, Van Horn, & Harris, 2005). Lieberman and colleagues have described "angels in the nursery," meaning that in almost any relationship a child may experience a growth-promoting force that emerges from loving care. Although much of their caretaking may not be positive for their child, there are often at least some caring behaviors provided even in abusive families. Building on the strengths and the positive parts of that relationship can be crucial for the child's development. Children who are fortunate, even in the midst of adversity, to receive experiences involving intense, shared emotions with a meaningful adult in their lives feel understood, accepted, and loved; such experience can ward off the "ghosts," or early negative experiences. Through positive, affirming caregiving, the child is provided with a sense of security and self-worth that can then be drawn on when the child becomes a parent to interrupt the cycle of maltreatment. Recognizing, uncovering, and supporting "angels" may be as important for interventions and therapeutic work as understanding and dealing with the "ghosts" that interfere with a parent's ability to nurture his or her own children.

Promoting Resilience in Children

In recent years, resilience has received worldwide attention. One group studying this issue, The International Resilience Project, has defined resilience as follows: "[A] universal capacity which allows a person, group or community to prevent, minimize or overcome the damaging effects of adversity." (Grotberg, 2003, p. 3). The International Resilience Project has developed this checklist for predictors of resilience in children:

- The child has someone who loves him or her totally (unconditionally).
- The child has an older person outside the home he or she can tell about problems and feelings.
- The child is praised for doing things on his or her own.
- The child can count on his or her family to be there when needed.
- The child knows someone he or she wants to be like.
- The child believes things will turn out all right.
- The child does endearing things that make people like him or her.
- The child believes in a power greater than seen.
- The child is willing to try new things.
- The child likes to achieve in what he or she does.
- The child feels that what he or she does makes a difference in how things turn out.
- The child likes him- or herself.
- The child can focus on a task and stay with it.
- The child has a sense of humor.
- The child makes plans to do things.

(Grotberg, 2003, p. 41)

For young children who are traumatized, it is crucial to emphasize resilience and strengths in the relationship with the parent rather than just weaknesses and problems (Masten, 2001; Masten & Obradović, 2006). All parents have strengths, even those in the most difficult circumstances. Using a strengths-based approach supports the relationship by supporting the parent as she is helped to be more in tune with, responsive, and emotionally available to her infant. Emphasizing resilience in development is consistent with Selma Fraiberg's wonderful statement, "working with young children is a little bit like having God on your side" (Emde, 1987, p. xix). By focusing on the needs of young children and putting resources where they can be used most effectively, human tragedy can be prevented.

BREAKING THE CYCLE

To best support the healthy development of very young children in the child welfare system, it is essential to provide immediate and ongoing education and training about trauma and its effects on infants and young children to service providers across systems that serve these children and their parents. In juvenile court and child welfare settings, an integrated, collaborative approach between agencies involved with the young child and family is essential for young children traumatized by abuse and neglect. This collaborative approach needs to focus not only on the legal imperative of "best interest of the child," but also on developing relationships across systems, such as early intervention and mental health, that address the social, emotional, and behavioral well-being of children 5 years old or younger.

From a preventive mental health perspective, child and family mental health needs are a crucial component of child-serving systems. At present, children under age 6 are seldom identified by primary care providers or child care providers as needing mental health services, and there is a concomitant scarcity of referrals to mental health programs. The stigma associated with mental health problems and the fear of labeling children at such a young age are powerful reasons for this situation, as is limited knowledge about the developmentally grounded mental health needs of infants and young children. These obstacles can be addressed and the essential needs of young children in the child welfare system can be better served by providing more accessible consultation, assessment, prevention, and therapeutic services in more comfortable settings, including homes, child care centers, Head Start and Early Head Start Centers, schools, family resource centers, and community centers. Services need to be extended to juvenile court settings to identify the needs of and find ways to provide support to vulnerable abused and neglected infants and young children that will assist them with their care and recovery leading to reunification or permanent placement.

It is also crucial to recognize that intervention and services will be most effective by addressing the parent–child relationship. Focus must be placed both on the young child's symptoms and problems with regulating and controlling his or her behaviors and emotions and the parent or caregiver so that the relationship, which is so crucial for healthy development, will be strengthened.

REFERENCES

Acra, C.F., Bono, K.E., Mundy, P.C., & Scott, K.G. (2009). Social competence in children at risk due to prenatal cocaine exposure: Continuity over time and associations with cognitive and language abilities. *Social Development, 18*(4), 1002–1014.

Baker, L.L., Jaffe, P.G., Ashbourne, L., & Carter, J. (2002). *Children exposed to domestic violence: An early childhood educator's handbook to increase understanding and improve community responses.* London, Ontario, Canada: Centre for Children and Families in the Justice System.

Bono, K.E., Dinehart, L.H.B., Claussen, A.H., Scott, K.G., Mundy, P.C., & Katz, L.F. (2005). Early intervention with children prenatally exposed to cocaine: Expansion with multiple cohorts. *Journal of Early Intervention, 27*(4), 268–284.

Boris, N.W. (2009). Parental substance abuse. In C. Zeanah (Ed.), *Handbook of infant development* (3rd ed., pp. 171–179). New York: Guilford Press.

Bowlby, J. (1969). *Attachment and loss, Volume 1: Attachment.* New York: Basic Books.

Bowlby, J. (1988). *A secure base: Parent–child attachment and healthy human development.* New York: Basic Books.

Brooks-Gunn, J., & Chase-Lansdale, P.L. (1995). Adolescent parenthood. In M.H. Bornstein (Ed.), *Handbook of parenting, Vol. 3: Status and conditions of parenting* (pp. 113–149). Mahwah, NJ: Lawrence Erlbaum Associates.

Cassidy, J., & Shaver, P.R. (Eds.). (2008). *Handbook of attachment: Theory, research, and clinical applications* (2nd ed.). New York: Guilford Press.

The Center on the Developing Child, Harvard University. (2009). *In brief: The impact of early adversity on children's development.* Retrieved May 20, 2010, from www.developingchild .harvard.edu

Cicchetti, D., & Toth, S.L. (1997). Transactional ecological systems in developmental psychopathology. In J.S.S. Luthar, J.A. Burack, D. Cicchetti, & J.R. Weisz (Eds.), *Developmental psychopathology: Perspectives on adjustment, risk, and disorder* (pp. 317–349). New York: Cambridge University Press.

Dakof, G.A., Cohen, J.B., Henderson, C.E., Duarte, E., Boustani, M., Blackburn, A., Venzer, E., & Hawes, S. (2010). A randomized pilot study of the engaging moms program for family drug court. *Journal of Substance Abuse Treatment, 38*, 263–274.

Dakof, G.A., Quille, T.J., Tejeda, M.J., Alberga, L.R., Bandstra, E., & Szapocznick, J. (2003). Enrolling and retaining mothers of substance-exposed infants in drug abuse treatment. *Journal of Consulting and Clinical Psychology, 71*(4), 764–772.

DeBellis, M.D., & Van Dillen, T. (2005). Childhood post-traumatic stress disorder: An overview. *Child and Adolescent Psychiatric Clinics of North America, 14*(4), 745–772.

Dicker, S. (2009). *Reversing the odds: Improving outcomes for babies in the child welfare system.* Baltimore: Paul H. Brookes Publishing Co.

Emde, R.N. (1987). Foreword. In L. Fraiberg (Ed.), *Selected writings of Selma Fraiberg* (p. xix). Columbus, OH: Ohio State University Press.

Emde, R.N., & Robinson, J. (2000). Guiding principles for a theory of early intervention: A developmental-psychoanalytical perspective. In J.P. Shonkoff & S.J. Meisels (Eds.), *Handbook of early childhood intervention* (2nd ed., pp. 160–178). New York: Cambridge University Press.

England, M.J., & Sim, L.J. (2009). *Depression in parents, parenting, and children: Opportunities to improve identification, treatment, and prevention.* Washington, DC: National Academies Press.

Finkelhor, D., Turner, H., Ormrod, R., Hamby, S., & Kracke, K. (2009). *National survey of children's exposure to violence.* Washington, DC: U.S. Department of Justice, Office of Justice Programs, Office of Juvenile Justice and Delinquency Prevention.

Florida Center for Child and Family Development. (2007). *Building FASD systems* (Technical Volume 2). Sarasota, FL: Author.

Fox, N.A. (2009, November). Facts and myths about the effects of early experience on young children's development. Presentation at community forum, *With the child in mind: Brain development and best interests decisions.* National Scientific Council on the Developing Child, University of Calgary, Alberta, Canada.

Fraiberg, S. (1987). The muse in the kitchen: A clinical case study. In L. Fraiberg (Ed.), *Selected writings of Selma Fraiberg* (pp. 65–99). Columbus, OH: Ohio State University Press.

Fraiberg, S.H., Adelson, E., & Shapiro, V.B. (1975). Ghosts in the nursery: A psychoanalytic approach to the problems of infant/mother relationships. *Journal of the American Academy of Child Psychiatry, 14*(3), 386–422.

Grotberg, E. (2003). *A guide to promoting resilience in children: Strengthening the human spirit* (pp. 3–20). From the Early Childhood Development Practice and Reflection Series. Retrieved May 21, 2010, from http://www.leedsinitiative.org/uploadedFiles/Children_Leeds/Content/Standard_Pages/Levels_of_Need/Resilience_new.pdf

Harden, B.J. (2007). *Infants in the child welfare system: A developmental framework for policy and practice.* Washington, DC: Zero to Three.

Hart, B., & Risley, T.R. (1995). *Meaningful differences in the everyday experience of young American children.* Baltimore: Paul H. Brookes Publishing Co.

Huth-Bocks, A.C., Levendosky, A.A., & Semel, M.A. (2001). The direct and indirect effects of domestic violence on young children's intellectual functioning. *Journal of Family Violence, 16*(3), 269–290.

Jones, L. (2004). The prevalence and characteristics of substance abusers in a child protective service sample. *Journal of Social Work Practice in the Addictions, 4*(2), 33–50.

Kaufman, J., Yang, B.Z., Douglas-Palumberi, H., Crouse-Artus, M., Lipschitz, D., Krystal, J.H., et al. (2007). Genetic and environmental predictors of early alcohol use. *Biological Psychiatry, 61*(11), 1228–1234.

Keller, P.S., Cummings, E.M., & Davies, P.T. (2005). The role of marital discord and parenting in relations between parental problem drinking and child adjustment. *Journal of Child Psychology and Psychiatry, 46*(9), 943–951.

Kelly, S.J., Day, N., & Streissguth, A.P. (2000). Effects of prenatal alcohol exposure on social behavior in humans and other species. *Neurotoxicology and Teratology, 22*(2), 143–149.

Kendler, K.S., Myers, J., & Prescott, C.A. (2007). Specificity of genetic and environmental risk factors for symptoms of cannabis, cocaine, alcohol, caffeine, and nicotine dependence. *Archives of General Psychiatry, 64*(11), 1313–1320.

Khantzian, E.J. (1997). The self-medication hypothesis of substance use disorders: A reconsideration and recent applications. *Harvard Review of Psychiatry, 4*(5), 231–244.

Kodituwakku, P.W. (2007). Defining the behavioral phenotype in children with fetal alcohol spectrum disorders: A review. *Neuroscience & Biobehavioral Reviews, 31*(2), 192–201.

Koenen, K.C., Moffitt, T.E., Caspi, A., Taylor, A., & Purcell, S. (2003). Domestic violence is associated with environmental suppression of IQ in young children. *Development and Psychopathology, 15*(2), 297–311.

Leslie, L.K., Gordon, J.N., Lambros, K., Premji, K., Peoples, J., & Gist, K. (2005). Addressing the developmental and mental health needs of young children in foster care. *Journal of Developmental and Behavioral Pediatrics, 26*(2), 140–151.

Lieberman, A.F., Padron, E., Van Horn, P., & Harris, W.W. (2005). Angels in the nursery: The intergenerational transmission of benevolent parental influences. *Infant Mental Health Journal, 26*(6), 504–520.

Masten, A.S. (2001). Ordinary magic: Resilience processes in development. *American Psychologist, 56*(3), 227–238.

Masten, A.S., & Obradović, J. (2006). Competence and resilience in development. *Annals of the New York Academy of Sciences, 1094,* 13–27. Retrieved December 15, 2009, from http://www.child-encyclopedia.com/documents/Masten-GerwitzANGxp.pdf

Mayes, L.C. (1995). Substance abuse and parenting. In M.H. Bornstein (Ed.), *Handbook of parenting: Vol. 4: Applied and practical parenting* (pp. 101–125). Mahwah, NJ: Lawrence Erlbaum Associates.

National Coalition Against Domestic Violence (NCADV) Public Policy Office. (2007). *Domestic violence facts.* Retrieved May 20, 2010. from http://www.ncadv.org/resources /FactSheets.php

National Scientific Council on the Developing Child. (2007). *The timing and quality of early experiences combine to shape brain architecture.* Working Paper #5, retrieved May 20, 2010, from www.developingchild.net

Osofsky, J.D. (2003). Prevalence of children's exposure to domestic violence and child maltreatment: Implications for prevention and intervention. *Clinical Child and Family Psychology Review,* 6(3), 161–170.

Osofsky, J.D. (2004). (Ed). *Young children and trauma: Interventions and treatment.* New York: Guilford Press.

Ostler, T. (2008). *Assessment of parenting competency in mothers with mental illness.* Baltimore: Paul H. Brookes Publishing Co.

Pears, K., Capaldi, D.M., & Owen, L.D. (2007). Substance use risk across three generations: The roles of parent discipline practices and inhibitory control. *Psychology of Addictive Behaviors,* 21(3), 373–386.

Putnam, F.W. (2006). The impact of trauma on child development. *Juvenile and Family Court Journal,* 57, 1–11.

Shonkoff, J.P., & Phillips, D.A. (Eds.). (2000). *From neurons to neighbors: The science of early childhood development.* Washington, DC: National Academies Press.

Singh, M.K., DelBello, M.P., Stanfrod, K.E., Soutullo, C., McDonough-Ryan, P., McElroy, S.L., et al. (2007) Psychopathology in children of bipolar parents. *Journal of Affective Disorders,* 102(1–3), 131–136.

Smyth, N.J., Miller, B.A., Mudar, P.J., & Skiba, D. (2003). Protecting children: Exploring differences and similarities between mothers with and without alcohol problems. *Journal of Human Behavior in the Social Environment,* 7(3–4), 37–58.

Suchman, N., Mayes, L., Conti, J., Slade, A., & Rounsaville, B. (2004). Rethinking parenting interventions for drug-dependent mothers: From behavior management to fostering emotional bonds. *Journal of Substance Abuse Treatment,* 27(3), 179–185.

Suchman, N., McMahon, T., DeCoste, M.S., Castiglioni, N., & Luthar, S. (2008). Ego development, psychopathology and parenting problems in substance-abusing mothers. *American Journal of Orthopsychiatry,* 78(1), 20–28.

Testa, M., & Smith, B. (2009). Prevention and drug treatment. *The Future of Children,* 19(2), 147–168.

Thompson, R.A. (2008). Early attachment and later development: Familiar questions, new answers. In J. Cassidy & P.R. Shaver (Eds.), *Handbook of attachment: Theory, research, and clinical implications* (2nd ed., pp. 348–365). New York: Guilford Press.

U.S. Department of Health and Human Services. (1999). *Blending perspectives and building common ground: A report to Congress on substance abuse and child protection.* Washington, DC: Author. Retrieved May 20, 2010, from aspe.hhs.gov/hsp/subabuse99/subabuse.htm

U.S. Department of Health and Human Services, Substance Abuse and Mental Health Services Administration, Office of Applied Studies. (2004). *Results from the 2004 national survey on drug use and health: National findings.* Retrieved May 20, 2010, from http://www.oas.samhsa.gov/ nsduh/2k4nsduh/2k4results/2k4Results.htm

U.S. Department of Health and Human Services, Administration on Children, Youth, and Families. (2005). Retrieved December 15, 2010, from http://www.acf.hhs.gov/

Wu, L., Ringwalt, C., & Williams, C.E. (2003). Use of substance abuse treatment services by persons with mental health and substance use problems. *Psychiatric Services,* 54, 353–369.

Zeanah, C.H. (Ed.). (2009). *Handbook of infant mental health* (3rd ed.). New York: Guilford Press.

2

Use of Evidence-Based Parenting Programs for Parents of At-Risk Young Children

When the court placed Pam, as an infant, with her grandmother, her mother was able to regain custody of her by completing a traditional parenting class model. Not surprisingly, there continued to be neglect and abuse in the home postreunification, and Pam was removed again. Pam's mother had learned little from the program she had attended, and what she had learned about the needs of her child were just ideas—she could not implement the developmentally appropriate strategies in her day-to-day life with her daughter. She reverted back to her inappropriate discipline practices and her less-than-nurturing relationship with Pam and eventually lapsed into neglectful behaviors that resulted in her daughter's reentry into the system.

Traditional parenting programs such as the one Pam's mother attended are defined as parent education-only classes and do not provide an interactive component for the parent and child to play together or opportunities for the parent to practice his or her newly acquired skills. In these classes, the teacher lectures to the parents about parenting activities. Pam's mother had been a school dropout with poor academic skills. She attended a typical middle school where lecture was the classroom format, and she had failed. Even so, she was placed in a traditional parenting class using this same presentation formula with expectations that she would learn. During her minimal participation in the classes, she had been inattentive and often needed discipline from the instructor. On more than one occasion, she was asked to put her cell phone away and to stop talking while the teacher was speaking. When she began the program, she was never assessed as to what she did or did not know about appropriate parenting or child development, nor was she reassessed at the end of the program to document progress or the lack thereof. The parenting agency had never seen her interact with infant Pam to assess whether she could use the skills presented to her. However, because her attendance was consistent—she had attended all eight of the parenting sessions—Pam's mother was given a certificate of attendance, which she presented in court as evidence of having successfully fulfilled her case plan requirement to complete a parenting program. On that basis, Pam's mother was given back custody of Pam.

Years later, history repeated itself. Pam was referred to parenting services to retain custody of her son, Victor. However, unlike her mother, Pam was enrolled in an evidence-based parenting program. The program had a structured weekly curriculum, including an interactive approach to the skills-building process. This allowed for hands-on activities and role-playing opportunities for Pam and infant Victor to participate in together on a weekly basis. In the parenting program, Pam learned concrete information and strategies related to day-to-day parenting issues she would face with Victor at his current stage of development and as he continued to grow. Pam's case manager had been able to select an evidence-based weekly parenting program for her that was designed specifically for parents of very young children. In Pam's case, the program chosen was the Nurturing Parenting Programs (Bavolek, 2007). The weekly program format consisted of a combination of parent-only discussion and role-playing time with group members led by a trained facilitator followed by a structured, facilitator-guided, interactive play time for Pam and Victor to play together in a nurturing environment. The instructor was able to follow Pam's progress each week.

The Nurturing Parenting Programs

The Nurturing Parenting Programs are a family-centered initiative designed to build nurturing parenting skills as an alternative to abusive and neglectful parenting and child-rearing practices. The long-term goals are to prevent recidivism in families receiving social services, lower the rate of multiparent teenage pregnancies, reduce the rate of juvenile delinquency and alcohol abuse, and stop the intergenerational cycle of child abuse by teaching positive parenting behaviors. The Nurturing Parenting Programs target all families with children ages birth to 18 years at risk for abuse and neglect. The programs have been adapted for special populations, including Hmong families, military families, Hispanic families, African American families, teen parents, foster and adoptive families, families in alcohol treatment and recovery, parents with special learning needs, and families with children with health challenges. The programs feature activities to foster positive parenting skills and self-nurturing, home practice exercises, family nurturing time, and activities to promote positive brain development in children birth to 18 years. Lessons can be delivered in a home-based setting, group-based setting, or combination of home and group settings. A National Institute of Mental Health study demonstrated the effectiveness of the Nurturing Parenting philosophy and implementation strategies in remediating current abuse and preventing the recurrence of abuse in 93% of the families completing the program (Bavolek, 1985).

Before even beginning the parenting program, a baseline/preassessment was completed with Pam and Victor, which included 1) Pam's completion of a parenting inventory measure, in this case the Adult-Adolescent Parenting Inventory–2 (AAPI-2; Bavolek & Keene, 1999); and 2) her participation in an observed, structured behavioral observation of her play with Victor. (See Early Childhood Relationship Observation Coding Scales [EC-ROCS] in Appendix G.) The structured observation and the parenting inventory were scored for Pam's strengths, strengths seen in the relationship, and areas needing help and support. The parenting facilitator also reviewed the dependency petition containing the allegations against Pam for her failure to care for Victor. This process allowed the facilitator and Pam to discuss her parenting strengths and weaknesses and to build a parenting program plan for Pam to meet her individual needs. Pam not only was assessed for her competencies but she was assessed within her relationship with Victor.

The Adult-Adolescent Parenting Inventory–2 (AAPI-2)

The AAPI-2 is designed to assess the parenting and child-rearing attitudes of adult and adolescent parent and nonparent populations. Based on the known behaviors of abusive parents, responses to the AAPI-2 provide an index of risk for practicing parenting behaviors known to contribute to the maltreatment of children. The AAPI-2 is the revised and renormed version of the original inventory first published in 1979.

Responses to the AAPI-2 provide an index of risk in five specific parenting and child-rearing behaviors:

- Construct A: **Inappropriate Expectations of Children**
- Construct B: **Parental Lack of Empathy**
- Construct C: **Strong Belief in the Use of Corporal Punishment**
- Construct D: **Reversing Parent–Child Roles**
- Construct E: **Oppressing Children's Power and Independence**

More than 20 years of research has established the inventory's solid levels of validity and reliability. The AAPI-2 has an assessed fifth-grade reading level. Responses to the AAPI-2 are presented in the Parenting Profile for each individual and for the group. Pre- and posttest Parenting Profiles present data to determine the effectiveness of the parenting program being offered (Bavolek & Keene, 1999).

During the course of the parenting program, Pam learned developmentally appropriate expectations for Victor. She was taught about the need to monitor his safety on an ongoing basis, whether he was in the bathtub or walking outside near the street. She learned how to use positive reinforcement and praise to increase the behaviors she wanted for Victor and to "catch him being good" rather then focusing on discipline and punishment.

During the interactive portion of the weekly parenting sessions, she learned how to guide Victor's behavior away from negative behaviors as a way to avoid punishing him. She learned how to communicate with Victor in ways that he could understand as a toddler, how to play with him and set boundaries, how to create routines for his daily care, and how to build his self-esteem and create trust in their relationship. Upon completion of the parenting sessions, the postassessment using the AAPI-2 and the behavioral observation were completed for a second time and a detailed parenting report of Pam's progress was submitted to the court instead of a mere certificate of attendance. (See Appendix B for Parenting Court Report Completion and Submission Guidelines.)

The parenting issues Pam faced are undeniably complex and embedded in inter-generational family characteristics for which there appear to be only limited solutions. The well-meaning practitioners associated with her mother's original case approached the issues facing the family in traditional but ineffective ways. Clearly, both Pam's mother and, subsequently, Pam needed parenting interventions that had evidence supporting their effectiveness and that gave them a reasonable opportunity to success-fully gain the parenting skills and knowledge they lacked.

To provide effective solutions, social workers, clinicians, judges, and other child welfare professionals must become educated about what treatment and intervention models work for which families. If the appropriate parenting and intervention pro-grams do not exist in the community, the child welfare system and its community-based partners must seek and develop programs that will lead to more successful outcomes for children and parents. How can one assess whether the services being provided to a child or his or her parents are effective in improving safety and well-being outcomes? How and why are these specific services chosen? How can a clini-cian, case manager, or judge determine whether a parent or child has benefited from a service or intervention?

Not knowing the answers to these questions can lead to misuse of the limited money the child welfare system has available to rehabilitate parents and support chil-dren. Ineffective services may waste the brief amount of time allotted by federal and state law[1] to rehabilitate families who often have chronic problems. More important, failing to provide an effective solution to the parents' problems can mean jeopardizing the safety and well-being of children by returning them to parents who are not adequately equipped to meet their children's basic physical, psychological, and developmental needs. The fact is that some services help, some services are actually harmful, and some services have no effect at all. In fact, the vast majority of prevention

---

[1]The Adoption and Safe Families Act (ASFA) of 1997 (PL 105-89) significantly reduced the amount of time a parent has to remedy the circumstances that brought the child into the child welfare system. Assuming the child welfare agency has appropriately made efforts to assist the family, judges are expected to make a decision about a child's permanent custody no later than 12 months after removal, although there is often a subsequent legal process before the court closes its case.

programs—more than 90%—have no evidentiary support to confirm or deny their effectiveness (Greenwood, 2006).

Stakeholders and consumers must start asking questions about the quality of the services available for the most at-risk parents with the most vulnerable young children. Research information is available that can help assess a program's validity and offer information about program effectiveness.

What Works for Parent Involvement Programs for Children?

Programs that address parenting take varied approaches. A 2009 Child Trends synthesis of findings from 67 rigorous evaluations of parent involvement interventions for children 6–11 years old identified cross-cutting themes of what works when intervening with high-risk populations (Mbwana, Terzian, & Moore, 2009). Three identified themes from this study that contribute to parental success are characteristically present in the Nurturing Parenting Programs, for example, the program that Pam and Victor successfully completed:

- The Nurturing Parenting Programs is a system of evaluated parenting skills training programs that are generally effective at improving child outcomes.
- The Nurturing Parenting Programs include parent–child involvement, an inherent program component that also tends to have positive impacts on child outcomes.
- The programs have a combined emphasis on the parent and child and generally will have positive outcomes.

Judges, case managers, clinicians, and community funding sources should demand programs with thematic components that science tells us increase program effectiveness and should lead community collaborations to introduce evidence-based services into the child welfare system at the local, state, and even national level.

 VIEW FROM THE BENCH
The Value of Evidence-Based Parenting Programs

In most child welfare and juvenile dependency court systems, attendance is the only measure of successful completion of a parenting program and there are no systematic assessments of parental progress or gain while in the program. Typically, there are *no* structured observations of parent–child interactions that demonstrate to the parenting program facilitator, case manager, or judge whether the parents are able to use their newly acquired skills during interactions with their children. There are no qualitative and quantitative measures to determine if insight has been gained and new practices and beliefs integrated. Successful completion is measured only by attendance, not by learning, understanding, or changing behavior.

When the parent comes into court holding her certificate of attendance from a parenting course, she has expectations that she has earned the right to have her

(continued)

children back. She may believe that she has learned from the program all she needs to know. The court, on the other hand, needs to be certain she *has* learned and must know *what* she has learned and if she has the ability to *use* what she has learned to enhance her relationship with her child. Findings of compliance with a mandate for a parenting class will require a more in-depth analysis than confirming mere attendance. Likewise, failing a parenting class cannot be based entirely on poor attendance. Although there are also parents who do not have the capacity to nurture a child and keep a child safe, the court must be able to discern the difference. If not, the system is clearly jeopardizing the child's safety and well-being.

WHAT DOES *EVIDENCE BASED* MEAN?

A growing body of research in the social and behavioral sciences has demonstrated that certain interventions, strategies, and approaches for working with children and their families are more effective than others to positively affect outcomes based on rigorous evaluations following prescribed formats. These programs need to meet defined criteria. These programs are called *evidence based*. Scientists refer to their evaluation designs as either *experimental* (a randomized controlled trial in which participants of similar characteristics are randomly assigned to the intervention or comparison or control group and data are collected and compared for both groups) or *quasi-experimental* (program participants are compared with a similar group of participants who did not receive the intervention but the groups were not randomized).

Not only are the results of the evaluations taken into account, but the evaluative process is also reviewed by peer scientists and/or experts in the field and the findings are typically published in peer-reviewed scientific journals. Programs that meet standards of effectiveness are then classified with various levels of evidence. Research suggests that, because of the greater effectiveness and efficacy of evidence-based programs and practices, families receiving these services will have less need for repeat referrals (Cooney, Huser, Small, & O'Connor, 2007).

A program is judged to be *evidence based* if 1) evaluation research shows that the program produces positive results, 2) the results can be attributed to the program itself rather than to other extraneous factors or events, 3) the evaluation is peer reviewed by experts in the field, and 4) the program is "endorsed" by a federal agency or respected research organization and included in their list of evidence-based programs. It is critically important that any system of evidence-based programs integrate the needs of culturally and linguistically diverse families within the child welfare system. Each family is entitled to having equitable access to programs of quality, delivered as needed in their own language, and tested or *normed*[2] for appropriateness with their cultural population. When the system of care does not have a robust array of interventions that meet these criteria, plans to design and implement culturally and linguistically matched programs must be a priority.

---

[2]*Normed* is a measure of a phenomenon generally accepted as the ideal standard performance against which other measures of the phenomenon may be measured.

Developing Culturally Appropriate Parenting Programs

In Miami-Dade County, Florida, parents whose children are in the dependency court system due to child maltreatment and/or neglect are often required to successfully complete a research-based parenting program with pre- and postassessments as part of the road to reunification, along with other services and programs. Approved providers working with families in the child welfare system provide parenting programs that meet the following criteria: evidence-based curricula, pre- and postassessments, parent–child behavioral observations, and the use of the AAPI-2 assessment tool in both English and Spanish. Few equivalent programs for Creole-speaking Haitian families existed, and there were no evidence-based parenting programs for this population in the National Registry of Evidence-Based Programs and Practices (NREPP). This represented a critical service need in the community. To assist Haitian family preservation, reunification, and permanency, Miami worked to integrate a Haitian parenting program curriculum with promising outcomes into the overall system of care for dependency court–involved families. With funding from the United Way of Miami-Dade, collaboration occurred among the child welfare community, the Haitian parenting program's developer, and the developer of the AAPI-2 to 1) test the efficacy of the curriculum with dependency court–involved Creole-speaking parents and 2) pilot a Creole version of the assessment tool.

WHAT DO PROFESSIONALS KNOW ABOUT EVIDENCE-BASED PRACTICES AND PROGRAMS?

Curious about the existence and awareness of evidence-based practices and programs in the child welfare system in Miami-Dade County, Florida, members of the nonprofit group Research and Reform for Children in Court, Inc., set out to answer the following questions (Lederman, Gomez-Kaifer, Katz, Thomlison, & Maze, 2009):

- Do practitioners understand what *evidence-based practice* means?

- What is the level of awareness by child welfare system professionals regarding how evidence-based practices effect positive change in families?

- How can evidence-based practices be best disseminated by professionals and judges making referrals for services in the child welfare system?

Although the answers to these questions are difficult to determine, they are important to the implementation of effective interventions, service delivery, and quality. To assess the perceptions, attitudes, and knowledge of evidence-based practices among those working in the child welfare system, a short survey instrument was developed. The goal of the survey was to identify child welfare professionals' level of understanding of evidence-based practice, to examine their attitudes about the use of evidence-based practice, and to target potential training and educational gaps in the community to improve existing systems and encourage the implementation of more evidence-based programs and policies.[3]

---

[3]The survey was administered at the 2008 Miami-Dade Community Based Care Alliance Annual Regional Child Welfare Conference, held in November 2008 in Miami, Florida. This conference drew more than 300 professionals who serve families in the child welfare system for training and discussion on current topics and practices in the field.

In Miami, 209 members of the child welfare community responded to the survey. The responses to the survey pointed to the need for further training in this area as well as a need to revise the criteria by which services for families involved in the child welfare system are selected.

Eighty-seven percent of the respondents who identified themselves as either *frontline child welfare professionals* or *service providers*—those who deliver direct services to families or engage in care management and investigative decisions—were *unable* to define *evidence-based practice* using the criteria outlined previously. Among child welfare workers, 92% of case managers, 90% of case manager supervisors, and 80% of child protective investigators were unable to define *evidence-based practice*. In addition, 97% of the *middle management* or *program specialists,* 60% of the *funders,* 50% of the *judges,* and all of those in the advocates group were unable to provide acceptable definitions of *evidence-based practice*.

Although 88% of the 209 survey respondents were unable to define *evidence-based practice,* 87% believed that evidence-based practice resulted in "better outcomes." Sixty percent of the respondents believed that evidence-based practices "improved collaborative decision making," and 52% agreed that "the Court thinks these are better programs" (Lederman et al., 2009). Thirty-five percent of the 209 respondents recognized that evidence-based practices are "cost effective" (Lederman et al., 2009).

Why Evidence-Based Programs and Practice Matter

The Caring for Children in Child Welfare (CCCW) study, a supplemental study to the National Survey of Child and Adolescent Well-being (NSCAW), surveyed service program managers and collected publicly available data in 78 counties nationwide to gather information about the organization, financing, and delivery of parent training services in each county. The study reported that "very little is known about the effectiveness of existing parent training approaches for families involved with child welfare services . . . [and] routine parent training has rarely been evaluated" (p. 7, Hurlburt, Barth, Leslie, Landsverk, & McCrae, 2007).

Of the parent training programs most used in child welfare, almost none was among those with the strongest base of empirical research, such as The Incredible Years (Webster-Stratton, 1992; used in only 1.4% of the counties), parent–child interaction therapy (Eyberg, 1988; used in 0.2% of counties), and parent management training (Kazdin, 2005; not mentioned in any county). Moreover, surveyed counties failed to use promising programs that at least have some rigorous evaluation or a strong theoretical base (e.g., Project 12-Ways [Wesch & Lutzker, 1991] was used in 0.2% of counties, Common Sense Parenting [Burke & Herron, 2006] was used in 0.1%). Of the parent training programs available in the counties, many did not have the appropriate intensity for the family's needs. In addition, child welfare agencies did not have strong authority over the delivery of training, and most of the programs in use did not have empirical research documenting the effect of parent training, nor did they have observational data with independent reports about parent–child behaviors (Hurlburt et al., 2007).

IDENTIFYING AND IMPLEMENTING EVIDENCE-BASED PARENTING PROGRAMS

Professionals from different disciplines who review Pam and Victor's case will no doubt see it from the perspective of their own field, experience, and training. Whether it be as a case manager, early intervention specialist, or treatment provider, the usual response is to prioritize, as a primary need for the family, that which the professional is most comfortable and capable of addressing. This has great potential to influence what programs and services are selected for a parent of very young children. Although professionals working in child welfare are focused on permanency and safety for the child as ultimate outcomes, the interventions they use as resources often are based on how their agency has historically served children and families or what the professional feels, on a visceral level, is best for the family. This often can result in a hit-or-miss set of services and outcomes.

Without some core understanding and community consensus *that science should inform practice,* communities may continue to provide lower quality, less effective services in a disjointed manner, based on subjectivity, habit, and accessibility. Bringing community partners and stakeholders to the table to learn about the value of evidence-based programs and practices is essential. Identifying and providing information about evidence-based programs for review and consideration and developing practical and effective referral pathways to evidence-based programs once established is critical. Implementing valid measures to assess participant progress is also essential. Communities also may want to ask the following questions before considering a new evidence-based parenting program:

- Is the program designed for parents with a wide age range of children?

- Does the curriculum have both a parent-only component and a parent–child interactive component so families can practice the skills they are taught?

- Is the curriculum available in multiple languages, if needed?

- Does the curriculum have documented evidence of effectiveness with child welfare families?

- What is the cost to be trained in the model? What is the cost for any required program materials?

- Will substance abuse and co-occurring mental health factors present a major issue with the parents who will be attending the parenting programs?

- What are the credentials of the current parenting provider work force, and what is its ability to deliver new programs to high-risk parents who also may have low literacy and functionality issues?

- How will the evidence-based programs be funded?

- How will successful completion be measured?

- How will the length and dosage of the evidence-based parenting program dovetail with the case timelines?

As each of the questions is answered, the stakeholders will be able to focus in more closely on what is realistic and most relevant to their community needs.

Where to Find Evidence-Based Parenting Programs

The following three federal web sites are excellent resources for learning more about evidence-based parenting programs:

1. National Registry of Evidence-Based Programs and Practices (NREPP), Substance Abuse and Mental Health Services Administration (SAMHSA): http://nrepp.samhsa.gov/

2. Office of Juvenile Justice and Delinquency Prevention (OJJDP), National Criminal Justice Reference Service (NCJRS): http://ojjdp.ncjrs.gov/

3. National Child Traumatic Stress Network: www.nctsn.org

The first two web sites contain information about federally designated *model programs,* including those designed for developing parenting skills among high-risk parents such as those found in the child welfare system. Both of these web sites provide a history of how the programs were selected and tested for scientific rigor; details about the programs' effectiveness; as well as information about facilitator training, costs for implementation, and accompanying assessment tools.

NREPP, which is posted on both the OJJDP and SAMHSA web sites, is a compilation of only those programs that have been rigorously evaluated with strong outcomes for the prevention and treatment of high-risk behaviors. The NREPP review process identifies programs by soliciting and identifying those with published and unpublished evaluations of their program outcomes. These reviews are then assigned to independent review teams based on the members' expertise. These teams review the data from the program and work to reach consensus as to the status that the program should be given: *effective, promising,* or *insufficient current data.* They then notify the program developer and give feedback as to their designation determination. It is those designations that are posted to help communities make decisions.

The National Child Traumatic Stress Network (NCTSN) is a federally funded network of independent grantees intended to serve as a resource on child traumatic stress for other professionals and the public. Information on children and trauma that relates to choosing the best programs includes the following:

*   Information on the various types of trauma

*   NCTSN products

*   NCTSN Learning Collaboratives and Learning Communities, the Network's approach to spreading, adopting, and adapting best practices across multiple settings

*   Fact sheets on empirically supported treatments for child traumatic stress

*   Information on creating trauma-informed and culturally competent child-serving systems

*   Facts and figures about child traumatic stress

Once program curricula or treatment models are identified, the providers can contact the developer for training and materials, including any accompanying testing materials that accompany the program curriculum to measure client progress.

Getting Started

Building an evidence-based system of care is not an easy process; there are no shortcuts. Different communities have different processes, and one size does not fit the needs of everyone in each community. However, knowledgeable community stakeholders and frontline providers can be part of the impetus for change. Some suggested steps follow:

*   An initial group of providers within the child welfare system, such as those who deliver parenting skills services, can start the discussion about evidence-based parenting programs by coming together and mapping the populations they

currently serve. The group should discuss the common risk factors associated with their families as well as group demographics, cultural and linguistic characteristics, and the age ranges of the children needing services. They also can identify previous barriers to services that can be anticipated, such as cost factors, retention, and transportation issues. This is an important first step.

- Each community can decide what they value as the core components of the programs they want to adopt. For example, a group can determine that, in addition to an evidence-based curriculum, the pre-post assessment portfolio should include a behavioral observation of the parent–child interaction as well as completion of paper/pencil measures (i.e., the AAPI-2) and weekly progress reports.

- Creating community-specific parenting program criteria at the start can reduce the overall number of potential programs for the stakeholders to review from the many programs that are detailed on the federal web sites. This will make it more manageable for the collaborative group to study the programs one by one, reviewing them and discussing the viability of each.

- When the work group has reached consensus on these criteria, each member can return to his or her agency to discuss the nuts and bolts of the change process needed to adopt a new evidence-based program. They can make contact with the curriculum developer for their program of choice, meet with their funders to identify training and implementation dollars, and lead discussions with existing parenting facilitators to reach agreement that extra training will be needed in the new model. Then, the community system of care can begin to retool their parenting programs. The work group can continue to meet monthly to serve as support to one another during the roll-out period. A communitywide orientation meeting also can be held for all parties working on dependency cases to become apprised of the process of changing to the use of evidence-based parenting programs to fulfill case plan requirements.

- Participating parenting providers will need to be monitored to be sure that programs are being delivered as designed. Any short cuts or modifications of the program design can affect the effectiveness of the program and fail to produce the desired outcomes. New stakeholders who want to deliver programs to these families should go through a vetting process. Programs that cannot maintain fidelity to the parenting program model and compliance with the group's stated expectations should not be permitted to serve child welfare–involved families.

Miami's Story:
Development and Implementation of the Dependency Parenting Provider Initiative

The Miami-Dade Community Based Care Alliance, the Miami Juvenile Court, Our Kids, Inc. (the lead agency for Miami-Dade's child welfare system), the Department of Children and Families, the University of Miami's Linda Ray Intervention Center, and the Louisiana State University's Health Sciences Center faculty worked together to develop

(continued)

requirements for parenting program providers that meet the unique needs of the child welfare population in their community. The goal of these efforts was to use the science of child development and parenting skills through evidence-based curricula that measure change and promote positive outcomes for children and families. Because of the nature of the child welfare system and the dependency court environment, there is a critical need to ensure that parents are equipped and able to incorporate parenting skills into their daily interactions with their children. Thus, behavioral observation rating measures and standardized, reliable, and valid pre- and postmeasures are required to help structure and capture information about a parent's ability to generalize what they have learned in a parenting program and for the purpose of accountability at the agency level. Furthermore, the behavioral observation and pre- and postassessments provide the judges and caseworkers with an opportunity to gain a better understanding of the parent–child relationship and the parent's ability to nurture and guide his or her child(ren).

The parenting classes and the behavioral observations are *nonclinical interventions*. All parenting curriculums are to be implemented as designed to ensure fidelity to the selected parenting program's model. The parenting program must be managed by an administrator whose role is to ensure program integrity and support the staff delivering the actual parent education. Each provider is expected to use parenting facilitators to teach the course, complete reports, and conduct the behavioral observations. Although the parenting class facilitators do not need to have clinical credentials, it is expected that they have the skill level and experience to deliver the curriculum successfully. The provider assumes responsibility for deciding on the credential and experience level of the facilitator to meet the program goals.

In the Miami model, all parenting program providers must agree to use the following core components for each participating family in order to become an "Approved Parenting Program Provider":

1. **Evidence-based curriculum** (discussed previously)

2. **Valid and reliable pre- and postmeasure:** These are measures that have been normed on the populations that are being served and have research data that have resulted in the measure being published as a standardized assessment tool. In Miami, all of the parenting providers use the AAPI-2 (see text box on AAPI for more information). Each parenting provider is expected to buy the necessary materials and to ensure sufficient staff training in the administration and interpretation of the AAPI-2.

3. **Behavioral observation of parents with their children (ages 0–5) are collected before starting the program (preservice behavioral observation) and again after they have completed the program (postservice behavioral observation). The behavioral observation is ONLY for parents with children ages birth–5 years old:** The parenting program facilitator at each provider agency is also responsible for the behavioral observations of parents and children ages birth–5 who are enrolled in the group they are teaching. The Early Childhood Relationship Observation Coding Scales (EC-ROCS) used for this purpose were developed by Dr. Joy Osofsky of Louisiana State University and Dr. Anne Hogan

of the Florida State University Center for Prevention and Early Intervention Policy (CPEIP) as an adaptation of existing clinical observational scales (see Appendix G). Training is provided by experienced clinicians trained directly by Dr. Osofsky in the procedural methods.

The lead child welfare agency, Our Kids, Inc., hosts a full-day behavioral observation training three to four times a year to ensure that all new facilitators are trained on the model. Use of the behavioral observation model ONLY applies to parents and their children who are 0–5 years old; no model has been developed for parents and children over 5 years old for the Miami system of care.

The preobservation provides a window into the strengths and weaknesses of the parent–child interactions and/or communications and helps determine what will need to be addressed in the parenting classes at the onset. The postobservation provides feedback as to the degree of integration of positive parenting skills and changes in the parent–child interactions subsequent to the completion of the parenting program. Parenting facilitators do not have to be licensed to complete the behavioral observation process. The same facilitator has the responsibility to complete all of the core components of the parenting protocol. In choosing a facilitator, the agencies take full responsibility that the person can successfully complete the tasks and follow the procedures to do so. The behavioral observations must be implemented in a way that ensures fidelity to the behavioral observation protocol.

Implementing Evidence-Based Parenting Programs

The National Implementation Research Center has developed meaningful information related to communities who want to build systems of evidence-based practices and need a path for the process (Barnoski, 2004; Fixsen, Blase, Timbers, & Wolf, 2001; Leschied & Cunningham, 2002). The essential *implementation* outcomes that communities typically want to reach are defined by Dean Fixsen as follows (Fixsen et al., 2005, p. 12):

- Changes in adult professional behavior (knowledge and skills of practitioners and other key staff members within an organization or system)
- Changes in organizational structures and cultures, both formal and informal (e.g., values, philosophies, ethics, policies, procedures, decision making), to routinely bring about and support the changes in adult professional behavior
- Changes in relationships to consumers, stakeholders (e.g., location and nature of engagement, inclusion, satisfaction), and systems partners.

Desirable outcomes are achieved only when effective programs are implemented well. The outcomes of implementation attempts can be categorized as *paper implementation* (i.e., putting into place new policies and procedures with the adoption of an innovation as the rationale for the policies and procedures) and *process implementation* (i.e., putting new operating procedures in place to conduct training workshops, provide supervision, change information reporting forms, and so forth with the adoption of an innovation as the rationale for the procedures).

Summary of Steps for Selecting and Implementing an Evidence-Based Parenting Program

1. Develop and put into place new policies and procedures for the new programs. Realizing that having the paperwork requesting that a parent be referred or even a judge mandating that a parent attend an evidence-based parenting program does not mean that the referral will be made or the services provided. It also does not mean fidelity to the model is assured over time in all cases. Plans to monitor programs—quality assurance—are a necessary system component.

2. Putting the new operating procedures in place, training the work force for implementation, providing supervision for the practice changes, changing the reporting mechanisms, and creating the culture of change toward evidence-based programs, from top down and from the bottom up, will require stakeholders and judges committed to the ongoing process.

3. Monitoring program performance to track implementation and assure that the outcomes are actually beneficial to the consumers, organizations, and systems is essential according to the evidence-based practice literature. Plan for this and build it in.

(Fixsen et al., 2005)

By integrating evidence-based parenting programs into the child welfare community, parents involved with the child welfare system will have access to a gold standard of programs that offer the best chances for successful outcomes. Communities will reasonably expect that positive outcomes can be obtained for families and that their outcomes can be sustained postparticipation. This may eliminate the need for parents to repeat programs. The assessment tools that measure outcomes of the evidence-based program will provide valid and reliable measures to document client progress and give the caseworker and the judge more accurate feedback about the parent's ability to care for his or her child.

VIEW FROM THE BENCH
Measuring Change

Before evidence-based parenting training was mandated in Miami, every parent who attended the traditional lecture-style classes successfully completed parenting training and was found in compliance with that task in their case plan. Some parents were even reunified based on that "successful completion." Now judges are provided with information to help them ascertain whether a parent has made progress and to what extent. Comparing the parent's pre- and postparenting scores from the AAPI-2 allows the judge to see whether learning has occurred. It also gives the judge the ability to determine whether the parent is at high, medium, or low risk for continuing the abuse. Dr. Bavolek has encouraged the judiciary in Miami to pay particular attention to the AAPI-2 construct that looks at empathy when evaluating parent progress and risk to the child, as a lack of empathy is a red flag for being an abusive parent.

Finally, the court has an objective measure of learning and an evaluation of individual strengths and weaknesses. Through the narrative and observational scales provided to the court, the judge can determine whether a parent was able to use what he or she learned when interacting with his or her child. The report also recommends further intervention for some parents who cannot or did not learn enough to reduce their risk to their child. For the first time, judges are able to make more informed decisions about the safety of children by looking at the outcomes of these measures as they evaluate visitation and custody determinations.

Engaging Parents of Young Children in Evidence-Based Parenting Programs

Convincing a young mother that, this time, her participation in a parenting program will be different requires practitioners to make extra efforts to establish trust with their clients. Practitioners must recognize the complexity of the tasks parents must accomplish to regain or retain custody of their children. A variety of strategies exist that can help parents of young children in community-based services and programs and that encourage sustained compliance and are considered best practices for family engagement.

Family Engagement

Family engagement is a prerequisite for helping each family to achieve its goals. Key elements include the following:

- Listening to each family member
- Demonstrating respect and empathy for family members
- Developing an understanding of the family's past experiences, current situation, concerns, and strengths
- Responding to concrete needs quickly
- Establishing the purpose of involvement with the family
- Being aware of one's own biases and prejudices
- Validating the participatory role of the family
- Being consistent, reliable, and honest
- Engaging and involving fathers and paternal family members

(Child Welfare Information Gateway, University of Denver, Institute for Families, 2005)

Approaching the families from the onset in strengths-based ways that confirm their role in their children's lives whenever possible will help professionals start to build the relationships they need to work successfully with the children and their families across diverse cultures and family systems. The following core set of characteristics will maximize success along the way.

1. **Be family centered.** Parents need to be involved in developing activities and programs that pertain to their family's needs from the beginning. They need to feel comfortable explaining the barriers they will face as participants and what aspects of the program will be of interest to them. They also can explain the

motivators that will keep them coming to the program. This will help professionals design programs that matter to families and that will keep them coming.

2. **Treat the parents with respect.** Bring a sense of respect to interactions and communication with the parents. Although information about the case—allegations against the parents, the case plan components, and the tasks the parents will need to complete—is available to providers, often this information has not been presented clearly to the parents by a caseworker or an attorney. Parents' perspectives and feedback about what they are experiencing in their lives must be at the core of plans for rehabilitation. It is therefore essential for providers to start by acknowledging parents as a source of information.

3. **Keep the parents informed.** Be sure discussions about programs, treatment plans, and assessment findings are explained to parents in meaningful ways. Any uncommon terms or concepts should be explained in ways that make sense to parents. Allow parents the space to ask questions and state their opinions. Professionals should be responsive, giving parents the time to express themselves and treating them with dignity and patience when they are responding.

4. **Acknowledge the parents' concerns.** During the parents' participation in a parenting program, they may feel comfortable enough to discuss problems regarding their child's development with the parenting program facilitator. They might express concern that by enrolling their child in early intervention services the child will be labeled *developmentally delayed*. The parents may be concerned that the child will be treated differently and looked down on by others. Assure the parents that this information is kept confidential and will not be shared with others except with those involved with their case. Explain how assigning a category or label to a child's area of needs is the only way that the government will pay for the services to the child, thereby saving the parent from having to pay. Let the parents know that with the services the child is likely to improve and that labels do not follow the child into elementary school.

5. **Educate the parents.** Give families the tools they need to become good consumers of children's services. Taking the time to meet with parents to discuss the core components of quality child care will help them be more active participants in choosing programs for their child. Be cognizant of the fact that once families learn what quality child care looks like, they will rightfully demand it for their child. Once parents have the tools to identify quality, providers will need to be prepared to respond appropriately when parents raise concerns about safety and quality.

6. **Create incentives for participation.** Find opportunities to provide incentives that validate compliance and quality participation by the parents. For example, parenting programs may offer family meals or snacks, connect families with resources at the holiday season, or help parents gain access to food or transportation vouchers as incentives when parents are productive to help cement the relationship with the family. Caseworkers can discuss the program with their clients in a supportive manner, explaining to them that programs of this type, in coordination with compliance with other mandates of their case plan, can give them greater access to programs where they can be successful. Caseworkers can work with the families to help them with challenges of transportation, where needed, so that attendance can be consistent.

7. **Be strengths based.** "Catch them being good" is a phrase that should be applied to parents whenever possible. Finding opportunities to praise parent participation while still setting high expectations over time for compliance will often keep parents involved in program services. This praise may be the first time they have heard something positive about themselves. Finding even the smallest strength in the parent of a young child can be used to scaffold their level of buy-in and participation to new heights. This will help them focus on their positive parenting attributes and build confidence in their parental abilities. It will also keep them coming back to learn more and continue to receive support.

Moving the mindset of a large system of care toward integrated evidence-based thinking and implementation of quality parenting programs is a Herculean task and is best set on course by the collaborative efforts of social workers, case managers, clinicians, legal and lay child advocates, funders, and community parenting providers in concert with the child welfare agency managing the system. Coming together through professional associations, established interagency agreements, and court-led work groups provides options to communicate and dialogue about change.

Engaging Fathers

So often, when writing or speaking about the child welfare system, the discussion centers around only mothers. The reason for this oversight is the simple fact that many more mothers come into the courtroom and work with the child welfare agencies in an attempt to regain custody of their children. Fathers are therefore overlooked and often underestimated. These "forgotten clients" (Lamb & Sagi, 1983) must be actively engaged in the child welfare court and social services process. When fathers are actively involved in the dependency case, chances for reunification and subsequent family support improve (Sonenstein, Malm, & Billing, 2002). Engaging fathers must become a new priority for all child welfare professionals and judges.

In a 2006 Urban Institute report titled "What About the Dads?" (Malm, Murray, & Geen, 2006), fathers of children in the child welfare system are referred to as "out of sight, out of mind." The report examined nearly 2000 child welfare cases, and the results were not surprising. Their data revealed that although 88% of fathers' names were in the court case files, only 55% of fathers had been contacted by the agency, and only 30% of fathers had visited their children since the children were placed in out-of-home care. The report also indicated that even though 50% of nonresident fathers who had been contacted expressed interest in having their child live with them, placement with the father was the goal in only 4% of cases (Malm et al., 2006).

The sad reality is that the absence of fathers in the child welfare system is redolent of their absence in general in the lives of children. In fact, 24 million children in America (34%) live in homes without fathers. Almost half of all fathers do not live with their children, and 50% have no contact with their children at all. Children under age 5 living with single mothers are 20 times more likely to live below the poverty level than families with a father present (Sonenstein et al., 2002).

There are many personal and institutional barriers to overcome to engage fathers on a greater level. The judge may be discouraged by a father's perceived lack of concern or lack of participation in the dependency proceeding. Child welfare workers too often do not search thoroughly and in a timely manner for fathers. Researchers have identified a systemwide bias against fathers in the child welfare system (Malm et al., 2006). Anecdotal information suggests that, too often, fathers object when child support is ordered in court, telling the court their child is being taken care of. For some fathers, "being taken care of" often refers to the fact that paternal relatives are acting as daily caregivers for the child with the father dropping by from time to time with diapers. This attitude from some fathers can lead to judges and child welfare professionals becoming frustrated and sometimes ambivalent about engaging the father. This should not, however, be used as an excuse by the courts.

The definition of a *responsible father* varies across cultures. Some men have been raised to believe that being a responsible father begins and ends with providing financial support for the child. Some fathers believe that as long as a family member is caring for the child, they need not do anything themselves. Other fathers have been taught that their primary role is to discipline the children.

Perhaps many of the fathers in the child welfare system do not know how to be a good father because they did not have the experience of a hands-on, nurturing father when they were growing up. In designing interventions or when interacting with fathers, it is important to understand these fundamental premises in order to override perceptions and stereotypes and help children connect with their fathers when it can be a safe, productive experience (Bronte-Tinkew, Horowitz, & Metz, 2008).

Even when professionals and judges understand the various cultural roles that define fatherhood, it is just as important to try to get fathers to participate in programs that teach parents what children need and how they can be part of their child's development and success. Teaching fathers about the joys of fatherhood and the crucial importance of a child's healthy relationship with his or her father are essential tasks for communities hoping to break the cycle of intergenerational abuse and abandonment of parental responsibilities. At this time there is very little research specifically about noncustodial fathers in the child welfare system. There is even less research regarding effective practices that enhance father involvement in case planning, permanency efforts, and father-focused interventions (Sonenstein et al., 2002).

Although there is agreement that involving fathers in the life of a child is critical, research indicates that it is not whether the child is living with the father that is most important but rather that the father is involved and supportive of the child (Durham's Partnership for Children, 2007). Even if the father is incarcerated or lives in another city, it is the quality and extent of his involvement in the child's life that makes the difference (Raichel, 2009). Focusing on fathers as critical adults in the lives of young children will take deliberate action and change in the child welfare system. Children will continue to suffer if fathers continue to be forgotten clients.

WHEN AN EVIDENCE-BASED
PARENTING PROGRAM IS NOT ENOUGH

As described in Chapter 1, the needs of parents of very young children in the child welfare system differ in terms of their chronicity and severity. For this reason, there will be cases when even evidence-based parenting classes will not be sufficient to change a parent's behaviors and beliefs that are harmful to his or her children. In these cases, clinical interventions delivered to the child–parent dyad by a trained, licensed mental health specialist will be necessary. Clinical models for such evidence-based treatment can be found through the federal agencies' model program listings on their web sites, as mentioned earlier in this chapter. A discussion focused on one highly effective clinical intervention, Child–Parent Psychotherapy, follows in Chapter 3.

REFERENCES

Adoption and Safe Families Act (ASFA) of 1997, PL 105-89, 111 Stat. 2115–2136.

Barnoski, R. (2004, January). *Research brief: Outcome evaluation of Washington state's research-based programs for juvenile offenders* (pp. 2–20). Olympia, WA: Washington State Institute for Public Policy.

Bavolek, S.J. (1985). *Nurturing parenting programs for the prevention and treatment for child maltreatment*. Park City, UT: Family Development Resources, Inc. www.nurturingparenting.com

Bavolek, S.J. (2007). *Nurturing skills for families*. Ashville, NC: Family Development Resources.

Bavolek, S.J., & Keene, R.G. (1999). *Adult-Adolescent Parenting Inventory, Version 2 (AAPI-2): Administration and developmental handbook*. Park City, UT: Family Development Resources.

Bronte-Tinkew, J., Horowitz, A., & Metz, A. (2008). *What works in fatherhood programs? Ten lessons from evidence-based practice*. Washington, DC: U.S. Department of Health and Human Services, Administration for Children and Families Office of Family Assistance, National Responsible Fatherhood Clearinghouse.

Burke, R., Herron, R., & Barnes, B. (2006). *Common Sense Parenting: A proven step-by-step guide for raising responsible kids and creating happy families* (3rd ed.). Boys Town, NE: Father Flanagan's Boys Home/Boys Town Press.

Cooney, S.M., Huser, M., Small, S.A., & O'Connor, C. (2007). Evidence-based programs: An overview. What works. *Wisconsin Research to Practice Series, 6*. Madison, WI: University of Wisconsin–Extension.

Durham's Partnership for Children: A Smart Start Initiative. (2007). *Fatherhood initiative: Determining a course of action for Durham County, NC. Executive summary*. Durham, NC: Author.

Eyberg, S.M. (1988). Parent–child interaction therapy: Integration of traditional and behavioral concerns. *Child and Family Behavior Therapy, 10*, 33–48.

Fixsen, D.L., Blase, K.A., Timbers, G.D., & Wolf, M.M. (2001). In search of program implementation: 792 replications of the teaching-family model. In G.A. Bernfeld, D.P. Farrington, & A.W. Leschied (Eds.), *Offender rehabilitation in practice: Implementing and evaluating effective programs* (pp. 149–166). London: Wiley.

Fixsen, D., Naoom, S., Blasé, K., Friedman, R., & Wallace, F. (2005). *Implementation research: A synthesis of the literature*. Tampa, FL: University of South Florida, Louis de la Parte Florida Mental Health Institute, The National Implementation Research Network (FMHI Publication #231).

Green, A. (2008). Policy and practice reform to engage non-resident fathers in child welfare. *Child Court Works, 10*, 1–3.

Greenwood, P.W. (2006). *Changing lives: Delinquency prevention as crime-control policy* (pp. 49–84). Chicago: University of Chicago Press.

Hurlburt, M.S., Barth, R.P., Leslie, L., Landsverk, J.A., & McCrae, J. (2007). Building on strengths: Current status and opportunities for improvement of parent training for families in child welfare. In R. Haskins, F. Wulczyn, & M. Webb (Eds.), *Child protection: Using research to improve policy and practice* (pp. 81–106). Washington, DC: Brookings Institution.

Kazdin, A.E. (2005). *Parent management training: Treatment for oppositional, aggressive, and antisocial behavior in children and adolescents*. New York: Oxford University Press.

Lamb, M.E., & Sagi, A. (1983). *Fatherhood and public policy*. Mahwah, NJ: Lawrence Erlbaum Associates.

Lederman, C., Gomez-Kaifer, M., Katz, L., Thomlison, B., & Maze, C. (2009, Fall). An imperative: Evidence-based practice within the child welfare system of care. *Juvenile and Family Justice TODAY*, 22–25.

Leschied, A.W., & Cunningham, A. (2002). *Seeking effective interventions for young offenders: Interim results of a four-year randomized study of multisystemic therapy in Ontario, Canada* (pp. 3–29). London, Ontario, Canada: Center for Children and Families in the Justice System.

Malm, K., Murray, J., & Geen, R. (2006). *What about the dads?: Child welfare agencies' efforts to identify, locate and involve nonresident fathers. Final Report*. Washington, DC: U.S. Department of Health and Human Services and Administration for Children and Families, Administration on Children, Youth and Families and Children's Bureau.

Mbwana, K., Terzian, M., & Moore, K. (2009). What works for parent involvement programs for children: Lessons from experimental evaluations of social interventions. *Child Trends fact sheet* (Pub. #2009–47, pp. 1–21). Washington, DC: Child Trends.

Raichel, J. (2009). Engaging and involving fathers in a child's life and in the child welfare case. *Protecting Children, 24*(2), 23–33.

Sonenstein, F., Malm, K., & Billing, A. (2002). *Study of fathers' involvement in permanency planning and child welfare casework*. Washington, DC: The Urban Institute.

University of Denver, Institute for Families. (2005). Increasing father involvement in child welfare. *Perspectives on Practice, 1*(2), 2–4.

Webster-Stratton, C. (1992). *The Incredible Years: A trouble-shooting guide for parents of children ages 3–8 years*. Toronto: Umbrella Press.

Wesch, D., & Lutzker, J. (1991) A comprehensive 5-year evaluation of Project 12-Ways: An ecobehavioral program for treating and preventing child abuse and neglect. *Journal of Family Violence, 6*(1), 17–35.

3

Healing the Infant–Parent Relationship

It was clear to the parenting facilitator and case manager that Pam needed more than an evidence-based parenting skills program delivered in a group format. Having never been nurtured or lovingly cared for as a child herself, she needed training on how to have a healthy, supportive relationship with her own infant in a one-to-one setting. Pam and Victor were referred to an evidence-based, child–parent, relationship-grounded psychotherapy program (Child–Parent Psychotherapy [CPP]) to try to repair their relationship and to build Pam's capacity to nurture her son. In this model, the clinician would work with just Pam and Victor to focus on their needs in weekly sessions over the course of several months.

At the initial structured assessment of the play interactions between Pam and Victor, the infant mental health clinician observed that Pam's attempts to show affection to Victor were rough and highly intrusive. Pam tended to tease Victor with the toys, and he would become frustrated. Pam did not know how to play with Victor, instead pushing on the mat while he was playing and trying to stand him on his head. In her first parent–child therapy session, she essentially either teased Victor or played with the toys herself and ignored her son who was left to play by himself.

As the sessions each week with Pam, Victor, and the therapist progressed, the therapist noted vast improvements and progress in Pam's work on building a responsive relationship with Victor. Early on, Pam showed neutral or "bland" affect and facial expressions toward Victor and had difficulty showing positive emotions, shown by fun and joy in her interactions with Victor. However, as the sessions progressed she made great strides. After 25 weekly sessions of CPP over the course of 6 months, Pam was able to understand Victor well enough to know when he wanted attention or how he wanted to play; she was able to maintain eye contact with Victor, and she softened her tone of voice with him and even laughed with him rather than teasing as before. She more frequently used positive guidance and discipline strategies in response to his behavior rather than threatening him with coarse language and abruptness. A strong bond had begun to develop between Pam and Victor with observable smiles and laughter and clear enjoyment in their joint play. Pam had learned to smile at her infant and to understand why that was important. Previously, these were foreign concepts to her. Pam and Victor's positive interplay and enjoyment increased, and being in the relationship gave them both support and enjoyment. The one-to-one guidance in a specialized intervention model had been the method for their continued improvement. Their community had built a process for them to gain access to an evidence-based intervention to meet their needs.

UNDERSTANDING CHILD–PARENT PSYCHOTHERAPY

Young children develop in relationships and use parents or caregivers to help them grow in positive ways. If the parent–child relationship is positive, they learn that relationships can be trusted—that when they cry, they will be picked up; when they are hungry, they will be fed; and that the environment is safe to explore. They also learn from their parents or caregivers how to control their behaviors and emotions and which behaviors and emotions are acceptable. Through CPP, young children who are abused and neglected have the opportunity to learn trust in relationships, which behaviors and emotion will bring them positive attention, and how to have their needs met. CPP, which engages both the child and parent together, is the relationship-based treatment program that has been implemented in Miami (Lieberman & Van Horn, 2005, 2008). CPP is evidence based and designed to support the child–parent relationship through interventions for children ages birth–5 years who are showing mental health or behavior problems, including symptoms of posttraumatic stress. CPP is especially helpful for children who have been maltreated and who have been exposed to trauma, following the assumption that the young child has been harmed in the relationship through abuse and neglect and must be healed in the relationship. Abuse and neglect leads to lack of trust and difficulties in attachment that can best be addressed by repairing the damage that has been done to the relationship. Together with the caregiver, the therapist works to help the child create a new narrative including an understanding that the caregiver will keep him or her safe. The therapist helps both the child and the parent understand the maladaptive behaviors that resulted from the trauma and helps the child develop more positively, building on the strengths of the parent.

CPP is based on the premise that the child's relationship with the mother, father, or primary attachment figure represents the most important "port of entry" or opportunity for intervention to help support the child's development in all areas, with particular focus on social and emotional development. Furthermore, CPP works with the parent and child to facilitate increased emotional and behavioral regulation. These issues are particularly important for children who have been traumatized by exposure to abuse and neglect and as a result are unable to show emotions and behaviors in appropriate ways; these children usually have increased aggressive or withdrawn behaviors. CPP has been shown to be effective in several studies (Lieberman, Ghosh Ippen, & Van Horn, 2006; Lieberman, Van Horn, & Ghosh Ippen, 2005; Toth, Maughan, Manly, Spanola, & Cicchetti, 2002) and is considered evidence based by the National Child Traumatic Stress Network (NCTSN; www.nctsn.org).

Working with Different Cultures in Child–Parent Psychotherapy

Attention to the cultural values of the parents in the context of the family is an integral component of the intervention plan. By addressing each family based on their unique cultural background and language, the CPP professional weaves the family's cultural values into all the principal components of the intervention. CPP uses a flexible approach, with clinicians encouraged to modify their engagement strategies depending on the needs and background of the family while still maintaining the core components of the model. Cultural issues are addressed in the CPP treatment manual, and CPP clinicians must be open to learning about cultural practices that may be very different from their own (Lieberman & Van Horn, 2005). For example, the clinician may need to be aware that in certain cultures it important to first meet and address the head of the family before working directly with other family members. In other cultures, modesty in dress may be highly valued, and the therapist may show respect for the family's culture by being mindful to dress conservatively when in the presence of that family.

Cultural rituals also may be important in helping a family gain a sense of safety and normalcy following a traumatic event. Clinicians may help a family identify particular aspects of their cultural heritage that may promote healing following a trauma. Examples may include attending worship services or seeking guidance from a spiritual advisor. Many cultures utilize song or dance as a way to celebrate or mourn; culturally appropriate expressions of emotion through song or dance may be especially helpful as they may serve to reestablish a feeling of physical regulation after a traumatic event.

Core Components of Child–Parent Psychotherapy

Joint sessions are carried out with the child and parent in the playroom together and are centered on the child's free play with carefully selected therapeutic toys. CPP psychotherapy is different from other interventions, in which the therapist may work with the child alone to help the child cope with trauma or overcome behavior problems or may work with the parent alone to teach skills to deal with the child's behavior. CPP asserts that working with one member of the dyad is not as effective as working with both the caregiver and the child. The child's development occurs within the context of the family; and although a child may benefit from the support of a therapist whom they see for a limited amount of time each week, the child is more likely to thrive if the parent gains the skills to provide support for the child on a consistent basis.

Toys are selected to promote cooperative play and to facilitate the child's ability to express his or her feelings about a traumatic event. Toys that encourage cooperative play and positive interactions between caregiver and child may include books to read together, balls to bounce back and forth, and toy food and dishes that can be used to play house or go on a picnic. Toys that are appropriate to help a child create a trauma narrative include human and animal figurines; toy doctor's kits; and toy ambulances, police cars, and fire trucks.

The focus during play is on the child's trauma experience and on the child–parent interaction, with individual sessions scheduled for the parent as needed to provide parental guidance and help support the parent's relationship with the child. Children who have experienced trauma use play to try to make sense of the traumatic event. The play may be a direct expression of the trauma (e.g., a child who has witnessed a homicide uses human figurines to recreate the event), may be a symbolic representation of the trauma (e.g., a child who has witnessed a homicide repeatedly hits and jumps on a large stuffed animal as an indirect representation of the traumatic event), or may represent the child's emotional state surrounding the event (e.g., a child who has witnessed a homicide may be fearful and anxious and not be able to play with any of the toys in the room but frenetically runs and throws toys around the room).

During CPP, the work involves helping the parent understand the developmental and emotional meaning of the child's behavior to increase parental understanding and empathy. For example, children who have experienced interpersonal violence sometimes imitate the aggressor. If a young child curses at her mother during a therapy session, the mother may respond by bursting into tears and stating that the child hates her and is just like the boyfriend who abused her. The therapist may help the parent understand that the child does not know the meaning of the words. As the therapist and the parent talk about where the child learned that kind of language, the parent may begin to describe an event during which her boyfriend cursed at and physically threatened both herself and the child. During this discussion, the therapist may ask the mother to talk about how she felt during this situation. The therapist may then talk to the child, helping the child label the scary feelings that she had when her mom and the mother's boyfriend were fighting.

A focus of the intervention is helping the parent to understand his or her child's emotions, including those that are "dysregulated" due to exposure to trauma. Parents often come to treatment and say that their child is "bad." They may state that the child cannot sit still, is aggressive, and behaves disrespectfully. The therapist and parent may discuss how trauma can be dysregulating to children, and the therapist may reframe the child's behavior as a response to the trauma rather than willful disobedience.

An additional focus of the intervention is on maladaptive child behaviors and parenting patterns that are punitive, harsh, or developmentally inappropriate. CPP also helps both the parent and child in the relationship understand the mistrust and misunderstandings that have resulted from the earlier traumatic experiences of both child and parent.

CPP fosters joint parent–child activities that promote mutual pleasure and the child's trust in the parent. Simply playing can be very therapeutic for parents and children who have not had the opportunity to be relaxed in each other's company. Activities that involve physical affection are important to children who have been physically abused and may have learned to fear touch.

A variety of intervention strategies are used that are individually tailored to the needs of the child and the parent. These strategies include developmental guidance, role modeling, emotional support, crisis intervention, assistance with problems of living, and insight-oriented intervention. CPP starts with the most simple and direct intervention strategies. More complex interventions such as those designed to help the parent gain insight into his or her behaviors and feelings and those of the child are used only when simpler interventions are not successful in producing child improvement.

Intervention Strategies Used with Child–Parent Psychotherapy

Clinicians trained in CPP have a variety of intervention modalities available to them. Depending on the needs of the young child and the parent, each of the strategies described here is likely to be used at some point in the treatment.

Care Management

One modality, care management, is used when a family needs help connecting to resources to meet their practical needs. Care management may include helping a mother find safe housing for herself and her children or helping a grandmother find an appropriate day care for the grandchild who has recently come into her care. For many families, once basic needs, specifically regarding safety, have been met, the problems that brought the family into treatment may dissipate. For example, many children are referred to treatment as a result of aggressive behavior. When young children do not feel safe, they have difficulty controlling their behaviors; aggression is one way of responding to an environment that feels chaotic or unsafe. For some children, as soon as they are placed in a safe environment—for example, one where they do not hear frequent gunshots or police sirens—their aggressive behavior decreases.

Playtime

Play is a modality that often is used in CPP. When caregivers and children play together, they have fun and enjoy each other's company. For many families, especially for families with children with behavior problems, enjoyable caregiver–child interactions are a rarity. During difficult times, some caregivers focus on negative events rather than positive experiences, and many parents are surprised when a therapist states, "Look how much fun your child is having with you." When CPP increases the amount of positive engagement that a caregiver and child have, both the caregiver and the child look forward to more of these experiences. Thus, the caregiver may praise his or her child more and do more fun things with the child than they did before the intervention, and children may respond to their caregivers in a more positive manner. Often, when children find that they can get positive attention from their caregivers, the children's negative behaviors decrease.

Understanding Child Development

Some families require more complex interventions, including the therapist's interpreting the caregiver's or child's behavior. For example, some caregivers who have had a long history of abuse expect that they will continue to be abused. These caregivers may project this expectation onto their young children so that when a child displays age-appropriate behaviors (e.g., saying "no" or having a temper tantrum), the caregiver experiences this as a direct attack and either avoids the child or is harshly punitive toward the child. In these cases, the therapist helps the caregiver understand that the child's behavior is not meant to attack the caregiver but is a typical part of the child's development. The therapist further helps the caregiver see that her expectations of the world may affect how she views and interacts with the child.

Speaking for Baby

Incorporated in CPP work with the parent–child dyad is "speaking for the infant" as an additional intervention to help sensitize the caregiver to an infant's feelings (Carter, Osofsky, & Hann, 1991). This therapeutic strategy allows the therapist to express what the infant may be feeling in words to help the parent understand what the infant's play and behaviors may mean. Often, it is very difficult for parents who experienced poor parenting and other adversities themselves to be empathic with their infant's feelings. Also, many do not know how to understand what behaviors and emotions may mean. "Speaking for the infant" incorporated into dyadic CPP therapeutic interventions provides a strategy to help the parents gain understanding and empathy for their children and is an indirect way to influence changes in parenting behavior. Many parents do not understand how important it is to talk to or smile at their infant. So the clinician can talk for the infant, saying, "I love it when you talk to me and sing to me, Mommy" or "When you hold me and rock me, I feel much better." Speaking for the infant can be used as an indirect way to educate the parent by saying, "It may seem like I am big enough to do things on my own, but it really helps when you help me." Such interventions can dramatically change the parent's understanding of the child and of the meaning of behaviors and emotions.

Play Therapy

Play therapy may be used as an adjunct to CPP to allow children the opportunity to play out and work through trauma. At times it is very difficult for parents to see and be with their children while they play out traumatic experiences during therapy. In these cases, after the parent is helped by the therapist to understand the child's need to play out the trauma, the therapist supports the parent in returning to play with the child and in creating a new way of being together and building a more positive relationship. Play therapy with the additional support of the therapist also may assist the child in learning more about how to regulate his or her behaviors and appropriate expression of emotion.

Psychoeducation

Another main component of the work with parents involves parental *psychoeducation*, a process that helps the parent to understand typical developmental issues for his or her child as well as to learn skills for nurturing and caring for the child. Psychoeducation also allows the parent to ask questions about his or her child. Parental guidance and other work with the parent includes teaching and modeling appropriate expectations and interactions relative to the child's developmental needs. Parental guidance may be beneficial when a parent acts with good intentions but not in the most appropriate way to achieve an end. For example, parents who want to help their children grow up to be independent and strong may encourage their children to master tasks before they are developmentally ready. This may occur when a parent allows her toddler or preschool-age child to watch horror movies and then becomes frustrated when the child has nightmares or wants to sleep in the parent's bed. In this case, developmental guidance may include validating the parent's wish for her child to be fearless but also helping the parent to empathize with how her child is feeling. Asking the parent to remember how she felt about scary movies when she was younger may help the parent to realize that her own child is not ready for such experiences. The therapist may explain to the parent that the child will actually learn to be brave by feeling that she is protected and safe as a young child. Exploration and raising awareness of the parent's own unresolved issues from childhood that might be interfering with attachment and her attitude toward her child is also stressed (Fraiberg, Adelson, & Shapiro, 1987).

Although many interventions teach parenting skills, CPP focuses on the unique aspects of the child. Clinicians trained in CPP do not teach or lecture to caregivers about general child development; rather, they collaborate with the parent and work together to understand the child and how to best meet the child's needs.

When Pam and Victor were referred for CPP, they first participated in a relationship-based assessment to determine their strengths and areas of need. (See Appendix G for Sample Child–Caregiver Relationship Assessment.) Once their treatment plan was formulated in conjunction with the infant mental health therapist, they began to participate in the weekly CPP sessions. During the assessment, observations of Pam and Victor's interactions were made during free play, structured play with four increasingly difficult tasks for Victor, and a "staged" brief separation and reunion between Pam and Victor. During the observations, focus was placed on the affect (i.e., mood and facial expressions and body language) of both Victor and Pam, how they played together (whether there was reciprocity or back-and-forth play), how Victor handled the transitions from one toy to another and whether his mother helped him, whether Pam was able to follow his lead and choice of toy and facilitate the play, and whether they seemed to enjoy being together and playing together. Initially, Pam did not know how to play with Victor. Furthermore, being a victim of chronic abuse, she had learned mainly negative ways of interacting, relating, and being with people and so had little capacity to enjoy playing and nurturing her own child. As explained in Chapter 1, parenting comes naturally, but it comes naturally the way you learned it, and Pam did not have an opportunity to learn positive parenting (Docherty & Kirk, 1995).

Pam was not aware of Victor's developmental level and what he was capable of doing. This lack of knowledge about developmental milestones that is so common in young mothers resulted in her doing inappropriate things with him (e.g., trying to have him stand on his head, teasing him, being intrusive, being generally insensitive to his needs and wants). Pam, like so many other young mothers, became involved in playing with the toys herself rather than focusing her attention on her son.

Through play, it was possible to focus on Victor's trauma experience in relation to Pam's trauma experience and to focus on building positive elements in the child–parent relationship. The process involved translating the developmental and emotional meaning of the child's behavior to Pam to increase parental understanding and empathy. As Victor responded more positively to Pam, she showed much more positive affect, smiling at her infant and enjoying the mutual, reciprocal play. Pam was learning more about Victor and herself and how positive interactions allowed her to have fun with Victor. She also learned more about Victor's developmental needs and how to meet them.

CPP allowed Pam and Victor the opportunity to develop a positive relationship that would facilitate not only his development but also her capacity as a mother and an adult. Despite the many improvements in Pam and Victor's relationship, however, the CPP clinician realized the importance of "leaving the door open" for a young mother like Pam who had experienced so much abuse herself in case later dilemmas resulted from developmental issues that emerged as Victor grew older.

VIEW FROM THE BENCH
How CPP Helps with Reunification

Some of the young parents I see in court do not know how to play with their infants. When they are asked as part of an assessment to sit on the floor in the playroom and engage their infant, they are puzzled and disconcerted. In court, these same parents are adamant in their beliefs that they are good parents and that an insidious injustice has resulted in the removal of their infant. The parents believe that parenting is not very onerous.

Learning to parent when one only has experienced abusive and neglectful parenting is quite complicated. Becoming nurturing and acting unconditionally and with empathy cannot be learned in a book or a class or by watching a video. It must be caringly and patiently modeled, as our infant mental health therapists do in CPP. Because of CPP, I have reunified families who, when I first saw them in court, I believed to be so harmed and hopeless that termination of parental rights was inevitable. Now every family and young child has a chance.

RELATIONSHIP-BASED EVALUATIONS

To learn more about how the parent and young child relate to each other and to guide implementation of CPP, an observational method, the modified Parent–Child Early Relational Assessment (Crowell & Fleischmann, 1993), is conducted at the time of referral and before the initiation of treatment. After this assessment, a determination is made regarding whether the most appropriate referral is for evidence-based parenting training, CPP, or both programs. Parental informed consent is obtained for the assessment. The modification of the original Parent–Child Relationship Assessment by Dr. Amy Dickson of the Louisiana State University Health Sciences Center (LSUHSC) Harris Program for Infant Mental Health is structured as shown in Table 3.1.

Table 3.1. Modification of the original Crowell relationship assessment adapted by Dr. Amy Dickson of the LSUHSC Harris Center for Infant Mental Health

Prior to assessment	Parents or caregivers are given instructions about the assessment, told what to expect, and informed that they will receive further instructions between each episode. Individual tasks are demonstrated to the parent or caregiver.
Free play (8–10 minutes)	Instruction: "Play with the child as you would at home."
Cleanup (no more than 5 minutes)	Instruction: "Have the child clean up, helping him or her if you feel your child needs help."
Bubbles (3–5 minutes)	Instructions: "Use the bubbles to play with your child."
Task 1 (2–4 minutes)	Specific task instructions are given. (This task is slightly below the child's developmental level. Although the caregiver is not told, the child will likely be able to complete the task independently.)
Task 2 (2–4 minutes)	Specific task instructions are given. (Task is slightly below or at the child's developmental level.)
Task 3 (3–5 minutes)	Specific task instructions are given. (Task is slightly above or at the child's developmental level.)
Task 4 (3–5 minutes, if used)	Specific task instructions are given. (Task is slightly above the child's developmental level. Although the caregiver is not told, the child will likely need help to complete the task.)
Separation (no more than 3 minutes; have parent take the bubbles)	Instructions: "Leave the toys out so that the child can see the task toys and then leave the room as you would at home."
Reunion (3 minutes)	Instructions: "Knock on the door, call the child's name, and step all the way into the room." The parent and child return to play.

This chart was developed by Dr. Amy Dickson.

During the assessment, the clinician carries out a careful observational assessment of the parent and infant or toddler, including *positive affect or emotions (e.g., smiling, laughing); depression and withdrawal; irritability, anger, or hostility; intrusiveness on the part of the parent, behavioral responsiveness of parent to child and child to parent;* and *emotional responsiveness of both child and parent,* including the caregiver's ability to create a positive, warm, and supportive emotional environment for the child. Clinicians also observe the caregiver's discipline strategies during the structured task. Positive behaviors include modeling the correct behavior and praising the child for success. Negative behaviors include shaming the child or physically threatening the child. In addition to these behaviors, the enthusiasm expressed by the young child in playing with his or her parent or caregiver also is observed. Emotions are scored using a 5-point scale. During the brief separation and reunion, caregivers' and children's behaviors are rated. Observations of the caregivers include the following: *sensitivity in comforting the child, minimizing distress,* and *helping the child return to play and exploration.* Observations of the children include the following: *ability to self-soothe, ability to be comforted in response to parental support,* and *return to play after the separation.*

In Pam and Victor's case, the relationship-based assessment enabled the therapist not only to see Pam's weaknesses in relating to Victor, but also to identify her strengths. Even if parents lack the ability to be nurturing and developmentally sensitive to their infants and toddlers, they often show some strengths when relating to their children. During the evaluation, the therapist was encouraged by Pam's ability to explain to Victor what the various toys were and to give him ideas about how to play with them. Her communication style with Victor was helpful and animated and showed as a strength; Pam seemed to be enjoying telling Victor stories and encouraging him to play. Although Pam did not yet see a clear role for herself in the play, she was able to encourage that important behavior and opportunity for learning in her son. Furthermore, the fact that she talked to Victor as they played was important for encouraging his language development, especially when her words were positive and reinforcing of his behavior. Pam's strengths that were noted in the observational assessment were used in later therapy sessions with Pam and Victor.

Miami's Story:
How Child–Parent Psychotherapy (CPP) Was Implemented in Florida

In 2000, the Florida legislature funded a 3-year, multisite Infant and Young Child Mental Health Pilot Project, designed to provide earlier identification, better evaluation, and more effective treatment services for high-risk children. The children in the project were either at risk for out-of-home placement due to abuse and neglect or were already in the child welfare system and judged dependent by the state, but were those for whom parental rights had not yet been terminated. The primary goals of the pilot project were to reduce the occurrence and recurrence of abuse and neglect, enhance the child's developmental functioning, and increase expeditious permanent placements. A secondary set of goals was to develop a model for intervention and treatment that could be replicated in different sites, to document the components of quality infant mental health interventions, and to evaluate their effectiveness. Three sites were chosen for the pilot: Miami, Sarasota, and Pinellas County.

The Miami site involved a collaboration between the Miami Juvenile Court and the Linda Ray Intervention Center at the University of Miami. The target population was infants and toddlers in the dependency system due to abuse or neglect. Although the Miami team had much experience working with courts, child welfare, early intervention, and child care, the nexus with infant mental health clinical professional expertise had not yet been built. Therefore, the court and the university program identified the need for intensive training for the infant mental health clinicians at the Linda Ray Intervention Center by a clinical team from the LSUHSC Harris Program for Infant Mental Health. The LSUHSC Harris Center has a long history of providing clinical training, both in New Orleans and nationally, in both infant mental health relationship-based assessments and a relationship-based treatment model. Based on the needs of the young children and their families, the need for relationship-based assessments and evidence-based CPP treatment, it was decided that the partnership would focus on training in these two areas. The goal was to not only train the infant mental health clinicians to carry out relationship-based assessments and CPP treatment, but also to broaden the program components with the goal of sustainability and expansion in Miami.

Following the Florida Infant and Young Child Mental Health Pilot Project, the Miami site was committed to continuing this model of infant mental health relationship-based assessments and treatment for dependent children. To do so, they obtained additional funding for ongoing collaboration between the juvenile court (Judge Cindy Lederman), the University of Miami's Linda Ray Intervention Center (Dr. Lynne Katz), and the LSUHSC Harris Center for Infant Mental Heath (Dr. Joy Osofsky), with national, state, and local funding. With the leadership of Dr. Lynne Katz, Judge Lederman, and their colleagues, multiple funding was obtained from District XI of the Department of Children and Families, the Office of Juvenile Justice and Delinquency Prevention through a Safe Start Promising Approaches grant award, the Head Start Bureau, Administration for Children and Families, and via a partnership with the local Miami-Dade Community Action Agency as part of the Early Head Start Child Welfare Initiative. The intervention and treatment model developed and implemented by the Miami Infant Mental Health team partners established the first Early Head Start Juvenile Court collaborative in the United States. The collaboration demonstrated an effective way to provide evidence-based services to families with the goals of breaking the intergenerational cycles of abuse and neglect and helping the young children achieve permanency.

The model requires extensive engagement services necessary to maintain the therapeutic work. In most cases, 10 hours of the clinicians' time is spent achieving 1 hour of services because of the families' many needs. Engagement hours involve case management that may include help in finding child care, assistance with housing, and education on child development and parenting. All of these interventions contribute to parental growth and the success of the program. The therapist may also include in her activities home visiting, visiting the child at child care, helping to arrange transportation, or communicating with the child welfare department. Additional services may be required for the family including treatment for substance abuse, domestic violence, mental illness, and parent or child cognitive impairments that could interfere with the parent's ability to parent effectively.

ENGAGING PARENTS AND THEIR INFANTS IN CLINICAL INTERVENTIONS

Clinically engaging a parent who has lost her child, at least temporarily, to the child welfare system as a result of maltreatment, who herself may be abusing substances or who may suffer from mental illness, is a daunting task. Why should the parents trust a mental health professional whom they fear is going to report each and every behavior they observe related to their child back to the court? Why should they trust this person when they have never learned to trust anyone earlier in their lives? They know from past experience that if they allow themselves to trust, they may end up disappointed. The professionals who truly want to help parents such as Pam need to embody certain personal and professional qualities if they are to successfully engage and work with parents and young children in the child welfare system.

Treatment Engagement with Caregivers of High-Risk Children

The high rates of dropping out and other engagement problems are significant concerns in the delivery of mental health and other services to high-risk families. Even in home-based services, where transportation and other logistical barriers are eliminated, many families do not participate fully in services. Whereas compliance is often described as "going through the motions," engagement or full participation is positive involvement in the helping process (Yatchmenoff, 2005). There are two primary components of

(continued)

engagement: 1) behavioral (i.e., the quality of client performance on tasks necessary within treatment or services to achieve outcomes) and 2) attitudinal (the emotional investment and commitment of a participant showing that the task is perceived as worthwhile and beneficial) (Karver et al., 2005). Successful engagement models have practitioners using the following tools to engage parents (Staudt, 2003):

- Establishing treatment relevance and/or acceptability
- Addressing daily stressors
- Creating a therapeutic alliance
- Examining and addressing external barriers
- Addressing cognitions and beliefs about treatment

Empathetic Listening

Clinicians, child welfare professionals, and others who work with high-risk families and parents who maltreat their children must be able to be empathic, no matter how bad the circumstances. They must tap into their own personal, clinical, and empathic skills, often with the help and support of reflective supervision (Weatherston & Osofsky, 2009) to not pass judgment on the parent and what he or she has done to his or her child. Some practitioners cannot help responding to these parents negatively, believing that they themselves could parent this child so much better than the abusive, neglectful, drug-abusing parent before them; however, it is important for the therapist to remember that the goal is not to show that he or she knows how to be a better parent but to help the parent improve his or her own parenting abilities. Therapists must be able to be good and "active listeners" and be able to "hear and hold" the traumatic stories and experiences of the parent. Often the stories are difficult to hear and may provoke anger and frustration in the therapist. Child welfare workers may experience very similar emotions. That is the reason that reflective supervision is so important for this work.

Creative Problem Solving

Therapists, together with child welfare professionals and others who interface with the child and parent, also need to be creative and good problem solvers, as the care management and "engagement" issues with these families often take much creativity and persistence. They need to not get discouraged when a mother does not show for an appointment. Being "court ordered" to attend a session or meeting does not ensure that appointments will be kept. The therapist who is successful in this work must be able to work with multiple systems, not be overcome with frustration with the bureaucracy, and relate well to people from many different backgrounds, different levels of experience, and different approaches to their work.

Patience

Therapists and child welfare professionals must be patient; often the parents will take one step forward and two back as they work to regain custody of their child. The therapist also must be realistic and set clear limits and boundaries because parents in these circumstances often will try hard to test their providers and push them away like they have done with everyone else in their lives. It is important to recognize that the parent's relationship with the infant mental health therapist may be the first positive relationship they have ever had with a professional.

Therapists will have to be aware that every appointment may not be kept or begin on time. For example, when it is raining or snowing, it is likely that a parent who must wait outdoors for multiple buses may be late or may not appear at all. Therapists are encouraged to plan their schedules so that they will have other paperwork or supplemental activities to do if a client does not come for the appointment.

Many factors including poverty, stress, and family dysfunction can continue to interfere with the parent's progress toward gaining insight and skills related to parenting his or her child. In the course of working through the tasks of a case plan, a mother may relapse and may need additional support to return to her "recovery" track. A therapist also needs to be aware—as a professional who is still human—of her personal "triggers" that may be set off by some of these parents. For example, if the therapist has a young child the same age as the abused and/or neglected child of the parent they are trying to treat, strong emotions may emerge toward the abusing parent. Therapists who are successful in working with high-risk, maltreating families need to be aware of their own personal reactions to the parent or child and be comfortable dealing with them in a trusting supervisory relationship.

Honesty

Engaging families may be at odds with the therapist's need to present reports on the parent's progress in court hearings. (See Appendix B for a sample Infant Mental Health Therapist Court Report.) Some reports may be positive; however, when they are not, it is very easy for the parent to feel disrespected and betrayed by the therapist. Therefore, it is crucial, no matter how horrible the circumstances of the case, that parents feel respected and empowered; they have to be able to *trust* the clinician, and the clinician, in turn, needs to apprise them honestly as to the evaluation of the parent's progress prior to appearing in court or writing a report. There is nothing worse for a parent who may have been feeling betrayed and disrespected by their family of origin than to also feel betrayed or revictimized by the court-ordered service providers. Parents too often are surprised by information that is shared in court by service providers who have not shared the information with them first. This, of course, causes anger and lack of trust in the professional and can result in client "no-shows" after the court hearing. No matter how negative the information to be shared at the court hearing, the clinician must first discuss it with the client openly and honestly, with sensitivity and empathy, in preparation for the court appearance. Parents report feeling less betrayed when this is done. If a client does become angry as a result of a negative court report, the therapist must be willing to process this anger with his or her client. Failing to do so will create a barrier to further treatment success. Many parents involved in the child welfare system have never had the opportunity to process their anger in a safe environment; in previous relationships, anger has most often resulted in the termination of a relationship. Discussing angry feelings is often very difficult for them.

Empowering

Parents need to be empowered so that they understand that they are responsible for their progress and that their progress or lack of progress will be reported to the court.

Most parents are used to blaming the "system" or someone else and have difficulty accepting responsibility for their actions. Again, dealing with these issues with parents must be done with empathy and sensitivity. It is important to remember that when the therapist reports findings to the judge at a court hearing in front of the parent, it is always good practice to start the court report and discussion with something positive, no matter how small. Again, it is crucial that all information has been discussed with the parent prior to the court hearing.

Enormous rewards can result when a mother or father is able to trust his or her therapist. The parent must believe that the therapist has his or her child's best interest at heart and is willing to work together successfully to facilitate regaining custody of the child. Working with a child and parents to heal their relationship can be very rewarding for the therapist. It is not just that the parent is able to have the child back but, even more, that the young child is able to have his or her parent back and that this parent is able to nurture and support the needs of the child.

The process of providing access to clinical interventions involves not only the parents and the young children but also requires that community partners who are working with the family check in frequently with each other about the progress being made by the family across different programs. This will help keep the momentum of family engagement moving forward as tasks are completed and more skills are gained by the parents. There will be challenges to keeping the family coming to their intervention programs, whether it be transportation issues, parent work or school schedules, health crises needing attention, or need for assistance with housing sustainability and basic necessities. The community providers who can maintain open communication with and accessibility to each other will provide the most seamless overall care and support for the family.

CPP, focusing on healing and helping the relationship between parent and child, builds on the strengths of both members of the dyad—the mother or father's desire to regain custody of his or her child and be the parent he or she always hoped to be and the amazing strength of the child who, when being nurtured, can help bring out the best in the parent. Relationships can be healed, first with trust and then with learning and persistence. This therapeutic opportunity may be the very first chance that this parent has to learn something about him- or herself and how to be a parent.

REFERENCES

Carter, S., Osofsky, J.D., & Hann, D.M. (1991). Speaking for baby: Therapeutic interventions with adolescent mothers and their infants. *Infant Mental Health Journal, 12*, 291–302.

Crowell, J.A., & Fleischmann, M.A. (1993). Use of structured research procedures in clinical assessments of infants. In C.H. Zeanah (Ed.), *Handbook of infant mental health* (pp. 210–221). New York: Guilford Press.

Docherty, N., & Kirk, M. (Directors). (1995). *Frontline: When the bough breaks [Television series]*. Canada: Canadian Broadcasting Corporation.

Fraiberg, S., Adelson, E., & Shapiro, V. (1987). Ghosts in the nursery: A psychoanalytic approach to the problems of impaired infant–mother relationships. In S. Fraiberg & L. Fraiberg (Eds.), *Selected readings of Selma Fraiberg* (pp. 164–196). Columbus, OH: Ohio State University Press.

Karver, M.S., Handelsman, J.B., Fields, S., & Bickman, L. (2005). A theoretical model of common process factors in youth and family therapy. *Mental Health Services Research, 7*, 35–51.

Lieberman, A.F., Ghosh Ippen, C., & Van Horn, P. (2006). Child–parent psychotherapy: 6-month follow-up of a randomized controlled trial. *Journal of the American Academy of Child & Adolescent Psychiatry, 45*, 913–918.

Lieberman, A.F., & Van Horn, P. (2005). *Don't hit my mommy! A manual for child–parent psychotherapy with young witnesses of family violence*. Washington, DC: Zero to Three.

Lieberman, A.F., & Van Horn, P. (2008). *Psychotherapy with infants and young children: Repairing the effects of stress and trauma on early attachment.* New York: Guilford Press.

Lieberman, A.F., Van Horn, P., & Ghosh Ippen, C. (2005). Toward evidence-based treatment: Child–parent psychotherapy with preschoolers exposed to marital violence. *Journal of the American Academy of Child and Adolescent Psychiatry, 44,* 1241–1248.

Staudt, M.M. (2003). Helping children access and use services: A review. *Journal of Child and Family Studies, 12,* 49–60.

Toth, S.L., Maughan, A., Manly, J.T., Spanola, M., & Cicchetti, D. (2002). The relative efficacy of two interventions in altering maltreated preschool children's representational models: Implications for attachment theory. *Developmental Psychology, 14,* 877–908.

Weatherston, D., & Osofsky, J.D. (2009). Working within the context of relationships: Multidisciplinary, relational, and reflective practice, training, and supervision. *Infant Mental Health Journal, 30,* 573–677.

Yatchmenoff, D.K. (2005) Measuring client engagement from the client's perspective in non-voluntary child protective services. *Research on Social Work Practice, 15,* 84–96.

4

Supporting the Development of Very Young Children

As Victor approached 2 years of age, his great aunt with whom he was living noticed that he was saying fewer words than she remembered her other nieces and nephews had spoken at the same age. Although he was able to follow directions when she asked him to pick up a toy or bring over a book for her to read to him at bedtime, he rarely initiated words and was unable to label common items in his environment, such as *car* or *dog.* Victor's aunt brought her concerns to her pediatrician, whose response was, "He's a boy; they are slower to speak" and, "He'll say something when he has something important to say; don't worry." But Victor's aunt continued to worry and brought her concerns about his language development to his caseworker, seeking a referral that would supply her with answers in response to her concerns about Victor's development. Victor's caseworker was able to identify the "portal" in the community where she could initiate the process of having Victor tested to see whether his aunt's concerns about his language development were valid and in need of attention.

The reality is that young children such as Victor in the child welfare system have a higher incidence of developmental delays than do children in the community as a whole. Whereas the rate of young children requiring special education services due to developmental delays outside the child welfare system stands at approximately 10% of the total population, the rate for children in the child welfare system is higher, ranging upward of 25%–35%, on average (Casanueva, Cross, & Ringeinsen, 2008).

Integrating Developmental Screenings at Primary Care Facilities

The addition of a simple and systematic screening among children in foster care doubled the detection rate of developmental disabilities in a population that is at high risk for developmental problems in a University of Rochester Medical Center study (Jee et al., 2010). Results point to the fact that universal screening is feasible in a busy pediatric practice.

In 2007, Starlight Pediatrics changed its standard of care to include sending foster families a brief, nondiagnostic screening questionnaire (Ages & Stages Questionnaires® [ASQ-3™]; Squires & Bricker, 2009) a week before well-child visits. When called to be reminded about their appointment, the families also were reminded to bring the completed questionnaire. The vast majority of the questionnaires were completed before or at the visit (96%), which researchers concluded meant the task was feasible for families. It generally took providers less than 5 minutes to score and review the questionnaires with families during their visit (Jee et al., 2010).

More important, the questionnaires helped providers detect twice as many potential developmental disabilities as they found before the screening was implemented (58% versus 29%). The questionnaires also teased out more delays in problem-solving, personal-social, and fine motor skills than had previously been detected (Jee et al., 2010).

FEDERAL ENTITLEMENTS FOR INFANTS AND TODDLERS

Maltreatment of children ages birth–3 years can have deleterious effects on their development, effects that can be addressed by early intervention. The federal Keeping Children and Families Safe Act of 2003 (PL 108-36) amended the Child

Abuse and Prevention Treatment Act (CAPTA; PL 93-247) to require that states develop "provisions and procedures" for referring child maltreatment victims to early intervention services. The legislation targets children younger than age 3 who are involved in a case of child abuse or neglect that is substantiated by the child welfare system, and it specifies delivery of early intervention services funded under Part C of the Individuals with Disabilities Education Act (IDEA; PL 108-446; 21 USC §106[b][2][A]). Part C services are intended to enhance the development of infants and toddlers with disabilities and minimize infants' potential for developmental delay. These services also can be an entrée into special education services when compromises to development are enduring (Casaneuva et al., 2008). This prevalence rate means that it is critical for professionals working with this young population to understand their role as first observers of the children in their caseload.

The point of entry for many communities to gain access to early intervention is through the local public schools or Early Steps programs. Federal entitlement programs for young children (newborn–3 years old) and preschoolers (3–4 years old) have been established. Their express purpose is identifying children with developmental delays early on so that interventions can be put in place that will help increase the child's preparedness for school entry at age 5. Part C of IDEA is a federal grant program that assists states in operating a comprehensive statewide system of early intervention services for infants and toddlers with disabilities, ages birth–2 years, and their families. Congress established the Part C (early intervention) program in 1986 in recognition of "an urgent and substantial need" to

- Enhance the development of infants and toddlers with disabilities

- Reduce educational costs by minimizing the need for special education through early intervention

- Minimize the likelihood of institutionalization and maximize independent living

- Enhance the capacity of families to meet their child's needs

---

Individuals with Disabilities Education Act

The Individuals with Disabilities Education Act of 1990 (PL 101-476) and its predecessor statute, the Education for All Handicapped Children Act of 1975 (PL 94-142), arose from federal case law holding that the denial of free public education to children with disabilities constitutes a deprivation of due process. It has grown in scope and form over the years, having been reauthorized and amended a number of times, most recently in December 2004 (PL 108-446). Its terms are further defined by regulations of the U.S. Department of Education, which are found in Parts 300 and 301 of Title 34 of the Code of Federal Regulations.

States have some discretion in setting the criteria for child eligibility of early intervention services, including whether to serve at-risk children. As a result, definitions of eligibility differ significantly from state to state. States also differ concerning which state agency has been designated the lead agency for the Part C program. However, in most communities the local school system can assist by directing families to the appropriate agency. Once referred, the early intervention team at the agency will schedule an appointment for the child and the family during which psychosocial information will be gathered and the early intervention team members with varied expertise will assess the child's developmental areas to determine whether the child is progressing on a normal trajectory for his or her age. Depending on the results of the assessment, which takes place within 45 days of receipt of a referral, the child may or may not meet eligibility as needing services to close any developmental delays.

Early intervention services assess multiple developmental domains when children are referred, including the domains of gross motor development (large muscles that affect walking, crawling, and sitting), fine motor development (small muscles that are used to pick up and grasp items), cognition (levels of understanding), language (both receptive and expressive), socioemotional status, and self-help skills such as feeding and dressing.

This screening and assessment process may have different pathways in different communities. For Victor, as a child within the child welfare system, the standard process to determine his levels of functioning began with a comprehensive *level of care* (LOC) *assessment* conducted by a licensed clinician. The multifaceted assessment included observations of Victor in multiple settings, the gathering of collateral information from his home environment and his child care program, home visits to observe Victor with his foster family, and use of multiple assessment measures including the ASQ-3™ screening tool (Squires & Bricker, 2009) to initially identify developmental areas that might be delayed and may require further in-depth assessments. Results of the initial ASQ-3 screener and extensive observations of Victor in multiple settings indicated that Victor showed *potential* developmental delays in his language development and socioemotional development. In both his home and school settings he spoke noticeably less than his playmates and often got angry and upset when others could not understand his needs or requests.

The results of the LOC assessment were passed back to the caseworker, who made the referral to the Early Steps program in Victor's community for a full assessment by a multidisciplinary team to confirm the existence of his delays. Victor's delays of 25% in producing language that was developmentally appropriate for his chronological age met the criteria for speech and language services. His socioemotional functioning was determined to be within typical ranges for his age, and it was determined that those needs could be met through behavioral strategies and more positive reinforcement at home and at his child care program.

In addition to the early intervention entitlements available to Victor and his family, the Adoption and Safe Families Act of 1997 (ASFA; PL 105-89) requires that states ensure that the physical and mental health needs of children in care are met. This gives juvenile judges the power and responsibility to monitor compliance with ASFA and to make sure children receive early intervention services when needed. The most recent reauthorization of the CAPTA (PL 93-247) requires that children younger than age 3 who have a substantiated case of abuse or neglect be referred for screening for early intervention services. This welcome new provision has the potential to identify, treat, and ultimately reduce the disproportionate delays documented by the research (Jee et al., 2010). Dependent children have a right to this screening; it is no longer optional. (See Appendix D for the Miami Juvenile Court Order for Early Intervention Services Evaluation Through Part C of IDEA and Miami Juvenile Court Order of Referral to Healthy Start.) It is hoped that this new provision will increase children's readiness to learn when school begins. The early intervention community, child welfare professionals, and the judiciary must work together to make sure children with delays are identified and receive the services to which they are entitled.

VIEW FROM THE BENCH

In my desk on the bench I have three drawers. The bottom two drawers contain children's books—some new, some old—all donated by our public library, our Early Learning Coalition, and kind individuals. My top drawer is the treasure drawer that contains small toys and candy. When I invite children to come up to the bench and navigate the treasure drawer, I speak with them and carefully observe them. I have seen children unable to control their impulses when asked to choose something from the treasure drawer. One small boy almost became wild, furiously grabbing everything in the drawer. No one had questioned his behavior before or realized that something might be wrong. One day, I watched a small boy approach the bench whose head was clearly misshapen, and no one could tell me if he had received medical care. I have observed children who communicate with grunts and have not been evaluated for speech delays. And some days I see children who appear to have never seen a book before. I address all of my observations about the needs of these children with the parents, caseworkers, and lawyers in the courtroom. We work together on educating the parent and initiating the process for professional evaluation. Thankfully these children have been brought to court, giving me a firsthand perspective of their special needs.

EARLY INTERVENTION SERVICES AND SUPPORTS

The multidisciplinary early intervention team, which included an early intervention teacher, a speech therapist, a physical therapist, and occupational therapist, determined that Victor would be eligible for speech therapy three times per week and weekly consultation support from an infant mental health therapist. The services could be delivered in the *natural environment* of his Early Head Start program during his regular school day.

Natural Environments

Part C of IDEA requires "to the maximum extent appropriate to the needs of the child, early intervention services must be provided in natural environments, including the home and community settings in which children without disabilities participate" (34 CFR §303.12[b]).

By definition, natural environments mean *"settings that are natural or typical for the child's age peers who have no disabilities"* (34 CFR §303.18).

The exception to the rule reads

> The provision of early intervention services for any infant or toddler with a disability occurs in a setting other than a natural environment that is most appropriate, as determined by the parent and the individualized family service plan team, only when early intervention cannot be achieved satisfactorily for the infant or toddler in a natural environment.

The provision of early intervention services taking place in natural environments is not just a guiding principle or suggestion; it is a legal requirement.

The multidisciplinary team who determined that Victor was eligible for services met at the onset of this process with his aunt and an educational surrogate, a knowledgeable member of the community who volunteers to assist in helping the team make appropriate educational decisions for a child in out-of-home care. The surrogate was appointed by the local public school system to represent Victor's educational needs. Together with an early intervention staffing specialist, they developed the mandatory individualized family service plan (IFSP) that outlined the results of Victor's assessment, his levels of functioning, and the plans for intervention services to address his speech and language delays and his socioemotional issues (see Appendix F for a sample IFSP). The IFSP constitutes a legal document between the early intervention program, the public school system, and the parent or guardian for services. Through the IFSP development process, Victor's aunt, the educational surrogate, the caseworker, and the early interventionist from the Early Steps program worked as a team to plan, implement, and ultimately evaluate the services being proposed to meet Victor's needs.

For some young children, the areas of delay also may be physical or cognitive and may entitle them to everything from physical therapy or occupational therapy to a nutritionist for a number of sessions weekly. They also may qualify for a special center-based program or home visitation program. In each case, the child and the family or guardians are at the core of the decision-making process. For the initial meetings as well as the quarterly and semiannual review meetings, case managers as well as the court-appointed special advocate or guardian ad litem volunteers and children's attorneys are welcome to attend along with the foster family or relative caregivers and the parents so that everyone working on behalf of the child is aware of the child's needs and the intervention plans. The logistics of having the child gain access to the services may require planning and cooperation among these members, including the caseworker.

Over the course of Victor's participation in language development services at his child care program, both the teachers and his aunt began to see an improvement in his expressive language. He was using more words to request what he wanted, and he would repeat words when labels for objects were provided to him. Soon he began linking two or three words together as a precursor to creating full sentences. With more and more progress in language development, he was observed to be calmer and less prone to using temper tantrums to get what he wanted. His speech therapist was pleased with his progress and language acquisition and taught both his teachers and his aunt how to elicit and support his development in this area.

Provisions in IDEA provided for transition planning by Victor's teachers, the educational representative, his caseworker, and his aunt as Victor approached 3 years old that would allow him to continue speech therapy services through the Part B entitlement portion of IDEA that focuses on children ages 36 months to 4 years old. This offered a continuum of early intervention for Victor that carried him through until his entry into kindergarten. In Victor's world, the opportunity to increase his language through quality speech and language services opened the window toward development of the skills he would need to be successful when he entered kindergarten.

Therapies for Young Children

What occupational therapy practitioners actually do in early intervention settings depends on the goals a family has for their child. The practitioner evaluates the child and then identifies things that parents and caregivers can do throughout the day to reinforce a skill and improve sensory processing or enable new learning. For example, parents might be concerned that their child cannot pick up her food to finger feed. An occupational therapy practitioner can work with her family to identify times during the day that the child can practice isolating her index finger and grasping small things. Together, the practitioner and parents might develop strategies to adapt meal times with larger bits of food for easier grasping, provide opportunities to press buttons on the television remote, and work on pointing to pictures during the bedtime story routine at night. Incorporating work on skills into regular daytime routines is a central tenet of occupational therapy. Occupational therapy practitioners support and encourage the parents' relationship with their child. The time a family spends working with a child in between an occupational therapy practitioner's visits is vital (Opp, 2009).

Speech-language pathologists (SLPs) also have a central role in providing services and supports for families and their infants or toddlers with disabilities as members of the early intervention team. The appropriately certified and licensed (as applicable) SLP is qualified to address delays and disabilities in communication, language, speech, emergent literacy, and feeding and/or swallowing. Effective communication is fundamental to all aspects of human functioning, particularly learning and social interaction. The development of communication skills begins at birth. Families with infants and toddlers (birth–36 months) who are at risk for or have disabilities should receive developmentally supportive care: 1) prevention; 2) screening, evaluation, and assessment; 3) planning, implementation of, and monitoring intervention; 4) consultation with and education for team members, including families and other professionals; 5) service coordination; 6) transition planning; 7) advocacy; and 8) awareness and advancement of the knowledge base in early intervention. These roles should be implemented in accord with the following guiding principles: Services are family centered and culturally and linguistically responsive; services are developmentally supportive and promote children's participation in their natural environments; services are comprehensive, coordinated, and team based; and services are based on the highest quality evidence that is available (American Speech-Language-Hearing Association, 2008).

Pediatric physical therapists assist in early detection of health problems and use a wide variety of modalities to treat disorders in the pediatric population. These therapists are specialized in the diagnosis, treatment, and management of infants, children, and adolescents with a variety of congenital, developmental, neuromuscular, skeletal, or acquired disorders and/or diseases. Treatments focus on improving gross and fine motor skills, balance and coordination, strength and endurance, and cognitive and sensory processing and/or integration (Stuberg & DeJong, 2007).

HOME VISITATION OPTIONS

The early intervention model for service delivery for Victor was speech therapy delivered at his school. This is just one option for early intervention. For many young children meeting eligibility under Part C, the service model is provided through home visitation. Home visitation models such as the evidence-based Nurse–Family Partnership model (Zielinski, Eckenrode, & Olds, 2009) are designed to help young women take better care of themselves and their infants. First tested in 1977, the model targeted first-time parents with nurses as in-home visitors. The program's goals were 1) to improve child health and development by reducing the amount of dysfunctional caregiving provided to infants; and 2) to improve the mothers' life courses by helping them develop a vision for their futures, plan future pregnancies, and stay in school and find employment. Long-term data from a 15-year follow-up of participating families include lower incidence of child abuse and neglect in children up to age 15 and an 83% increase in work force participation by low-income, unmarried mothers by the time their child was 4 years old (Goodman, 2006). Mary Dozier's home visiting program model, for example, provides 10 weekly in-home intervention sessions aimed at enhancing the ability of children to regulate attention, behavior, and physiology and to develop secure attachment to their primary caregiver (Dozier et al., 2006). Although findings are mixed, at best, with respect to the effectiveness of home-visiting programs in preventing child neglect, evidence is mounting that these programs can positively affect parenting practices and to a lesser extent children's cognitive development (Isaacs, 2008). It is also known, however, that fidelity to these program components is essential to achieve the same outcomes. Often, funding or training is comprehensive enough to allow the interventionists to replicate the models.

Early intervention programs typically have the capacity to deliver special education services to young children in their homes when they have more complex health or developmental needs and/or when barriers prevent them from attending a center-based program.

DISABILITY OR DELAY WITHIN A CULTURAL CONTEXT

It is important to understand that families of children of diverse cultures and languages may not identify a certain set of behaviors or symptoms as being descriptive of a delay. For instance, families often see their child's "condition" as temporary or something that will remedy itself over time. Families will vary in how much weight they will give to early intervention professionals as a result. This underscores the need for culturally normed tools for assessment and intervention as well as a good understanding of a child's culture beyond accessing translators. For instructional strategies and assessments, professionals should implement multicultural practices that respect the child and the family (Danesco, 1997).

Miami's Story:
Linking the Early Intervention Community
and the Child Welfare System

The high incidence of developmental delays identified among young children in the child welfare system should compel communities to come together to discuss linkages across the systems. In Miami, a judicially initiated Early Care and Education Workgroup was formed to initially teach judges about the early intervention entitlements available for the children they were seeing in their courtrooms needing developmental services. Once the information was available to them via a series of trainings by early intervention professionals, there was an immediate rush to refer every child birth–3 years old for an assessment by the Early Steps program as a matter of course.

The high volume of referrals overwhelmed the Early Steps intake department, necessitating a series of ongoing meetings to plan a more organized approach to the process. The level of care assessors incorporated the ASQ-3™ screening measure into their comprehensive assessment process. That allowed an initial screening to be completed to see whether the child potentially showed developmental delays in any areas. The LOC assessment then linked back to the caseworker for the child, who, depending on the results, was able to send on a Part C referral for further assessment that had accompanying documentation to support the need for an assessment. This type of procedural process can be established in any community once the early intervention and judicial/child welfare communities come together to determine where linkages can be made.

Using Genograms with Families Involved with Early Intervention Systems

The *genogram* is a visual representation of the family tree. It often includes three generations and shows how different members are biologically and legally related from one generation to the next. The common elements in a genogram include the following:

1. Relationships among family members to an "index" member
2. Demographics of family members
3. Strength of ties among members
4. Patterns of illness and causes of death among members
5. Types and dates of significant life events in family members' lives
6. Significant life stressors for family members

The genogram (or set of genograms) is a convenient way to summarize several characteristics of a family. In striving for efficient and effective communication with our colleagues, the genogram provides a useful approach for describing families. Preparation of a genogram also often offers special insight into patterns of health, illness, and health-care behavior. Genograms usually cover three generations. Typically, they involve the person being interviewed, his or her siblings, and either his or her children and parents or his or her parents and grandparents. As many generations as are considered relevant or interesting can be added. Basic data include—for each person on the genogram— name; current age or age at death (or date of birth and date of death); cause of death; occupation; marital or relationship status and history of same; and conflictual, overclose, and distant relationships. Questions such as, "What physical or emotional problems do (did) this person have?" can be asked. One can distinguish immediate from extended family on the genogram by drawing a circle around members of the immediate family. One also can add nonrelatives (besides spouse or significant other) to the drawing. One example might be a live-in caregiver for an elderly grandfather, both of whom live with the individual. The purpose of the genogram is to help organize thoughts, detect family patterns, and present complex material in a concise and understandable way.

Source: McGoldrick, Gerson, & Shellenberger, 1999.

REFERENCES

Adoption and Safe Families Act (ASFA) of 1997, PL 105-89, 111 Stat. 2115–2136.

American Speech-Language-Hearing Association. (2008). *Roles and reponsibilities of speech-language pathologists in early intervention: Position statement.* Retrieved May 27, 2010, from http://www.asha.org/docs/html/PS2008-00291.html

Casanueva, C.E., Cross, T.P., & Ringeinsen, H. (2008). Developmental needs and individualized family service plans among infants and toddlers in the child welfare system. *Child Maltreatment, 13,* 245–258.

Casanueva, C., Martin, S.L., Runyan, D.K., Barth, R.P., & Bradley, R.H. (2008). Parenting services for mothers involved with child protective services: Do they change maternal parenting and spanking behaviors with young children? *Children and Youth Services Review, 30*(8),
861–878.
The Child Abuse Prevention and Treatment Act, PL 93-247, 42 U.S.C. 5116 *et seq.* As amended
by the Keeping Children and Families Safe Act of 2003, PL 108-36.
Danesco, E.R. (1997). Parental beliefs on childhood disability: Insights on culture, child development, and intervention. *International Journal of Disability, Development, and Education,
44*(1), 41–52.
Dozier, M., & Bernard, K. (2009). The impact of attachment-based interventions on the quality
of attachment among infants and young children. In *Encyclopedia on early childhood development* (pp. 1–5). Montreal, Quebec, Canada: Centre of Excellence for Early Childhood
Development.
Dozier, M., Peloso, E., Lindhiem, O., Gordon, M.K., Manni, M., Sepulveda, S., & Ackerman, J.
(2006). Developing evidence-based interventions for foster children: An example of a ran-
domized clinical trial with infants and toddlers. *Journal of Social Issues, 62*(4), 767–785.
Education for All Handicapped Children Act of 1975, PL 94-142, 20 U.S.C. §§ 1400 *et seq.*
Goodman, A. (2006). *The story of David Olds and the nurse home visiting program: Grant results
special report.* Princeton, NJ: Robert Wood Johnson Foundation.
Individuals with Disabilities Education Act (IDEA) of 1990, PL 101-476, 20 U.S.C. §§ 1400 *et seq.*
Individuals with Disabilities Education Improvement Act (IDEA) of 2004, PL 108-446, 20
U.S.C. §§ 1400 *et seq.*
Isaacs, J.B. (2008). *Impacts of early childhood programs (Research brief #5): Nurse home visiting.*
Washington, DC: Brookings Center on Children and Families/First Focus.
Jee, S.H., Szilagyi, M., Ovenshire, C., Norton, A., Conn, A.M., Blumken, A., & Szilagyi, P.G.
(2010). Improved detection of developmental delays among young children in foster care.
Pediatrics, 125(2), 282–289.
McGoldrick, M., Gerson, R., & Shellenberger, S. (1999). *Genograms: Assessment and intervention*
(2nd ed., pp. 199–234). New York: W.W. Norton.
Opp, A. (2009). *Occupational therapy in early intervention: Helping children succeed.* The American
Occupational Therapy Association. Retrieved May 27, 2010, from http://www.aota.org/
Consumers/WhatisOT/CY/Articles/40021.aspx
Squires, J., & Bricker, D. (with Twombly, E., Nickel, R., Clifford, J., Murphy, K., Hoselton, R.,
Potter, L., Mounts, L., & Farrell, J.). (2009). *Ages & Stages Questionnaires® (ASQ-3™): A
parent-completed child monitoring system* (3rd ed.). Baltimore: Paul H. Brookes Publishing Co.
Stuberg, W., & DeJong, S. (2007). Program evaluation of physical therapy as an early interven-
tion and related service in special education. *Pediatric Physical Therapy, 19*(2), 121–127.
Zielinski, D.S., Eckenrode, J., & Olds, D. (2009). Nurse home visitation and the prevention of
child maltreatment: Impact on the timing of official reports. *Development and Psychopathology,
21*, 441–453.

5

Early Care and Education Settings that Support Child Development

At Early Head Start (EHS), Victor received quality early childhood education services interspersed with speech therapy services from the early intervention program two times per week. In addition, his teacher had a weekly consultation with an infant mental health therapist. These components created a wraparound best practice model for Victor's development. Children such as Victor often may spend 8 hours a day in child care, which speaks to the need for them to be enrolled in quality programs with staff who understand what they are going through. Sometimes the hours in child care are the most stable, stimulating, and consistent times in the lives of these children, but sometimes they may not be. We cannot automatically assume that every child care program can meet the needs of children in the child welfare system. There are many questions that need to be asked by the professionals working with a child and his or her family when trying to determine the quality of a child care program and whether the program is a good fit for the child.

Resources are available to educate professionals and families about making good choices for early childhood services. Systems of care that are built on quality, evidence-based programs include the essential need for infants and toddlers to be enrolled in responsive early childhood programs. Research tells us that the quality of early child care has long-term effects on children's development. Belsky and colleagues (2007) examined children's functioning from age $4\frac{1}{2}$ years through the end of sixth grade for a sample of 1,364 children from the National Institute of Child Health and Human Development (NICHD) child care study data. Their study results indicated that although parenting was a stronger and more consistent predictor of children's development than early child care experience, higher quality child care predicted higher vocabulary scores. For a child with language delays such as Victor, it could be anticipated that the quality child care experience at EHS coupled with speech therapy intervention and a stable home environment with his aunt combined to help move his development forward on a positive trajectory.

Victor's progress in the area of language development, once he was linked to early intervention services, illustrates the need for communities to develop mechanisms that provide early access to quality services and settings for vulnerable children to ameliorate or reduce their incidence of delays. Quality early care and education programs are a critical part of the package needed to support healthy development in the early years and, ultimately, school readiness by age 5. The federal government has recognized the need for community providers to collaborate on behalf of young children through programs such as Head Start and EHS and, in fiscal year 2002, put funds in place for an initiative focusing on infants and toddlers in the child welfare system linking them to quality programs and practices.

The Early Head Start/Child Welfare Services Initiative

The EHS/Child Welfare Services (CWS) initiative was a joint effort established in 2002 by the Office of Head Start (formerly known as the Head Start Bureau) and the Children's Bureau (CB), Administration on Children, Youth and Families (ACYF). Funding was provided through Title IV-B, subpart 2 of the Social Security Act—Promoting Safe and Stable Families (PSSF)—to enhance the capacity of the sites to serve these children. When the EHS/CWS projects were funded in the Fall of 2002, the referral of infants and toddlers by CWS to early intervention services was not a routine practice.

Specifically, the EHS/CWS initiative has done the following:

- Highlighted certain models and approaches to the provision of early childhood services that may be particularly effective in addressing the needs of children and families involved in the child welfare system

- Confirmed the promise—and critical importance—of fostering partnerships between EHS programs and CWS agencies to effectively identify and serve families currently in the child welfare system or at future risk of maltreatment or out-of-home placement

- Demonstrated the potential of collaborations with other community social and health service organizations to strengthen the nexus of supports and services available to special target populations (e.g., caregivers with mental health or substance use disorders)

- Revealed ongoing challenges to serving CWS-involved families and to building effective interorganizational partnerships that must be addressed if similar early childhood initiatives are to achieve their full potential to promote the safety and well-being of infants and toddlers

(James Bell Associates, 2009)

Victor and Pam received their clinical services as part of the EHS/CWS initiative and Victor was enrolled in his EHS program through the same initiative. The initiative helped begin to build overall community capacity for quality early care and education access with enhanced services. In most communities, however, there are insufficient slots for the number of children who could benefit from an EHS experience, resulting in children having to wait for services until they are older or to attend inferior child care programs.

Professionals working in communities with quality programs have come to understand that simply removing maltreated young children from their adverse environments and placing them in a good foster home is insufficient intervention. This approach fails to recognize the young child's need for developmentally appropriate environments outside the home to support the child's progress over the early years. In turn, collaborative early care and education programs can provide services to the child and his or her parent or guardian that can help the parent or guardian better understand the child's capabilities and accommodate the child's needs. Understanding what are developmentally appropriate expectations for an infant or toddler can contribute to making the child less difficult to manage, prevent further maltreatment, and support healthy child growth and development and school readiness. Early care and education settings with high degrees of parent participation can develop a safety net for the young child who is building trusting relationships.

The EHS/CWS initiative illustrated that communities can build capacity aimed at the following:

1. Improving the quality, effectiveness, provision, and availability of therapeutic services to children in the child welfare system who experience traumatic events through a seamless continuum of referral, assessments, and treatment managed by the experienced staff of the community stakeholder body

2. Engaging a dedicated and expert body of professionals, community providers, and consumers who have the ability to participate in building a network of centers, programs, and constituencies to improve services to children in the target

population who have experienced traumatic events; this body of knowledge will have applicability to additional populations across sites to promote cost-effective best practices

3. Providing community training regarding the impact on individuals, families, and communities of child traumatic stress and of effective therapeutic interventions to prevent the occurrence of serious negative consequences of childhood trauma

4. Increasing the community's ability to expand services for traumatized children in the target age range who currently go underserved due to lack of funding for early intervention and treatment through existing sources; such collaborations of community mental health providers and agencies providing early intervention integrating the treatment model and intervention strategies can leverage community resources (James Bell Associates, 2009)

Miami's Story:
The Child Welfare Partnership with EHS

The federal EHS/CWS initiative offered an opportunity for CWS-involved infants and toddlers from 24 communities across the nation to receive an array of services that they typically would not receive through CWS, including health and developmental screenings through early intervention service providers. The overall purpose of the EHS/CWS initiative was to enhance and expand the service network for CWS-involved children and families and to provide more intensive supplemental services in local communities that could benefit child welfare populations. The initiative was built on the assumption that intensive collaboration and coordination between EHS programs and local CWS agencies would provide some of the most vulnerable children and families with access to child development, parenting, health, and family support services available through EHS. These enhanced services with providers coming together and planning a seamless referral process for toddlers to attend the special EHS took time to build and systematize. Each community could choose the integrated service model that was practical for their community.

In Miami-Dade County, the EHS/CWS initiative was a collaborative partnership established between Community Action Agency (the conduit agency that encompasses EHS), the Juvenile Court, the University of Miami's Linda Ray Intervention Center, and the local community-based CWS providers. The EHS/CWS funding allowed 24 target children in the child welfare system identified in court as needing specialized mental health services to attend EHS and concurrently linked them and their primary caregivers to a therapist trained in the Child–Parent Psychotherapy treatment model (discussed in Chapter 3) from the University of Miami's Linda Ray Center. These families completed an average of 25 dyadic therapy sessions.

Child welfare system care management and permanency goals were tracked along with the parents' and children's therapeutic goals. Outcomes of the EHS/CWS overall project underscore the acquisition of valuable new knowledge that is relevant to the service and policy goals of the Children's Bureau, the Office of Head Start, and EHS programs in general as well as to the broader fields of early childhood education and child welfare (James Bell Associates, 2009).

A key component of the EHS/CWS initiative in Miami was the development of processes and procedures that linked systems and practitioners. Ongoing communication among the caregivers who worked with the child and parents, the EHS educational and social work staff, the Linda Ray Center infant mental health therapists and enrollment specialists, and the child welfare case manager demonstrated that multidisciplinary partners can work together on an ongoing basis to integrate services for families. Information was exchanged during quarterly team reviews and formal or informal meetings. Each provider was able to give feedback on the child's progress at EHS as well as the progress being made to improve the infant–parent relationship, with all working toward the related goals of permanency and well-being for the child. In addition to the social work care management component at EHS, the Linda Ray Intervention Center clinicians and support staff communicated both informally and through formalized meetings with relatives, parents, and the providers regarding progress. They were able to do this effectively as a result of having had opportunities for cross training on the needs of children who have been victims of abuse and/or neglect, joint planning, joint program development, improved coordination of program records, and communications with community partners and administrators of all the agencies that were assisting the parent–child dyad (Cohen, DeSantis, & Katz, 2004). Finally, and critically, the information from the Early Head Start program was related to the juvenile court judge via a formal court reporting document and/or a court appearance by either the IMH therapist, the EHS teacher, or both. (See Appendix B for a Sample Early Head Start Court Report.)

QUALITY CHILD CARE ENVIRONMENTS

Given economic realities in recent years, many communities may not have access to specialized service dollars for initiatives such as the EHS/CWS project. This, however, does not mean that linkages between the child welfare system and early intervention services cannot be made. EHS, Head Start, and community providers of early care and education programs also can come together and network for quality services for the infants and toddlers in the system of care.

One practical approach to creating quality early care and education services is to focus on increasing the use of high quality child care centers serving infants and toddlers in the child welfare system. Communities can begin by asking the following:

- Which centers serve this population of children and are these programs licensed?

- Are they accredited? If so, by what accreditation organization?

- Have the caregivers at these child care programs received any training about maltreated infants and toddlers?

- Are the child care programs communicating with the other service providers working with the family?

- What are the standards expected that define quality child care for all children and for children in the child welfare system specifically?

The National Association for the Education of Young Children (NAEYC) is the largest, most prominent body addressing the area of early childhood education quality and developmentally appropriate practices. NAEYC adopted a position statement in 1993 addressing violence in the lives of children that has served as the mainstay for advocacy efforts around quality and reform for early childhood programs serving young children who have been victims of or who have been exposed to violence. NAEYC set out two major goals in this position paper: 1) to decrease the extent of violence in all forms in children's lives by advocating for public policies and actions at the national level and 2) to enhance the ability of educators to help children cope with violence, promote children's resilience, and assist families by improving professional practice in early childhood programs.

These messages resonate with professionals making child care placement decisions for young children in the child welfare system. Of critical importance when looking at quality of child care is a trusting relationship with the preschool or primary school teacher. Most teachers of young children, however, have not been trained to help children cope with the effects of violence or maltreatment. It is critical, therefore, that early childhood teachers receive training on the developmental consequences of stress and trauma, protective factors, making themselves emotionally available to the children in need, and understanding how they can support therapeutic strategies provided by clinicians outside of the classroom. Use of ongoing consultation services to support the teacher's mental health responses when children enrolled in their classrooms are victims of violence and as a mechanism to provide daily strategies to support the child victims is becoming an increasingly important component of early childhood programs (NAEYC, 1997).

Victor was particularly fortunate to be attending an EHS program in his community. Federal regulations for Head Start and EHS outline specific performance standards that must be met related to children's mental health issues and developmentally appropriate practices and that recognize that all children, including children such as Victor, experience stress and trauma in their lives and need informed teachers and educational programs that meet their needs.

Head Start Performance Standards for Child Mental Health

Head Start Performance Standards for Child Mental Health include supporting the integration of working collaboratively with parents for issues related to parent education by

- Soliciting parental information, observations, and concerns about their child's mental health

- Sharing and discussing staff observations of their child and future potential issues regarding their child's behavior and development, including separation and attachment issues

- Identifying and determining with parents appropriate responses to their child's behaviors

- Discussing how best to strengthen nurturing supportive environments and relationships in the home and at the program

- Helping parents better understand mental health issues

- Supporting parents' participation in any needed mental health interventions

- Grantees and delegate agencies must secure mental health services frequently enough to allow for timely and effective identification of intervention responses to family and staff concerns about a child's mental health.

(Performance Standard 1304.24[a][2]).

- Head Start and EHS must design and implement program practices that are
  - Responsive to the identified behavioral and mental health concerns of an individual, child, or group of children
  - Assist with providing special help for children with atypical behavior or development
  - Use other community mental health resources, as needed.

(Administration on Children, Youth, and Families, Performance Standard 1304.24[a][3][i–iv])

In all communities, Head Start and EHS must—at a minimum—be licensed but also must adhere to standards of adult–child ratio according to the age of the children, safety, teacher credentials, professional development mandates, and safe environment both inside the classrooms and in outdoor play areas. Child care centers also can go beyond minimal licensing standards to become accredited by accreditation bodies such as NAEYC. However, there still exist child care settings that are not regulated or licensed due to religious affiliation exemptions or kin providing child care to family members. Research tells us that without standards of care, we can do children a disservice and even harm them. The largest longitudinal national study of child care quality is the National Institute of Child Health and Human Development study of Early Child Care and Youth Development initiated in 1989. Multiple researchers worked cooperatively to design the study and, in 1991, enrolled a diverse sample of children and families at ten locations across the U.S.

In one study sample, children (ns = 595–856, depending on the assessment) were recruited at birth and assessed at 15, 24 and 36 months of age. Multiple features of the child care experience were modestly to moderately predictive. Analyses that adjusted for maternal vocabulary score, family income, child gender, observed quality of home environment, and observed maternal cognitive stimulation indicated that the overall quality of child care and language stimulation, in particular, was consistently but modestly related to the child's cognitive language outcomes at 15, 24, and 36 months of age (NICHD, 2000).

Certainly, child care quality alone is not the single determinant of child outcomes. The NICHD study also has addressed the impact of the relationship between early infant–mother attachment and children's social competence and behavior problems in preschool. In another study sample examined from the NICHD data, the relationship between early infant–mother attachment and children's social competence and behavior problems during the preschool and early school-age period were examined in more than 1,000 children under conditions of *decreasing, stable,* and *increasing* maternal parenting quality. Infants' Strange Situation attachment classifications (categories of attachment included *secure, insecure, disorganized*) predicted mothers' reports of children's social competence and teachers' reports of externalizing and internalizing behaviors from preschool age through first grade. These relations appeared to be mediated by parenting quality; the main effects of attachment classification disappeared when effects of parenting quality were controlled (NICHD, 2006).

VIEW FROM THE BENCH
Why Quality Early Care and Education
Is Critical for Young Children in the Child Welfare System

In an effort to obtain a firsthand view of the quality of early care and education being provided to very young children in dependency court, I visited a number of child care centers and was horrified by what I observed. One of the teachers was working on removing holiday decorations in her classroom while eight to ten toddlers were sitting on the floor. The 2- and 3-year-old children were sitting in a circle, silent. When they spoke she told them to be quiet. If they moved, she yelled at them. One little girl started to cry after being yelled at and the teacher yanked her off of the floor by her arm and carried her by her arm, in the air, to the "time out" seat where she was deposited. The children were ignored by the teacher except for the occasional "no" or "stop that." The children remained in their place on the floor, afraid to move or speak while she worked, alone, on adding paper to the bulletin board and got herself something to drink as they watched. After observing this class for several minutes, I visited the infant room, where an infant was still strapped in his car seat on the floor when I arrived close to 9:30 a.m. I immediately reported this center to the Department of Children and Families as I left, disheartened. I had been told about the conditions in some of our child care centers by guardians ad litem who visited their children there. It was worse than I imagined. This center was located in one of Miami's most impoverished neighborhoods where the children really need a few hours of caring, stimulation, and nurturing during their day. Why do we as a society allow the children who are most in need to be treated with such cruelty, indignity, and indifference?

Interactions also were observed. For example, when parenting quality improved over time, teachers rated children with insecure infant–mother attachments lower on externalizing (acting out) behaviors; when parenting quality decreased, teachers rated insecure children higher on externalizing behaviors. In contrast, children classified as securely attached in infancy did not appear to be affected by declining or improving parenting quality (NICHD, 2006). For Victor, child care quality was a critical component as a stabilizing influence during the period when he and his mother, Pam, worked toward improving the quality of their relationship. No doubt the quality of his EHS program, supplemented by the early intervention services, contributed to Victor's developmental progress and a reduction in acting-out behaviors as reported by his teacher over time. (See Appendix E for a sample Our Kids of Miami-Dade and Monroe, Inc. Protocol for Child Care Placement.)

There are resources available to professionals who will be involved in choosing a child care placement for a child to help sort out the good from the bad child care centers. Early Learning Coalitions, such as the one in Miami-Dade and Monroe Counties in Florida, for example, have developed a checklist for families and other professionals to utilize when observing a child care center. This checklist can be helpful in determining where to place a young child for child care (Early Learning Coalition, Miami-Dade County, Florida, 2009).

Checklist for Selecting a Quality Child Care Program

Look and listen. You can tell a great deal by observing and listening to what is going on in the classroom or home. Do the children seem happy and are they enjoying activities? Do the teachers seem to be loving, nurturing, and responsive to all children in their care? Are problems handled promptly and appropriately? Do the teachers seem like people you can trust with the health, happiness, and well-being of your child? Is this a place where you would feel good about your child spending many hours each day?

Ask questions. If you have any questions or concerns, write them down as they occur to you. Ask for an opportunity to have your questions answered or your concerns addressed.

Pay attention to your instincts. You know your child best. Pay attention to any feelings of uneasiness you may have experienced during site visits or interviews. Keep in mind the following questions:

- Could you picture your child in this setting?
- Were the toys and activities you observed the kinds your child would enjoy?
- If your child accompanied you on your visit, what was his reaction?

Keep in mind that children respond in their own unique ways to new situations. Also, do not rule out other factors that could influence your child's reaction (e.g., being hungry, being tired, having a natural fear of new people or places). Trust your instincts and your ability to make wise decisions for your child.

When cost is a factor, carefully weigh the pros and cons of each teacher and facility that you visited. Decide which facility satisfies the greatest number of your priorities at a rate that you can afford. Keep in mind that the highest cost does not always guarantee the best teacher and facility. Likewise, the least expensive rates do not necessarily mean poor teachers and facilities.

Do your best to make a good choice. Now that you have done your homework and some careful thinking, you are ready to make your choice. Remember, selecting and placing your child in an early learning program is just the beginning. You will want to talk to your new teacher often and make occasional visits to ensure that your child is safe and happy and that your decision was the right one.

(NAEYC, 1997)

Early care and education programs for infants and toddlers need to be monitored with an effective system of public regulation. Core qualities should include the following: 1) a holistic approach to addressing the needs of children and families that stresses collaborative planning and service integration across traditional boundaries of child care, education, health, employment, and social services; 2) systems that recognize and promote quality; 3) an effective system of professional development that provides meaningful opportunities for career advancement to ensure a stable, well-qualified work force; 4) equitable financing that ensures access for all children and families to high-quality services; and 5) active involvement of all stakeholders—providers, practitioners, parents, and community leaders from both public and private sectors—in all aspects of program planning and delivery (NAEYC, 1997).

Avoiding Cultural Missteps When Working in Early Childhood Environments

Young children in child care today reflect their culturally and linguistically diverse communities. Early childhood professionals must be cognizant of the uniqueness of the children and their different backgrounds and pay special attention to being responsive, nonjudgmental, and inclusive in both the daily activities at school and in their interactions with the families. Celebrations, literacy activities, and class discussions focused on learning about the children's varied cultures should take place throughout the school year rather than just during a single month designated for one group or another. Books should reflect the stories that will have meaning for all children, and children should see their own faces and families as they turn the pages.

Emerging literacy activities, such as labeling classroom items with word names, should have the words in the languages of all the children. Art projects should incorporate materials familiar to the children's cultural environments. Cultural missteps do happen, however, even with the best of intentions. But when teachers are open to inquiry about the cultures of their students, these can be part of their professional learning experience.

One example of such a misstep occurred in a Miami early childhood classroom. Children were happily stringing bracelets of colored macaroni as an art activity when a parent volunteering in the classroom voiced her dismay. She explained to the teacher that in her culture, using food for art play was offensive, given that so many people she knew did not have enough food for their children. The teacher had never thought of this and apologized to the parent for being unknowingly insensitive.

REFERENCES

Belsky, J., Vandell, D., Burchinal, M., Clarke-Stewart, K.A., McCartney, K., Owen, M., et al. (2007). Are there long-term effects of early child care? *Child Development, 78,* 681–701.

Cohen, E., DeSantis, J., & Katz, L. (2004, July). *Early intervention with children in substance abusing families in the child welfare system.* Workshop presented at the national conference on substance abuse, child well-being, and the dependency court, Baltimore.

Early Learning Coalition, Miami-Dade County, Florida. (2009). *Child care checklist.* Retrieved May 27, 2010, from http://www.elcmdm.org/Parents/childcare/Checklist.pdf

James Bell Associates. (2009). *Early Head Start-Child Welfare Services Initiative—Final synthesis reports: volumes I and II.* Submitted to the Children's Bureau, Administration of Children, Youth and Families. Arlington, VA: Author.

National Association for the Education of Young Children. (1997). *Licensing and public regulation of early childhood programs: Position statement.* Retrieved May 27, 2010, from http://www.naeyc.org/files/naeyc/file/positions/PSLIC98.PDF

NICHD Early Child Care Research Network. (2000). The relation of child care to cognitive and language development. *Child Development, 71*(4), 960–980.

NICHD Early Child Care Research Network. (2006). Infant–mother attachment classification: Risk and protection in relation to changing maternal caregiving quality. *Developmental Psychology, 42*(1), 38–58.

6

Developing a Coordinated System of Care

It was 4:30 in the afternoon when the child welfare agency transporter arrived at the parenting provider agency with Pam's son Victor, who was 22 months old. The toddler's anxious
cries could be heard echoing down the hall as he was carried to the clinic room for his
weekly appointment for supervised Child–Parent Psychotherapy with the infant mental health
specialist and his mother, Pam. Victor was distressed, sweaty, and frantically looking around,
his eyes searching furtively for someone familiar in an unfamiliar setting. The transporter
remarked casually that he had been crying like that since 2:00 p.m. when he had picked the
child up from his foster care home. And, he added, for the last 2 hours the infant had been
in the car, traveling with him to other appointments, taking some other older children to and
from their scheduled dental appointments. Although the transporter was carrying Victor's dia-
per bag, which had been sent by the foster parent with a bottle, pacifier, and some toddler
snacks for the trip, he never looked in the bag. Shortly afterward, Pam arrived, and she
found her son crying inconsolably, flushed and sweating, unable to make eye contact or be
comforted. Their therapy session was scheduled to last for 1 hour and Victor was inconsolable the entire time.

Every day, in both small and large ways, there are examples of system disconnects
that negatively affect young children in foster care. Coordinating something that
seems simple—transportation—is often a challenge for providers, putting undue additional stress on a young child. The key is putting the pieces together of a coordinated
system of care for these children that supports rather than harms them. Successfully
developing agency collaborations, coordinating logistics, and creating memoranda of
agreement that dictate policies and procedures are part of the necessary activities to
support cross-system functionality. Examining these components of the system of care
to be sure there are no gaps can also link the labor-intensive work of the frontline professionals. These interagency connections can reduce duplication of services and provide programs that are part of an effective continuum for families. A good system can
create a seamless pathway for a family to move through their case process.

Day after day, the nitty-gritty details related to logistics, scheduling, and program limitations can make or break the system, dishearten families, and even do
emotional harm to the children along the way. Professionals who are aware of the
anticipated challenges of providing family-centered practice and who have a plan to
prevent the disconnects will be the most effective service partners and have the greatest chance of helping their families succeed.

The stress experienced by Victor when he was transported for a supervised treatment session not only made Victor anxious but also made the therapeutic session
unproductive. Pam was frustrated by her own inability to soothe Victor after his
ordeal and internalized his mood and distress as being her fault. It was, however, a
system integration failure that caused Victor's stress and made the transportation
experience traumatic for him.

Child welfare professionals, community providers, and clinicians working in the
trenches of the child welfare system everyday often ask, "Are we doing right by the
children to bring them into this system at all?" "Does the system process harm them
even more?" "Wouldn't they sometimes just be better off if they were left in their
homes?" A community may develop evidence-based programs and practices and
have the best intentions; however, they are not effective if no one gains access to them
and if there are barriers as simple as transportation keeping families from attending.
Likewise, these very programs will not fully meet the needs of children and parents
if they are unable to effectively interface across agencies, if they compete for clients
because of monetary needs rather than because they are the best program for the

family. Quality programs and practices are of no use if parents are inappropriately referred for services that they do not need or from which they cannot benefit.

Unfortunately, in many child welfare systems, service provision is fragmented, care management is really *crisis* management, and the dependency judges find themselves having to take on the role of case coordinator in addition to being the judicial decision maker. Thoughtful, focused planning and strategizing about how to best support the developmental, social, and emotional needs of the child may be part of the courtroom discussion; however, it often may take second place to the many logistical and practical challenges of ensuring basic safety, complying with legal requirements, and dealing with constant emergencies for the families. It is well known that an integrated, coordinated system of care is not only better for children and their parents but also promotes more effective outcomes and eases the burdens on clinicians, community service providers, and case managers. The ultimate goal is to create and implement a system that is less traumatic and more healing. It is the responsibility of all involved in the system to make this happen. Coordinating the system of care in juvenile and family court provides the best opportunity to succeed in breaking intergenerational cycles of abuse and neglect affecting maltreated infants and young children (Lederman & Osofsky, 2004, 2008; Lederman, Osofsky, & Katz, 2001; Osofsky et al., 2007).

Pam and Victor's story illustrates the urgent need for the child welfare system and the court to not only focus on the emotional health and relationship needs of infants and toddlers everyday but to work to build strong and seamless linkages between the court and community providers. This can reduce children's stress rather than increase the young child's traumatic experiences. Getting the ball rolling is the hardest part.

Providers often recognize the need for improved service integration; but often they do not know how to change their familiar patterns, and old habits continue. For systems change to occur, it is important for all systems to understand that providing support and continuity for the child is crucial. With this focus in mind, determinations have to be made initially about the contextual framework that will result in a particular child and family's needs being met. All systems need to understand the current policies and research from the field that support both efficient progress of the case plan and the well-being of the child at the same time. Institutionalization of evidence-based programs and practices is crucial at the community level as is a collective understanding of the pathways that work for families to gain access to programs that support their young children during their ordeals.

THE NEED FOR JUDICIAL LEADERSHIP

Judicial leadership is an essential aspect of the systems-change process in the child welfare arena. When a judge invites system and community stakeholders to the table, they come. Judges are able to use their positional power and authority to create legitimacy around the process and to ensure that things get done. Judges who are willing to literally come down from the bench and take a proactive leadership role can be visionaries. They have a vision of what the final outcome should be and can act as stewards or keepers of this vision. As such, they are essential for steering the course of the change process and for bringing aboard other essential players (Dobbin, Gatowski, & Maxwell, 2004).

Once a revised system of care, or part of the system of care, is developed, the judge serves as the overseer of the implementation process, holding community and child welfare systems stakeholders accountable for working together and continually pushing the vision forward. A judicial leader also will help his or her colleagues recognize the value of "doing business differently." An informed and educated judge who is knowledgeable about the developmental needs of young children, who understands the impact of family violence on young children, and who sees the value of evidence-based programs and best practices can get his or her colleagues excited and prepared for a new way of doing business.

Finally, for an integrated, coordinated system of care to function, juvenile dependency judges need to make timely and concise judicial decisions that will ensure infants and their parents are referred to evidence-based programs with integrated, nonduplicative, well-informed care management support. Judicial expectations of effective family engagement, with a focus on the young child's emotional well-being and developmental support, can create the will for enhanced training and practice by child welfare professionals, community service providers, and clinicians. An open and welcoming courtroom environment and an educated, engaged judge is an essential component of any responsive system of care for infants and parents in the child welfare system. Such a comprehensive model that includes consultation to develop systems change, training for the clinical and parenting components, and ongoing consultation to ensure quality and fidelity to the models also can work toward building sustainability of the systems change.

Judges must be brought into the system planning process early and in a leadership role to maximize their effect. This can be easier said than done. Although some jurisdictions are blessed with judges who are passionate about evidence-based practice and system integration and about traumatized infants and their parents, there are many more judges who believe that being a change agent is not in their job description. Encouraging judges to take up the mantle of systems change may require judge-to-judge mentoring and exposure to social science research.[1]

VIEW FROM THE BENCH
Approaching a Judge to Discuss Systems Change

Judges are human beings, despite the robes and the power they have as constitutional officers. They may seem unapproachable, but they are not. They are bound by codes of ethics and professional responsibility that restrict their actions in many ways, but they are infused with the responsibility to promote the administration of justice.

If you have a choice, look for a judge who is active in the community: That is the sign of a jurist who sees a more expansive role for the judiciary. Approach the judge with a letter setting forth your credentials and your goals. Remember that judges receive letters every day from dissatisfied litigants, from providers seeking business, and from people asking the judge for something. Make your letter different.

Follow up with a telephone call to the judge's assistant and make an appointment to meet with the judge. Remember, judges cannot speak privately to anyone involved in any case before them. "Ex parte" communications are clearly unethical, and the judge can be disciplined for speaking to a party involved in a case outside of the courtroom when all parties are not present. This explains why judges generally may be reluctant to speak on the telephone with someone they do not know.

If all else fails, invite the judge to an event for your organization or professional association. Recognize the judge for his or her service to the community and engage the judge in your vision for how you can work together to promote the administration of justice.

---

[1]Chapter 7 delves more fully into the role of the courts and judges in improving outcomes for very young children.

CONVENING THE COLLABORATION AND CREATING CONSENSUS FOR CHANGE

Collaboration is more than just bringing stakeholders to the table—collaboration is more than "cooperation." Collaboration involves giving collaborators a meaningful role, a strong voice and a real opportunity to make a contribution. Meaningful collaboration emerges over time and multiple interactions through which trust and mutual respect develop among members. (Dobbin et al., 2004, pp. 51–52)

Once a judge has been identified and contacted, the dialogue for change can begin. The judge should convene the core group of key people to assist with leading the change effort. This core team must then determine who to bring into the collaborative process. Determining who should be invited to participate in the collaboration and keeping members engaged in the process, even during challenging points, are essential tasks.

Stakeholders—those who have an interest in the overall well-being, safety, and permanency of children who have been maltreated—from across the child welfare system and community should be invited to participate. Stakeholders should be drawn from all levels and be reflective of the system: administration, the frontline, funders, community providers, and clinicians. This will allow for the greatest chance for developing a truly shared vision and systemwide reform (Dobbin et al., 2004). Community stakeholders, decision makers, and funders must be directly involved in all phases of planning, implementing, and assessing the effectiveness of the new system of care. This group must include not only the judge in the leadership role but also other representatives of the court; representatives from the child welfare system (e.g., protective investigations, foster care agencies, clinical providers); community mental health service providers; substance abuse treatment service providers; the school district; early intervention providers; health care providers; lay and legal child advocates; parents; child welfare legal services providers such as Head Start and Early Head Start (EHS); and early learning coalitions of child care providers, substance abuse providers, domestic violence specialists, and mental health and primary care providers.

The process of a systems change that supports infants and toddlers is initiated by introducing and educating the community stakeholder group to the social and emotional needs of infants and toddlers. Thus, the science of early child development becomes a driving force in the existing system and necessitates each partner reviewing and revising current practices. Training needs to be offered to help practitioners and community partners understand what young children need, how abuse and neglect has affected them, and what services can remedy and heal. The initial meetings of the collaborative should focus on the purpose of the collaborative, the goals it is trying to achieve, and how accomplishing those goals will move the community closer to the vision for an integrated system of care for young children and their parents. Logistical issues must be discussed and agreements must be reached. These include determining the structure of the collaborative (e.g., will there be committees or will the work be done by the group as a whole?); the frequency of meetings; how decisions will be made; information-sharing processes, and how the work of the collaborative will be accomplished (Dobbin et al., 2004). The collaborative should commit to a multidisciplinary approach in which government and nonprofit agencies are seen as partners, not adversaries, who share the common goal of improving the system and its outcomes.

Once these issues are decided, the substantive work of the group can commence. The first item of business should be to get everyone in the collaborative focused on the same vision. The judge and other key partners should share their vision about the ultimate system of care for very young children in the child welfare system. This can be accomplished through a training initiative focusing on young children's needs. In one community, a "Stop Court and Train" Day was developed, whereby the courts were closed and all professionals working in the system were mandated to come for a day of training and discussion. Training focused on realistic goals for responding to the needs of very young children, including the following:

- All infants and toddlers in the appropriate age range are screened for developmental delays, referrals for Part C evaluations are made when necessary, and appropriate early interventions (e.g.. speech therapy, occupational therapy, physical therapy) are put into place.

- Parents of very young children who are not bonded to their children or infants and toddlers who are exhibiting signs of depression and anxiety are offered early childhood relationship assessments and evidence-based, relationship-focused interventions such as CPP when needed.

- Parents of very young children have access to and participate in evidence-based, culturally and linguistically appropriate parenting programs that are geared toward parents with infants and toddlers. The emphasis of these programs is on improving empathy and awareness of their infant or toddler's physical, emotional, and social needs and understanding developmental milestones.

- Infants and toddlers are enrolled in quality early care and education environments such as EHS and accredited child care centers.

- Child welfare case managers, providers of the previously discussed services and interventions, and parent and child advocates are communicating regularly with each other and with the court through structured reporting tools.

- Each young child has a medical home with a practitioner who is specifically trained to work with very young children in the child welfare system and is aware of this population's unique needs.

- Transportation is not provided by a transportation "worker" but rather by one of the child's caregivers who is expected to, and given support to, accomplish this.

- Quality training and skills development (with pre- and postmeasures) specific to the needs of infants, toddlers, and their parents are available to and mandated for all child welfare case managers, foster parents, and relative caregivers, in varying degrees.

- The supportive theories of coparenting between biological families and foster parents are encouraged and protocols are developed for implementation.

MAPPING THE CURRENT SYSTEM OF CARE

After a training plan has been developed, the next step is to map the current system of care—to get an accurate and comprehensive picture of how services, interventions, and coordination currently operate and to identify the gaps in services or disconnects in gaining access to services among the multiple layers of stakeholders and providers. It is very helpful to ask all stakeholders to share verbally and in writing (using a brief questionnaire) about the services their agency provides for very young children and their parents involved with the child welfare system. One individual needs to be responsible for tracking the information shared and developing a grid of all information reported; and a group of people should be responsible for reviewing the grid and identifying overlays, duplication of services, the various points of entry into the service (how and from whom referrals and linkages are made), what the actual services are, the times and locations the services are provided, how the services are funded, what the various funding streams are and where they may overlap, whether programs are filled to capacity, and whether there are waiting lists. In all communities, a person with experience in system coordination work should be identified and asked to lead the process while working closely with the judge.

Information to be Gathered When Mapping the Current System of Care

Ask each agency in the community to compile the following information in order to create a systems map:

- A list of the program services at the agency; for each program, list whether the program is evidence based, the goals of the services, who the program is appropriate for (e.g., ages, language delivered), the length of program, and the total dosage of intervention and schedules

- A list of the facilitators, therapists, teachers, and so forth who provide the services, as well as their credentials

- Cost information if the services are not free to families; include information about sliding scales

- Sample memoranda of understanding or agreement that currently exists between agencies (See Appendix C for a sample Memorandum of Understanding for Cross-Agency Collaboration.)

- The protocols used to measure client progress over time that will provide accountability to the court

This process of compiling information will enable the community and the judge to identify gaps in services focusing on children younger than age 5, identify duplicated services, and begin discussing what parts of the system need to be built. (Miami Safe Start Initiative, 2005–2009; www.miamisafestartinitiative.org)

After gaining a full view of the existing system of services, the collaborative should examine more specific aspects of the selected programs and evidence-based practices or lack thereof. The group should review the length and frequency of the various programs, the times of day the sessions are given, where the programs are located in the community, and what transportation barriers can be expected for participants.

PLANNING THE NEW SYSTEM OF CARE

Once the mapping process is complete, the collaborative needs to begin planning the next steps that are consistent with the overall vision. Thoughtful and detailed planning is essential before launching an integrated process. That said, unanticipated issues will arise and the group need not plan for every possible contingency or extenuating circumstance. The goal is to create a functional, operational, and integrated system of care that is flexible while adhering to a set of agreed-upon standards and practices.

The planning stage is when the "nuts and bolts" will be hammered out. The collaborative should study the map of the current systems, discuss where gaps in services or processes exist, and identify programmatic and systemic strengths on which they can capitalize. These systems may include early intervention (as the majority of these children will experience some developmental delays as a result of neglect), child welfare (the system that oversees their placement, care, and care management), mental health professionals (who evaluate, intervene and provide therapeutic services for the infant, the parent, and the infant–parent dyad), early childhood educators (who oversee and provide quality child care to provide needed stimulation and reciprocal care), and parenting facilitators (who work with the parents and the infant–parent dyad to educate them on ways to optimize the child's development and provide support for the relationship). Discussion, planning, and decision making can center around the following questions:

- How will access to developmental assessments under Part C of IDEA be handled? Is the current process working for infants and toddlers in the child welfare system? Should a screening component (e.g., the Ages & Stages Questionnaires®, Third Edition [ASQ-3™]; Squires & Bricker, 2009) be put into place to help determine which children should be referred for full Part C evaluations? How will communication between the Part C evaluator and the child welfare system stakeholders be handled?

- When developmental delays are identified, who is responsible for ensuring that early intervention services are put into place? How can noncustodial parents, custodial parents, relative caregivers, and foster parents be brought into the early intervention plan for the child? Who will liaison between the early intervention providers and the child welfare professionals, other service providers, and the judge?

- How should referrals to the various community-based parenting programs be made? Should referrals be centralized through one agency that assigns the family to a particular service provider? How will reports be provided to the court and the parties and professionals in the case? Does the community want to monitor the quality of the programs, and, if so, how?

- Would it work best to expand the capacity of a number of providers to provide multiple services (e.g., early intervention, early care and education, infant mental health, parenting, health care) based on geographic location of the child? Is the community better suited to a system that has specialized service providers offering one or two of these services? Would a mix of both systems best meet the needs of the community?

- How will schedules and/or services need to be adapted to ensure that the young child will be at his or her best during the scheduled therapy sessions, interactive parenting course, or visitations? Will agencies need to focus on hiring and training additional staff or reallocate existing resources?

- How will transportation be coordinated and facilitated?

- How can current funding be maximized and leveraged to build or expand system components that are not sufficient to meet the needs of the population in care?

- What entity or agency will be responsible for ensuring coordinated case planning and service planning for very young children and their parents? Will regular case planning and permanency planning "staffings" be held to consistently revisit the case plan goal and family engagement efforts? How will communication among and within agencies be handled, and in what manner will information be conveyed to the judge?

- How have adult substance abuse, mental health, and domestic violence providers been engaged and educated about the needs of very young children and their parents? Have specialized services for very young children been developed within residential programs, and how will these programs coordinate with the other clinical and community services being provided to the child and parents?

- How is the pediatric community for primary health care and dental care being linked with the system of care for very young children?

- How will parental and sibling visitation be provided to infants and toddlers in a meaningful and compassionate way that prioritizes the importance of primary relationships for very young children as well as their need for consistent and stable schedules?

On a practical level, it is often the case, as discussed in the mapping process, that memoranda of understanding or agreement will be needed if business practices will change with this new, multidisciplinary, cross-agency collaborative approach. Such agreements should specify the components of the system that will interconnect in more efficient ways, how this will be done, who is responsible for what, and how a system of checks and balances or quality assurance will be established and operated. Protocols for program delivery—both within the agency and externally across agencies—will need to be reexamined. Mechanisms for exchanging confidential information must be determined. This knowledge needs to be available to all who interface and make decisions related to children and families in court, including judges, lawyers, child welfare, court appointed special advocates, and others involved in the child's case. Education and training is needed at each level within this system of care on the developmental needs of infants and toddlers, including the intricacies of early brain development—the effects of trauma, the importance of the attachment relationship, and the overall impact of trauma on the developing young child and family.

The collaborative will need to consider eligibility criteria for each component and how the referral process may need to be changed for young children receiving services. During this planning phase, it will be helpful to create decision-making trees at the provider level so the entire team is knowledgeable about the rule-in and rule-out criteria for services. Reporting standards meeting the needs of the court also can be developed in collaboration with the program stakeholders. Everyone should be inquiring about the developmental health of the child at each juncture and keep in mind that the concept of "one size fitting all" does not work with vulnerable populations of young children.

IMPLEMENTING THE NEW SYSTEM OF CARE

Changing systems takes an enormous amount of energy, focus, and work. There must be a collective understanding of *why* the work of systems building and systems change is important, with a buy-in from the community and the court. Community partners may be frustrated with the endless administrative and coordination details needed to start on a new path. Once established, there will be new challenges related to monitoring the quality of services, fidelity to systems integration protocols, and how best to manage nonperforming partners in the collaborative.

Rolling out a new and improved system of care should be done in small, measurable increments. Timelines for implementing new processes, programs, and protocols should be agreed on and progress should be revisited regularly—even weekly if necessary. Each component put in place should set the stage for a successful implementation of the next component. For example, when setting up a system for ensuring that all infants who enter care receive a screening using a tool such as the ASQ-3 (Squires & Bricker, 2009), this process could start as a pilot in one child welfare agency unit. The glitches in the referral process should be measured and ironed out, retested again with the same group, tweaked, and then expanded into other divisions or units. Internally, programs will likely need to follow the same path, initially taking a limited number of referrals to test out the referral, service, reporting, and feedback process. Change takes time, and changing for the better requires constant examination and reformulation to ensure that the system is running smoothly.

During the challenging time of implementation, it is crucial for the multidisciplinary collaborative to stay focused on the fact that an integrated system of care has the potential to reunify families that would never have been reunified without this multidisciplinary, coordinated approach. For families such as Pam and infant Victor, the less disjointed the system of care, the higher the likelihood that Pam will complete and benefit from her case plan and that the relationship between Victor and his mom will begin to heal and move forward on the right track.

ASSESSING PROGRESS AND CHANGE

With an eye toward creating a steady plan for systems development over time, communities can address the need for accountability and quality assurance when limited resources are available in the current economic environment. An important initial consideration is to develop a plan to monitor outcomes of families participating in the newly developed programs or systems linkages, not only to obtain feedback as to how the new mechanisms are working for them but also to see how access to higher quality services are affecting permanency outcomes as well as effecting changes in the parent–child relationships. Providers such as case workers and clinicians also will be important to survey to determine whether they perceive that the new systems are helping them do their work. A monitoring plan to capture improvements in outcomes should be developed at the onset so that these vital pieces of information can be collected. This is where a natural partnership can be developed with the data systems divisions of the court and child welfare as well as with universities and program evaluation agencies who are curious to explore the process of change and outcomes. Partnerships such as these may not require obtaining additional funding to both quantitatively and qualitatively evaluate a community's change process. The judge often can elicit interest in the work by inviting research and evaluation-focused stakeholders to the table. The invitation to evaluate progress and change in the court setting often fits nicely into a researcher's professional agenda.[2]

---

[2]Visit http://www.rr4cc.org for information about a nonprofit group working to partner with universities and researchers to promote evidence-based practices and programs.

What Infants and Toddlers Need from the System of Care

- Access to consistent, frequent visitations when in the child's best interest
- Access to developmentally appropriate assessments to determine developmental status and create pathways to early intervention when needed
- Linkages with community Part C programs that are timely and ability to connect with services if needed
- Creating linkages with quality child care programs and federal programs such as Head Start and EHS that acknowledge capacity issues and plan for interim services
- Creating pathways to a medical home for the young child that remains stable over the course of the case and afterwards
- Examining the opportunities for training frontline and supervisory staffs and funders in the community about the special needs of infants and toddlers

Miami's Story:
Designing and Implementing a System of Care
for Infants, Toddlers, and Their Parents

Since 2000, a judicially led process has evolved as a collaboration with stakeholders and community providers to move the child welfare system toward more effective services, communication, linkages, and training aimed at improving the lives of infants and toddlers. The process followed the path described earlier in this chapter.

In the beginning, the Miami Juvenile Court invited multidisciplinary experts to participate in a lecture series at the courthouse lobby during lunchtime to discuss the special needs of infants and toddlers. Lawyers, guardians ad litem, case workers, judges, and volunteers were encouraged by the court to attend the monthly sessions that focused on different topics related to the healthy development of young children. A judge always introduced the speakers, explaining that a new early childhood initiative was the court priority. Eventually, over the course of the trainings—in large part because of the persistence of the partners to keep their staff attending the workshops and the daily judicial insistence on asking about child development in every case involving young children—changes were made in the court settings.

Not only was there emphasis on the required legal procedures, but questions about early intervention, developmental delays, child care placements, and the infant–parent relationship also were asked in the courtroom regularly and it was expected that the parties to the case would have answers. The term *Part C*, the federal entitlement for young children identified as developmentally delayed, became a familiar rather than a foreign term to those in the courtroom. The culture of the Miami Juvenile Court transformed from ignoring infants and toddlers to focusing directly on them.

Everyone working with the cases recognized that, at times, the court was the first place that a developmental delay or mental health need was identified for young children. There was an awareness across all of the systems affecting young children in our

(continued)

community that the court was serious about helping the infants and toddlers who were never addressed before and that "everyone better get on board." Eventually, in the court-room setting where the judges also were able to have more informed case workers, lawyers, and others who interfaced in these young children's lives, dialogues about com-munication delays, developmental screens (e.g., ASQ-3; Squires & Bricker, 2009), and themes such as bonding and attachment became embedded in the court hearings dis-cussions. The process within the court setting and the overall child welfare practice was enriched by incorporating the science of early childhood development.

However, system change does not happen overnight. In fact, it was not until years after the initial push for change in Miami, coinciding with the transformation of Florida's child welfare system to a community-based (privatized) system, that reforming processes and improving programs became a community priority. The system stakeholders (case workers, judges, attorneys) had to shift their paradigm from being satisfied with *any* program to one that valued evidence-based practices and interventions. The parenting courses, for example, now required attendance at more sessions than the old 8-week programs and required more involvement by case workers, parents, and children. The related protocols and procedures expected more in-depth assessments of progress by the parents and interaction between parents and their very young children. Contracts with existing parenting providers were revamped by the funding agency to reflect the new requirements and mandates for evidence-based curricula. Parenting providers sought new training for their facilitators to deliver evidence-based parenting programs[3] and to adequately assess clients' progress in accordance with the new requirements. There was some dissent from current parenting providers in the community who accused the court of playing favorites.

CHALLENGES AND SOLUTIONS—LESSONS LEARNED FROM BUILDING COLLABORATIONS IN MIAMI

The collaboration of a multidisciplinary team for systems reform and integration has resulted in many advances in the approach, methods, and implementation of evidence-based programs and change in the way systems affecting young children in the child welfare system operate. Despite the significant advances made by the Miami team, it is still a work in progress. Any change is difficult, but change in a monolithic institution such as the child welfare system is extremely challenging. Collaboration and enormous effort have accomplished a great deal; however, often the challenges do not diminish with progress, but rather appear in different forms to be dealt with over and over again. Reform is not for the fainthearted or impatient.

Educating Cross-Disciplinary Partners

The first challenge to implementing a collaborative approach for any community is to accept the reason for change and the need to change to provide better services for

---

[3]The Dependency Parenting Provider Initiative and evidence-based parenting is discussed extensively in Chapter 2.

young children. It is also important to explain to the partners why the quality of their work is being questioned, especially when this is the way things have been done for decades. A common response is "We have all heard it before; we have always done it this way and no one has complained!" Thus, educating the community thoroughly enough to motivate change requires providing information about different ways of doing day-to-day work and finding ways to ask people to change the way they work by providing a credible explanation about what can be achieved if these changes are implemented. This education includes presentations on early childhood development, early intervention, developmental delays, and infant mental health, and education must continue for the programs to be implemented effectively.

Partnering with the Judiciary

For change to happen in the child welfare system, it is highly beneficial to have a proactive judge (or two) with the will to bring evidence-based practice into the courtroom and child welfare system. Programs that have existed for years will need to be told they have to completely change the way they handle their business or they will lose their court-referred clients. The court may need to inform the child welfare agency that the programs the agency is using are of questionable worth and, in fact, might be jeopardizing the safety of the children in care. The court will possibly need to take the position that sending troubled families to parenting programs that are not evidence based and only measure success by attendance does not fulfill the child welfare agency's duty to make reasonable efforts to reunify the family. Professionals working with young children in care need to know the law—that failure to meet the legal requirement of reasonable efforts means a loss of funding for the agency; with this legal power, the court will be able to eventually, with persistence, get their attention.

Monitoring Fidelity to the Model and Protocols

Although it takes a monumental effort for a community to map their services, develop new programs, and train stakeholders, the next step for a community is to create a quality assurance plan for monitoring compliance or fidelity to the chosen programs. Over time, some parenting programs may not be comporting themselves according to the agreed-on protocol. The programs may still be providing simple certificates of attendance to the court instead of submitting sufficient documentation of the results of the mandatory assessments. Communities need formal mechanisms by which to ensure fidelity to the selected models and ongoing monitoring, training, and retraining. This process will continue to evolve over time.

Promoting Collaboration Among System Partners and Stakeholders

Initially, the challenges, tasks, and barriers to creating a coordinated system will seem almost insurmountable. It is daunting to take on the multifaceted provider system, with its ingrained ways of doing business and providing services, quality assurance issues, traditional beliefs about the needs of young children, and lack of awareness of the impact of trauma. The existing systems may deemphasize the importance of quality programs, and there are typically few linkages between early intervention services, infant mental health services, quality child care, and the court.

On the positive side, becoming a responsive partner with the judge can give a provider immediate credibility and authority in the eyes of the court. However, despite the power of the court, when changes are expected to be made, there still can be defensiveness, disbelief, and grumbling that ripple through the system with all types of reasons emerging about why the requested changes cannot be made.

Juvenile court and the child welfare system are confusing and complex systems to those who operate on the outermost circle as community stakeholders. For providers, coming face to face with the judge for the first time in meetings rather than in the courtroom may make them feel uncomfortable about how to communicate, whether to express their opinions, or whether it is better to keep silent. Because judges are often in a leadership role and not engaged in the day-to-day challenges of systems integration, it is easy for miscommunication and misunderstanding to occur about what needs to happen next to solve a problem or challenge. (See Chapter 7 for more information about appearing in court and communicating with the judge.)

If the agencies do not comply initially with the changes that the judge and court have requested and continue with business as usual, more pressure will inevitably be placed on them. One of the strategies the judge and community partners can use to help make the needed agency change is to bring together experts, specialists, researchers, and community agencies serving young children for meetings, lectures, and/or brown bag lunches to provide support for the message that infants and toddlers need differentiated responses and that changes are needed in the systems to meet that need. A challenge is always finding the time to coordinate and attend the many meetings that need to be held to raise awareness. Being able to effectively change the systems requires much effort over time; however, the enthusiasm and drive of the judge in concert with community providers who support the change can provide the impetus for the team to find the time to support the work needed to meet the needs of the infants.

An early intervention community that is committed to making known to the court the special needs of infants in the system is critical; these professionals can lend their expertise to ensure that problem solving and decision making in child welfare cases is developmentally appropriate. With the leadership of the court, it is possible to raise the level of awareness that early intervention, as an example, is essential when children are at risk for developmental delays. Awareness can be raised about the fact that systematic assessments and specialized care management is needed for infants and toddlers and that evidence-based parenting programs and clinical interventions with the youngest of children have the greatest chance of changing the negative developmental trajectory of that child. A major challenge will be having sufficient time and energy to operate on many different levels and with multiple systems to meet the many needs and demands of the judge to create a much higher quality of care for young children in the child welfare system. Important initial inroads can be made to identify and link young children with services and existing entitlement programs.

For example, on one occasion in Miami, at the onset of such a systems change, the coordinator of Part C services (early intervention) called the judge to say that her fax was "burning up" as a result of the huge number of referrals for Part C assessments that were being sent from the court. After reassuring the director that the requests were the result of "initial enthusiasm and knowledge that Part C services are available for young children," a meeting was held with the judges. The goal was to craft a step-by-step screening and assessment process that would create a systematic, manageable prescreening process that would occur prior to a referral being faxed to

Part C for a full assessment. (See Chapter 4 for details of this process.)

Engaging the Provider Community

Although the process of change comes slowly, the incremental stages of systems change and coordination in Miami, for example, began to become evident over time. Stakeholders and funders discussed how budgets could be reallocated for program expansion and linkages for young children. Providers offered to provide an array of trainings orienting the community to resources such as early intervention services and CPP. Miami-Dade County's early learning coalition and subsidized child care network in concert with the Department of Children and Families licensing division agreed to provide lists of licensed, accredited child care centers to case managers. This helped them place children in quality child care. In another arena, the parenting program network of providers diligently worked on building an evidence-based set of curricula and adopted pre- and postassessment measures for detailing participant progress. Everyone agreed to the use of a standardized set of reporting templates that provided the information judges needed to evaluate parent progress. After enormous effort, the collaborative community partners were able to achieve an agreement from the programs who, without financial remuneration, agreed they would change the way they implemented programs and collected systemwide data on participant outcomes.

Working with Funders

In Miami, some of the community-based funders were impressed that programs were adding more accountability standards to their work and that the programs recognized, just as the judge did, that infants and toddlers linked to quality services experienced improved outcomes, as did the parents who successfully completed the evidence-based programs with their children. Trainings and workshops were held where funding agencies could come together and learn about the effectiveness of evidence-based programs. They learned that even though evidence-based programs may be more expensive to implement, chances of successful completion are greater for families. This could ultimately save dollars by reducing the need for families to repeat programs or enroll in programs that were less effective. Parsing out which funders were able to pay for which components was a challenge. In one case, an agency paid for the pre- and postassessments while another paid for the treatment sessions. It required hours of discussion, planning, and protocol development to work out the finances in some cases. However, once the system had retooled itself and families were benefiting from the change, there was a paradigm shift.

Availability of Mental Health Services

Infants, toddlers, and preschoolers ages birth–5 years have the highest incidence of maltreatment-related morbidity and mortality. At the same time, they also have the lowest access to mental health services. This is due to the widespread perception that providing therapeutic services for young children under 6 years of age is not essential, and that young children in this age group are not affected by trauma and are immune to mental health problems. A significant challenge to the availability and provision of services is that most providers—regardless of discipline and whether they are in community mental health centers or agencies, in private practice, or working for other public institutions—know little about doing evaluations and providing treatment services for these young children. Evaluations are deemed too expensive and unnecessary. Furthermore, there is a lack of training among service providers about the health, emotional, and behavioral manifestations of environmental adversity and traumatic stressors and about infancy and early childhood. A related challenge is that there are relatively few training programs where they can learn these skills. Fortunately, raising awareness has been much easier in the last decade, with increased evidence about the effects of trauma on brain development, greater knowledge about the science of early childhood development, and more data indicating that early intervention can make a significant difference. To raise awareness in the judicial and legal fields, evidence that early intervention can make a difference in reducing negative behaviors in adolescents such as violence, school dropouts, delinquency, substance use, and criminality is particularly relevant. Training played a key role in changing systems in Miami.

Even when training plans have been created and funders have come together in new ways to leverage their dollars, there still may be a lack of coordination between the systems of care and mental health service delivery. Children and families with multiple needs are overrepresented in primary medical care, child care and schools, family resource centers, domestic violence shelters, child protective services, and the legal system, but they are seldom referred for mental health services. It is for this reason that an integration of services is needed in this arena as well as through the strong hand of the court.

Once referrals are made in this area, another barrier is the significant lag time between initial identification of children's mental health or developmental impairment and the beginning of appropriate interventions, which may derail the child's developmental trajectory. Sometimes referrals for services just fall through the cracks. Without intervention, early delays and dysfunction only become progressively worse and more resistant to intervention. Again, the "muscle" of the juvenile or family court is key to making these changes happen as soon as a child is identified. Once they are identified, with an effective referral program in place, these young children can receive help immediately.

Recruiting and Developing a Competent Work Force

In Miami, like in so many other cities, there was very little availability of evidence-based programs or any infant mental health evaluation and treatment services. However, there was the growing will to make a difference, create integration across agencies, and somehow find a way to develop infant mental health providers to work with young children identified by juvenile court. Another piece of the collaboration was created by working with a senior infant mental health clinician and training colleague, who shared the commitment with Miami colleagues to create these services. Travel was required by both the trainers and trainees with ongoing didactic training in infant mental health with consistent supervision and consultation. Clinicians were identified who were willing to commit to undertaking intensive training and, once trained, to learn how to interface with juvenile court to bring information about relationship-based evaluations and treatments to the judge; this additional information allowed the judge to make more informed decisions about what was in the developmental interest of the young child related to treatment, visitation, and permanency decisions. The infant mental health and judicial collaboration provided increased information and, with that, better decision making about the child's best interests by the judge. At the same time, the collaboration increased the knowledge of the mental health professionals about how to bring relationship-based child development information to the court. A strong commitment of time and energy was made to providing education and training and to developing models for interaction with judges, lawyers, child welfare workers, court-appointed special advocates and guardians ad litem, and others who interfaced with juvenile court.

Although one program in Miami provides superlative services for the court, a continuing challenge is to gain the commitment of other agencies to provide high-quality evaluations and treatment services for maltreated infants and toddlers identified by the court. Although at times it has been possible to find financial resources for training, agencies and providers have been expected to do this difficult work in new ways for no additional resources. This has been challenging. Being successful requires discipline and adherence to high standards. Although this is not always

---

Culturally Competent Service Delivery

Cultural competence in the delivery of services is essential. Whether a professional is working as a case worker or an early childhood teacher, the effectiveness of both family support and family preservation services depends on the skills and ability of service providers to work closely with families from different cultures and ethnic backgrounds. To provide optimal support and assistance to families with children, practitioners must strive to be culturally competent, ensuring that services are respectful of and compatible with the cultural strengths and needs of the family.

The culturally competent professional is guided by the following principles:

- Respect for the client's home and family is of utmost concern.
- Local etiquette should prevail in the professional's behavior as he or she enters the family's environment.
- Careful work in establishing the role of the professional as a partner in helping is essential to establishing trust.
- The family remains in charge of their own lives while the professional motivates, facilitates, and creates a climate of respect and caring.

Becoming culturally competent is considered a lifelong process that requires continual study and effort (Olsen, Bhattacharya, & Sharf, 2006).

---

easy, there is no substitute related to outcomes for young children who have been maltreated and their families.

REFERENCES

Dobbin, S.A., Gatowski, S.I., & Maxwell, D.M. (2004). *Building a better collaboration: Facilitating change in the court and child welfare system.* (Technical Assistance Bulletin, Vol. 8, No. 2, pp. 51–88). Reno, NV: National Council of Juvenile and Family Court Judges.

Lederman, C.S., & Osofsky, J.D. (2004). Infant mental health interventions in juvenile court: Ameliorating the effects of maltreatment and deprivation. *Psychology, Public Policy & Law,* 10(1–2), 162–177.

Lederman, C.S., & Osofsky, J.D. (2008). A judicial mental health partnership to heal young children in juvenile court. *Infant Mental Health Journal,* 29(1), 36–47.

Lederman, C.S., Osofsky, J., & Katz, L. (2001). When the bough breaks the cradle will fall: Promoting the health and well being of infants and toddlers in juvenile court. *Juvenile and Family Court Journal, 52*(4), 33–38.

Olsen, L., Bhattacharya, J. & Sharf, A. (2006). *Cultural competency: What is it and why it matters.* Retrieved May 28, 2010, from http://www.lpfch.org/informed/culturalcompetency.pdf

Osofksy, J.D., Kronenberg, M., Hayes Hammer, J., Lederman, C., Katz, L., Adams, S., et al. (2007). The development and evaluation of the intervention model for the Florida infant mental health pilot program. *Infant Mental Health Journal, 28*(3), 259–280.

Osofsky, J.D., Putnam, F.W., & Lederman, C.S. (2008). How to maintain emotional well-being with working with trauma. *Juvenile & Family Court Journal, 59*(4), 91–102.

Squires, J., & Bricker, D. (2009). *Ages & Stages Questionnaires® (ASQ-3™): A parent-completed child-monitoring system* (3rd ed.). Baltimore: Paul H. Brookes Publishing Co.

7

Demystifying the Court Process

*How to Be an Effective
Advocate in Juvenile and Family Court*

The first time Pam entered the courtroom she was baffled, belligerent, and bewildered. Her infant had just been removed from her care and she did not understand why or how that could happen. Like many young parents, Pam was convinced she was a good parent. She learned from her mother that being a good parent did not require a great deal of effort. After all, Victor had clothing, a place to live, and was usually fed.

As the hearings progressed, with the assistance of her attorney, Pam gained a greater understanding of why she was in court, although she still thought it was unfair. She was treated with dignity. The judge took time to explain that what happened to Victor was not acceptable and explained why. At first Pam did not want to even listen. The judge tried, hearing after hearing, to make Pam trust her and to convince her that the goal of everyone working on the case was not to punish her or keep her child from her but quite the opposite. However, the judge was equally clear that Pam had to learn, take responsibility, and work hard to successfully complete her services. Many times she was told that Victor had to be her priority, without exception. The effect on Victor of Pam's missing a scheduled visitation was meticulously detailed by the judge so that Pam could almost feel Victor's disappointment and understand his anger when the mother he loves and waits for failed to appear. She needed to understand the impact of her actions on her son to facilitate change. Pam was not used to trusting anyone, so she was initially indifferent to the purported helping hands. Those working with Pam had to prove themselves, and they knew it.

Even small steps forward were praised. Pam's successes were highlighted and explained in terms of their effect on Victor. Pam needed to see what difference all of this made in terms of her relationship with her son—why praising Victor and showing affection to Victor would make a difference in their relationship. Watching Pam learn and grow and change her demeanor from defiance to realization as the case progressed was a gift to everyone involved.

In court, when Pam was asked what she was learning, she was able to articulate with great insight. She eloquently explained that she was learning that everything she did had an effect on her child. She said she learned to focus on her child instead of making everything about her own needs.

THE CHANGING ROLE OF THE COURTS

A new vocabulary has evolved to describe the changing role of the courts around the world. Terms such as *therapeutic jurisprudence* and *problem-solving courts* expand the vision and more accurately express the reality of what courts actually do. *Therapeutic jurisprudence* takes the law out of a legal vacuum and reminds the courts that law should take into account the consequences for the physical and mental health of the individuals and institutions it affects (Donnelly, 2009). In juvenile court, a true problem-solving court since its invention in 1899 in Chicago, success is determined by the ability to modify human behavior. The court is the catalyst and overseer of the healing process, and the judge is the conductor of that process in the courtroom and sometimes in the community as well by leading cross-system collaboration.

Problem-solving courts have emerged on the scene as an alternative to traditional courts where judges adjudicate legal issues. In traditional courts, the underlying problems that brought the litigants to court are not addressed and modification of behavior is not a remedy pursued. "[They] originated not in academia but from the efforts of practical, creative, and intuitive judges and court personnel, grappling to find an alternative to revolving door justice" (Flango, 2007, p. 41). Problem-solving courts change the role of the court from that of passive supervisor of the adversarial dispute resolution process to one of engagement in a team approach with attorneys, treatment providers, and program and court staff working toward a nonadversarial resolution of a shared problem.

Problem-solving courts transform the role of the court and require the jurist to expand his or her role both in the court and in increasing his or her knowledge beyond the law to other disciplines, including child development, social science, and research. Judges in problem-solving courts trade their typical role of objective referee for one of mentor and advisor and have a personal involvement in each case (Kozdron, 2009). This intensive, personal investment in each case enhances the power and responsibility of the judge.

Dependency Drug Court—Engaging Parents from the Bench

Research has shown that in drug court, the judge is often a key to success. The drug court judge's knowledge and temperament can determine whether parents engage and are motivated to become sober or walk away from help despite the consequences. The judge, acting as conductor, is highly engaged with each parent, tracking their progress, celebrating their successes, and refocusing them when they relapse. This motivational aspect is part of the parent's treatment and rehabilitation process (Senjo & Leip, 2001).

THE ROLE OF THE JUDGE IN CHILD WELFARE CASES: WHAT IS THE JUDGE THINKING?

The families who appear before child welfare judges around the country are desperately in need of so very much. Judges agonize about how to engage the mentally ill mother, how to persuade the chronic substance abuser to seek treatment, and how to convince a maltreated child that she is not at fault for her family's problems. How does one tell a hysterical 6-year-old that he cannot go home and why?

Judges may work with a child or a family for years, never giving up and hoping the improvements made are long lasting and transformative. But the devastation is personal when a reunified family comes back into the system or when a dependent child grows older, drops out of school, and becomes pregnant. Judges wonder, "How can I motivate this family to make lasting changes and halt the intergenerational cycle of abuse?" There is not a body of research instructive about how to be an effective juvenile dependency judge. Judging in juvenile and family court is more of an art than a science, although there certainly should be a more scientific approach to the decision-making process. The possibility of losing a child can be a powerful motivation for a parent. Judges that listen, engage, and motivate can wield great power for good.

The Role of the Judge

What is the role of the judge? U.S. Supreme Justice Benjamin Cardozo defined it this way:

> The work of a judge is in one sense enduring and in another sense ephemeral. What is good endures. What is erroneous is pretty sure to perish. The good remains the foundation on which new structures will be built. The bad will be rejected and cast off in the laboratory of years. Little by little the old doctrine is undermined. Often the encroachments are so gradual that their significance is at first obscured. Finally we discover that the contour of the landscape has been changed, that the old maps must be set aside and the ground charted anew. . . . (Cardozo, 1921, in Kaye, 2004)

Interestingly, judges are found to be happier in their judicial posts than their colleagues when they believe that they are more than neutral referees of the law who are more actively involved in the litigants' progress and are concerned about resolving the underlying problem that brought the litigant to the courthouse. They also are much more likely to believe that they are having a positive impact or helping the litigants in their court (Hora & Chase, 2004).

As the public brings more and more problems to the doors of the American courthouse, the justice system must adjust. The process of testing and retesting new ideas, remaining with and refining what is effective and rejecting what is not, keeps the law relevant and responsive to a changing world. Perhaps the next recognized role of a judge in a court of therapeutic jurisprudence is to act as community and courtroom conductor (Kaye, 2004). This requires the traditional role of the judge as a neutral umpire to be reenvisioned.

APPEARING IN COURT

The families who come into the courtroom in juvenile court come as a last resort with serious problems that have escaped solution. Decisions must be made quickly that can change the course of a child's life. Although the courtroom setting can appear chaotic and sometimes even sterile, judges want to help the children and families who appear before them. Judges, lawyers, and all who appear in court are limited by laws and rules. While witnesses are not expected to be well-versed in the law or the rules of procedure and evidence, it is important for non–legal professionals to at least be familiar with the court process and to understand that there are rules and laws that direct the proceedings. Case workers, social workers, clinicians, physicians, and others are considered witnesses—those with information pertinent to the disposition of the matter before the judge. Although the proceedings often are less formal in juvenile and family court, the professionals working with the family or those who are experts in their field are still expected to exhibit respect for the court proceeding, the judge, and the officers of the court.

The Court Process

A court is a place of prescribed rules and procedures. It is a forum where justice requires that every litigant be treated fairly and equally The adversarial nature of courts in America can be disarming and unfamiliar, especially for the clinician or social worker. In fact, they may find the atmosphere foreign and antitherapeutic. Although the rules may appear esoteric to those who are not legally trained (and sometimes to those who are legally trained), there is little room for deviation.

Most court appearances will be hearings where the judge is presiding. Occasionally, the witness may be called to testify in a trial where a jury is making the decision. This is rare in juvenile and family court because most matters are resolved by judges. The rules of evidence are the rules that determine what testimony the court can hear. The witness is not expected to know those rules, but adherence to those rules sometimes requires the proceedings to be disrupted by lawyers making objections and asking to address the judge in private. This is called a *sidebar*.

During the testimony of a witness, when a lawyer objects, the witness must immediately stop testifying and wait for the lawyers to argue to the judge why what was said should or should not be part of the record. The judge will listen, decide, and rule on the dispute. If a judge *sustains* the objection, this means that the question is not appropriate. The witness must wait for a new question to be presented before continuing. If a judge *overrules* the objection, the witness can continue as if the dispute did not occur. These disruptions can be numerous and lengthy, so the witness should not be embarrassed to ask for the lawyer to repeat the question the witness needs to answer. The witness should never answer a question he or she does not understand; it is always appropriate to ask for the question to be rephrased and repeated or clarified.

Not only will the lawyer who has called the witness to testify be asking questions of their witnesses (this is called *direct examination*), but the other lawyers will have an opportunity to ask questions as well (this is called *cross-examination*). Although cross-examination may be uncomfortable, it is a routine part of testifying in court, not a personal attack on the witness. If the witness and the attorney have prepared adequately, the witness should be prepared to handle questions on cross-examination.

The Appellate Process

The judge's rigorous adherence to rules of evidence is required by law. Failure to do so could result in a case being overturned. Final orders of dependency and termination of parental rights often are taken to a higher court to determine whether the trial court followed the law and made the right decision. This is called an *appeal*. It is, in effect, a second chance for the party who did not prevail in the trial to have the decision of the trial court reviewed before a higher court, called an *appellate court*. The appellate court will make a decision based on reading the transcripts of the trial and hearing argument from the attorneys. Witnesses do not appear in appellate court; however, the testimony that they provide at trial is reviewed by the appellate judges. Any mistakes made by the trial judge could result in the decision being overturned or in a new trial.

The appeal process is often very lengthy, sometimes taking months and even years waiting for the appellate courts to complete their review. Judges are therefore meticulous about following the law. In juvenile and family court cases, the length of time a case is in limbo waiting for the appellate court's decision can and does jeopardize permanency for children. Every judge in family and juvenile court is aware of the harm that can occur to children and families if the decision the trial court made is reversed by the appellate court and the case must be sent back to the trial court to enforce the decision of the appellate court. A common example of the impact of the appellate process is when parents who have had their parental rights terminated by the trial court are given additional opportunities to regain custody of their biological children based on the appellate courts reversal of trial court's decision to terminate parental rights. In essence, the case could start all over again while the children continue to wait for a permanent home.

Preparing to Testify or Present a Report to the Court

It is not necessary for a witness to know the rules to be an effective witness. However, in order to provide accurate and detailed information to the court, it is important for witnesses to prepare before testifying. Meeting with the lawyer who has requested the testimony is helpful. A pretestimony meeting allows the witness to anticipate issues that may arise during questioning. It also serves to educate the lawyer about the essential facts that are important to be brought before the court. Since a witness usually testifies by responding to questions or presenting a report, the questions asked by the lawyers must elicit the needed testimony. Leaving a court appearance without the information that the clinician or social worker needs to present can be frustrating for the witness and will leave the judge without pertinent information to make an informed ruling.

A clinician or social worker appearing as a witness in court must spend time preparing for his or her testimony by reviewing pertinent documents and records. He or she must know in advance if the court appearance will be a trial or a less formal and less lengthy hearing and know what matters the court must decide. Is the purpose of the hearing to seek a decision on visitation, placement, therapeutic needs of a child, or is the judge going to rule on termination of parental rights? The hearing may be formal with the witness on the witness stand being asked questions by the lawyers or judge or informal with the witness presenting a report. The witness will likely have a short period of time, usually only through answering questions, to make his or her opinions understood by the court.

A witness who is unprepared, who cannot answer basic questions that could have been anticipated, can seem indecisive and appear unknowledgeable. The court may find such a witness to lack credibility and give little or no weight to his or her testimony. Remember to bring the appropriate documentation, files, and reports to court. Ideally, the reports have been provided to the parties and the judge, when appropriate, prior to the hearing so they have had ample time to review progress and recommendations. In most instances, the judge has to be cognizant of managing his or her time in order to complete the daily docket. This often means that there is rarely enough time to spend on each case. Thus, witness preparation and confidence about the contents of the testimony or report is critical.

Testifying in Court

Witnesses who are well prepared will be most successful in responding to the questions of lawyers during the trial or hearing. All witnesses will first be sworn to tell the truth and then must wait to be questioned by the lawyers in court. Testimony should be succinct, but complete. Remember that the judge and lawyers have been trained in the law but not in child development, social sciences, or psychology. Do not use professional terms without explaining their meaning. Terms and concepts that the professional witness may use on a daily basis may be unfamiliar and esoteric to the judge, jury, and lawyers. This is especially problematic when appearing before a jury for a trial.[1]

When testifying, it is important to address the decision maker, not the lawyer asking the questions. Thus, the witness should look the judge or jury members in the eye when giving testimony. The judge considers the demeanor of every witness in determining the witness's credibility and in weighing the witness testimony. A forthright witness who does not equivocate is a good witness.

The testimony must be relevant to the issue being determined. One of the most common objections made by lawyers to testimony of a witness is relevancy. If the testimony does not directly relate to the matter being heard, the judge will not permit the testimony deemed not relevant to proceed and become a part of the record.

Narratives from witnesses during a trial or evidentiary hearing (more formal types of proceedings) are rarely allowed. So, the witness must make sure that what he or she wishes to say must come in a response to a question asked. It is natural to be afraid, intimidated, and nervous. If the witness has done adequate preparation, knows the matter to be decided, and listens carefully in court, the witness's perspective will be heard. The next time in court will be easier.

When testifying, the witness should be be honest and base statements on direct observations and interactions with the family as well as other objective facts and information that the witness has learned. It is important to be aware of and guard against any bias or self-interest. This can discredit a witness's testimony. The judge will want to know how much time the witness has spent with the child or family and the quality of the time together. If the witness is being paid for testimony, that information will be brought out in court. The witness should speak with conviction without appearing to be influenced by either party in court. There is nothing wrong with answering a question with "I don't know." This is a much better approach than making up an answer or answering a question outside of the witness's area of expertise or knowledge about the family. The court is likely to discount the testimony of a witness who does not tell the truth or who appears biased, and the court may never consider that witness to be credible or reliable again.

The judge, who must make decisions according to the legal standard "best interest of the child," needs factual reasons upon which to make that determination. Often, the judge has never seen the children who are the subject of the proceeding. Being specific and relating testimony to child development and child well-being will assist the judge in making a better informed decision. The judge and the lawyers are not the experts on child development, the witness is. So it is essential that the witness projects confidence about an area of expertise and is determined to make the expert opinion and the underlying factual reasons for it clear to the legal professionals.

Decision-Making Process

Judges are human beings who want to make the right decisions so that they can enhance the lives of the children and families in their courtrooms. The clinician, social workers, and other child welfare professionals are important partners in that endeavor. Articulate, well-prepared witnesses are an invaluable asset to the court, enabling the judge to make better, more informed decisions. Before testifying, it may be helpful to

---

[1]In most states, the hearings and trials in juvenile court are overseen only by a judge, who is the sole decision maker. However, in some states, the law allows for juries for particular types of adjudicatory hearings.

learn about the judge's background and experience. Some judges have well-documented philosophies about their work that can help the witness frame testimony.

In many juvenile and family courts, children are absent. The witness has a unique opportunity to fill that void by informing the court how decisions can be affected by child development; that is, what a decision will really mean in the life of a child. When an infant mental health therapist describes in detail that a 10-month-old infant repeatedly becomes inconsolable the moment her mother walks into the room, clings to the foster mother, and cries incessantly until she is picked up by the caseworker, the judge gains invaluable insight into the important relationships in the child's life and is better equipped to make visitation and reunification decisions. Conversely, when the infant mental health clinician describes how the young parent has begun to praise her infant using a more soothing tone of voice, and smile at her young child while learning to play together, the judge can visualize the improvement in the relationship.

The witness is crucial to a fair and healthy outcome if the witness has educated the judge. When professionals who appear in court have a clear understanding about the legal process and rules involved and are prepared for court, they have the best opportunity to enhance the court's ability to make intelligent, well-reasoned decisions on behalf of the children and families with whom they work. The professional's skill at demonstrating the needs of a child and her family can enhance the court's capacity to serve young children and their families knowledgably and well. Hopefully, what the judge learns from the witnesses appearing in court, day after day, will add to his or her body of knowledge and enhance future decisions as well.

REFERENCES

Cardozo, B.N. (1921). *The nature of the judicial process* (The Storrs Lectures series). New Haven, CT: Yale University Press.

Donnelly, M. (2009). Best interests, patient participation, and the Mental Capacity Act of 2005. *Medical Law Review, 17*, 1–29.

Flango, V.E. (2007). Problem-solving courts under a different lens. In C.R. Flango, C. Campbell, & N. Kauder (Eds.), *Future trends in state courts 2007* (pp. 41–45). Williamsburg, VA: National Center for State Courts.

Grace, M., Lederman, C.S., & Osofsky, J.D. (2002). Sharing child development expertise in court: Respect, rules, and roles. *Zero to Three Bulletin, 22*(5).

Hora, P., & Chase, D. (2004). Judicial satisfaction when judging in a therapeutic key. *Contemporary Issues in Law, 7*(1).

Karver, M.S., Handelsman, J.B., Fields, S., & Bickman, L. (2005). A theoretical model of common process factors in youth and family therapy. *Mental Health Services Research, 7*, 35–51.

Kaye, J. (2004). Delivering justice today: A problem-solving approach. *Yale Law and Policy Review, 22*, 125.

Kozdron, N.A. (2009). Midwestern juvenile drug court analysis and recommendation. *Indiana Law Journal, 84*, 373.

Osofsky, J.D. (2009). Perspectives on helping traumatized infants, young children, and their families. *Infant Mental Health Journal, 30*(6), 673–677.

Osofsky, J., Maze, C., Lederman, C., Grace, M., & Dicker, S. (2002). *Questions every lawyer and judge should ask about infants and toddlers in the child welfare system.* Reno, NV: National Council of Juvenile and Family Court Judges.

Parlakian, R. (2001). *Look, listen and learn: Reflective supervision and relationship based work.* Washington, DC: Zero to Three.

Resnik, J., & Curtis, D. (2007) Representing justice: The rise and fall of adjudication as seen from Renaissance iconography to twenty-first century courthouses. *Proceedings of the American Philosophical Society, 151*, 139.

Senjo, S., & Leip, L. (2001). Testing therapeutic jurisprudence theory: An empirical assessment of drug court process. *Western Criminology Review, 3*(1). [Online]. Available from http://wcr.sonoma.edu/v3n1/senjo.html

8

Understanding and Preventing Vicarious Traumatization and Compassion Fatigue

The first week that Amy, a veteran Early Head Start (EHS) teacher of children with special needs, began the new school year with Victor in her class, she familiarized herself with the particulars of his case. She read the dependency petition that outlined the allegations of his abuse and neglect. She and the EHS social worker read his story of neglect, abandonment, exposure to violence, and maltreatment, and she grieved for him. Her sense of connectedness to his pain brought tears to her eyes each day when she greeted him in the morning or as she placed him on the van to return "home" to his aunt. Amy's response was nurturing and supportive of Victor in the classroom, but she took on a personal sadness in her daily interactions. Her demeanor was sad and lethargic as she continued to think about what harm had been done to this little boy.

After an initial 2 weeks, she came to the EHS director with what she thought would be the perfect solution. She and her husband could adopt Victor, thereby ameliorating his pain and giving him a stable and loving home. Although this solution certainly seems on the surface to be generous and solution focused, as a way for Amy to ease her distress and ostensibly help Victor it is unrealistic and untenable. Professionals, though well-intentioned, do not typically adopt the children they care for every day who are in the foster care system. By thinking of that as the solution, they forget that the majority of the children in their care do have families that want to do right by them, who want to heal their issues so they can be reunified, and who love their children. They just do not know how to get where they need to go on their own. At the same time, early childhood professionals and their clinical, legal, and social service colleagues need ongoing support to channel their empathy productively and make sense of the pain they are internalizing in their work.

WHAT IS VICARIOUS TRAUMATIZATION?

Those who work daily with children who have been maltreated and their challenging families perform some of the most painful and frustrating work under the most adverse circumstances. They are surrounded by human suffering, deprivation, and impoverishment. How does the substance of their work and the toxic environments they work in affect their well-being? Those who do this work because they are passionate about protecting children and healing families often feel that they bear the ultimate responsibility for any harm caused to the child. The Herculean burden is overwhelming, and there is now empirical evidence that the suffering felt is real. The term for this suffering is *vicarious traumatization*.

Vicarious traumatization or *compassion fatigue* results from being exposed to traumatic events and material as a result of working with survivors or perpetrators of traumatic life events as part of everyday work. If a person engages empathically with victims or survivors, they are particularly vulnerable to compassion fatigue; this is the reason why individuals such as judges, child welfare workers, home visitors, and mental health professionals may become overwhelmed at times or experience burnout. (Figley, 1995; Pearlman & Saakvitne, 1995). Those individuals who measure their self-worth by how much they help others, have unrealistic expectations of themselves and others, are self-critical and perfectionistic, fear others will judge them if they show weakness, overextend themselves, or let work overtake their personal time are much more vulnerable. Figley (2002) studied secondary traumatic stress in health-care providers, journalists, attorneys, first responders, supportive services, military personnel, volunteers, and media personnel. Jaffe, Crooks, Dunford-Jackson, and

Town (2003) studied these reactions in judges. Both studies showed that all groups, in working with trauma day after day, experienced some degree of vicarious traumatization. Although some professional environments build in prevention, intervention, and coping strategies to help those who are affected by vicarious traumatization, many do not. In a setting where there is not even the opportunity to debrief after a traumatic event, the idea of vicarious traumatization or compassion fatigue often is neither admitted nor dealt with because it is perceived as a sign of weakness. Often, those who work in such settings find their own ways to cope and adjust, sometimes using maladaptive strategies such as self-medicating with alcohol to deal with stress. If their coping strategies are maladaptive, they may leave that type of work or, in some cases, be asked to leave if their performance suffers due to the situation being too stressful.

 VIEW FROM THE BENCH

Most judges in dependency court feel that they have the final and ultimate responsibility for the safety and well-being of the children under their jurisdiction. The buck stops on the bench. Every day, judges make decisions that could harm children and end their careers. The professional pressure is augmented by large caseloads, strict mandatory time standards pursuant to the Adoption and Safe Families Act of 1997 (PL 105-89), lack of resources, the need to monitor the performance of the other partners in the child welfare system, and the judges' duty to make hundreds of life-changing decisions every week in a matter of minutes. Stress is an understatement. All this is done in an environment where child torture and chronic neglect provide scenarios that can only be characterized as nightmares. One medical professional has used the term "soul murder" to describe what judges and child welfare professionals see every day in their work. Judges are public figures and constitutional officers who are afraid to show fear and frailty on the bench. The public cannot perceive the judge as weak or soft without jeopardizing the judge's career.

The truth is that judges are human, and most are parents. They feel the pain of presiding over child abuse and neglect cases. Telling the hysterical child why she cannot go home to mommy, making a custody decision that takes a child away from a mentally ill parent who loves her child but can never care for him, separating siblings, and terminating parental rights profoundly affect the judge. Judges new to the dependency assignment cry, have difficulty sleeping, and become depressed and anxious. Some confide in their colleagues when they feel it is safe to do so, but the court system provides no support.

At times, judges may seek psychological and psychiatric help on their own to continue their work. They strive to learn the balance—to always feel compassion but not to be incapacitated by it.

Unfortunately, for many who work in the child welfare system and with infants, toddlers, and young children affected by trauma, the cumulative effects of prolonged repeated exposure to the stories and situations experienced by these young children can affect the personal lives of those who work in the system. Experts who study the effects of work-related exposure to traumatized individuals have identified a number of common signs and symptoms indicating an individual may be suffering adverse effects.

Signs and Symptoms of Secondary Traumatization

- Cynicism, anger, or irritability
- Anxiety or new fears, e.g., about the safety of one's family
- Emotional detachment, depersonalization, or a sense of numbness
- Sadness or depression
- Intrusive imagery or thoughts about victims, patients, or clients
- Nightmares and difficulty sleeping
- Social withdrawal and disconnection from family and friends
- Changes in world view—sense of futility or pessimism about people
- Changes in spiritual beliefs
- Less self-care
- Increased physical ailments and illness
- Use of alcohol and/or drugs to "forget about work" or "relax"

From Osofsky, J.D., Putnam, F.W., & Lederman, C.S. (2008). How to maintain emotional health when working with trauma. *Juvenile and Family Court Journal, 59*(4), 91–102; reprinted by permission.

Depending on the discipline and the approach taken with young children and families, certain unique stressors and traumatic experiences may come up repeatedly; however, all individuals doing this type of work will share a common set of stressors as a result of processing the traumatic experiences of victims or perpetrators specific to the kind of work that they do. All will experience similar frustrations and problems in their day-to-day work, including burnout. Some frequently occurring events that add to stress are high caseloads, whether one is doing child welfare work, mental health services, or presiding in court in a busy jurisdiction; inadequate resources to meet demands, with an excessive workload and copious paperwork; little support in the institutional setting; and limited supervision or job support. If one experiences secondary traumatization, it may decrease one's ability to do the work objectively and empathically. Over time, one might see increases in absenteeism, impaired judgment in making decisions about a child or family, low motivation, poor quality of work, increases in staff turnover, and increased friction among staff. Vicarious traumatization of employees such as Amy at Early Head Start ultimately decreases their ability to work effectively in job settings.

The child welfare system involves the interaction of multiple bureaucratic organizations (e.g., child protection, judicial, law enforcement, medical and mental health) operating under somewhat different mandates and timelines with respect to processing cases. People in one organization frequently do not understand the roles, demands, requirements, and legal and institutional constraints that dictate what can be expected from others who work with the same children and families but for a different organization. Differences in professional orientation and training further complicate the process and impede the development of mutual trust and respect. Not infrequently, actions or inaction by members of one organization may increase the stress or complicate the jobs of members of another. As a case is shared and decisions are made across different disciplines and agencies, individuals may feel a loss of control while at the same time continuing to feel responsible for the outcome. Often, there is little or no feedback about the ultimate outcome of a case after it passes on to others in the system—and thus no indication of the success or failure of one's efforts. And even more painfully, the failures sometimes become front page news. Overall, working in the child welfare system can be highly stressful and increases one's risk for vicarious traumatization and burnout.

Common stressors leading to vicarious traumatization in child protection workers and social workers working with victims of crime include the death of a child on the worker's caseload, investigating a particularly horrendous abuse and neglect case, and frequent exposure to emotional and detailed accounts by children of traumatic events. For judges who must terminate parental rights, the first few times they make these decisions may lead to symptoms of distress. Younger children frequently play out a trauma repeatedly, which can be difficult for adults to see and experience. Other causes of extreme stress result from having to support grieving family members following a child abuse death and worries about continued funding of programs and adequacy of resources. For all who work in this area, stories of traumatizing events are all too common.

PREVENTING COMPASSION FATIGUE AND VICARIOUS TRAUMATIZATION: THE IMPORTANCE OF THE REFLECTIVE PROCESS AND SUPERVISION

Perhaps the most important message we can provide related to vicarious traumatization is that sometimes individuals who work in the child welfare system—be they judges, lawyers, child welfare workers, early interventionists, mental health workers, or others—must help themselves in order to do no harm.

The reflective process and reflective supervision can be extremely helpful and supportive for all individuals who work with or serve traumatized young children and their families (Osofsky, 2009). Reflective supervision is carried out regularly in a safe and trusting environment, allowing the therapist to share not only what he or she does but also how it feels to serve a particular family. Through this process, the supervisee can learn ways to build on the capacities, resilience, and resourcefulness of children and families and the idea that emotions and feelings are crucial to understand work with infants and families. Reflective supervision also allows the supervisee to learn that by pinpointing his or her own emotional responses (with appropriate boundaries), it is possible to recognize, understand, and respect the emotional responses of the infants, toddlers, and families being served. This approach is particularly important for supervisees who are doing infant mental health work. In a trusting environment, the supervisee feels free to express the anxieties, concerns, and feelings that may arise in the course of his or her work, which—with traumatized infants, young children, and families—may be very intense. If the supervisee has the opportunity to share and discuss these feelings in a safe environment, he or she will be better able to understand and to "hold," if needed, the intense feelings that arise during the course of the treatment of very young children and families. The supervisee is encouraged to talk about what he or she thought and felt in addition to what occurred in the session and what was said. Thus, issues of ambiguity that may come up in the course of the work are discussed in addition to areas of confusion for both the supervisee and the supervisor.

With very young children and their families, it is important to just "be there." It is this type of supervision that helps support the therapist to be emotionally available and responsive while providing effective intervention and care. In their work, Pawl and St. John (1998) elaborated on sensitive ways to support young children and families by just being there with the them rather than always having to do something. The open communication that occurs between supervisor and supervisee can serve as a model for needed communication between professionals and parents as well as parents and young children. However, it also must be recognized and accepted that healing occurs over time, and there may be an occasional need for time-outs from direct focus on trauma. Finally, issues of burnout, vicarious traumatization, and compassion fatigue need to be considered as an integral part of training and supervision. (Figley, 1995; Osofsky, 2009).

The best solutions often include the following:

- Finding strategies and opportunities for children in the child welfare system that bring joy to their lives during the course of the time they are in child care or early intervention settings each day

- Showing—through our affect and body language and by implementing individualized strategies for each child in our daily schedules, lesson plans, and routines—that the world can be fun, happy, productive, structured, and predictable

- Responding in nurturing, respectful ways to each child, giving them small-group learning opportunities and one-to-one moments to show them they are special and important

Curricula to enhance self-esteem—Dr. Becky Bailey's *Conscious Discipline* (2000) with "'I love you' rituals" as well as developmentally appropriate learning strategies such as the *HighScope* (Schweinhart, 2000) curriculum—support the need for children—even toddlers—to make decisions regarding their play choices throughout their day and to help them dispel feelings of powerlessness and dependence. In giving young children the tools they need, the early childhood professional will grieve less about their plights and be able to turn those feelings into supportive mechanisms imparted to the children that will be useful to the children in their future. Quality early childhood professionals—along with the other professionals and family members who are there for children in the child welfare system—can help and become attachment figures for the babies and toddlers in their care. One way to do this is to work hard at being in attendance at your program as often as possible, with infrequent absences. For young children, when their teacher is absent, they may wonder if he or she has abandoned them and whether they will return. To this end, early childhood professionals need to be "better than good" in response to the needs of the young children in their care. This does not mean professionals should grieve for the children they work with; instead, they should interact with them in joyful, positive ways—through daily interactions, music, art, dramatic play, literacy building, and individual one-to-one time and by coming to work prepared with a structure that supports routines each day. By following these guidelines, professionals will feel less of a sense of sadness about the children's situations and can serve more as a catalyst to help the children do well each day by providing supportive, developmentally appropriate, quality, evidence-informed practice at child care centers and early intervention programs. As professionals, it is important, too, that we uphold the ethics of confidentiality about each child's personal situation, never discussing their personal business with anyone not directly involved with the child's care. Their lives are not to be shared by name with our families or friends.

How, then, can early childhood professionals process their experiences with regard to the children in their care? Supervisors and lead teachers need to find times to schedule supervision and teacher planning days that allow for discussion of how teachers are feeling about the information they have learned about the children they care for. Staff need to brainstorm strategies to support the children and families with whom they work; this way, they know that they are contributing resources that will help to alleviate the stressors that affect their lives.

In summary, the following is a list of things professionals can do to mitigate vicarious trauma:

1. Praise a child welfare professional with whom you work.

2. Write a thank-you note to someone.

3. Take a few moments for self-reflection.

4. Confide in a colleague.

5. Do something nice for yourself.

6. Think about all the children and families you have helped.

7. Remember your success stories.

8. Do not be afraid to seek professional help.

9. Take some time for self-care including exercise, time off, and enjoyable activities.

10. Tap into your sense of humor.

11. Learn to say "no."

REFERENCES

Adoption and Safe Families Act (ASFA) of 1997, PL 105-89, 111 Stat. 2115–2136.

Bailey, B.A. (2000). *Conscious discipline: Seven basic skills for brain smart classroom management.* Oviedo, FL: Loving Guidance.

Figley, C.R. (Ed.). (1995). *Compassion fatigue: Coping with secondary traumatic stress disorder in those who treat the traumatized* (Brunner/Mazel Psychosocial Stress Series No. 23). New York: Brunner-Routledge.

Figley, C.R. (Ed.). (2002). *Treating compassion fatigue* (Psychosocial Stress Series No. 24). New York: Brunner-Routledge.

Jaffe, P.G., Crooks, C.V., Dunford-Jackson, B.L., & Town, M. (2003). Vicarious trauma in judges: The personal challenge of dispensing justice. *Juvenile and Family Court Journal, 54,* 1–9.

Osofsky, J.D. (2009). Perspectives on helping traumatized infants, young children, and their families. *Infant Mental Health Journal, 30,* 673–677.

Pawl, J.H., & St. John, M. (1998). *How you are is as important as what you do: In making a positive difference for infants, toddlers, and their families.* Washington, DC: Zero to Three: National Center for Infants, Toddlers and Families.

Pearlman, L.A., & Saakvitne, K.W. (1995). Treating therapists with vicarious traumatization and secondary traumatic stress disorders. In C. Figley (Ed.), *Compassion fatigue: Coping with secondary traumatic stress disorder in those who treat the traumatized* (Brunner/Mazel Psychosocial Stress Series No. 23) (pp. 150–177). New York: Brunner-Routledge.

Schweinhart, L.J. (2000). The HighScope Perry preschool study: A case study in random assignment. *Evaluation and Research in Education, 14*(3&4), 136–147.

Conclusion

The court was concerned that Victor had been in a stable, nurturing home with his aunt for almost 2 years and had not had regular contact with Pam. Reunification was uncertain. Some parents who have had their children removed want them back regardless of the circumstances; they are unable to distinguish their needs from what is best for their child. As the parent gains an understanding and awareness of child development and the importance of the basic principles of attachment and bonding, he or she may finally be able to elevate the needs of their child above their parent's own.

Pam was learning that being a good parent was quite difficult and that having a relationship with her child involved more than giving birth to him, clothing, and feeding him. She could see the quality of her relationship with her boys change as her interactions became more appropriate and child centered. The boys responded in markedly different ways to Pam's sensitivity than they had to her emotional unavailability.

When asked by the judge what she had learned through working with the IMH therapist in her Child–Parent Psychotherapy (CPP) sessions, Pam said, "I learned that my babies love me." Pam told the judge that she understood that Victor was in a loving and safe home and that he felt very happy and secure with his aunt, who had been his caregiver for 2 years. She acknowledged that the stability he had with his aunt was in his best interest. Taking his needs into consideration, she agreed to leave him in the permanent custody of his aunt. Everyone involved with Pam's case, from the judge to the caseworker to the clinician, lauded and supported Pam for making such a difficult decision and for putting the needs of her child first. Pam's own mother would never have understood.

When the concepts and practices discussed in this book, including the new terminology and the change of focus to infants and toddlers, were introduced to the juvenile court and child welfare community in Miami, there was confusion and concern. Why is the judge so focused on very young children who are nonverbal and could not possibly be as affected by maltreatment as their older counterparts? What is Part C and early intervention and why would a baby need occupational therapy? What is relationship-based Child–Parent Psychotherapy (CPP) and what is an infant mental health clinician? What is an evidence-based parenting program and why isn't the certificate of completion evidence enough of successfully completing the program? Besides, can learning really be measured?

The parents' lawyers were concerned about the impact of measuring outcomes on the ability of their clients to be reunified with their children. The guardians ad litem were concerned about the change from a focus on the child to a focus on the parent–child relationship. The Department of Children and Families administrators, attorneys, and case managers complained that the parenting programs they have been using for years had been working fine. Why now the shift?

MEASURING SUCCESS

Changing long-held beliefs and misconceptions about very young children and their families was an uphill battle. Trainings and education were helpful and necessary. However, nothing was as effective at raising understanding and awareness among system stakeholders as watching the interventions work. When the stakeholders began observing the positive outcomes made possible by using evidence-based practices focused on the unique needs of very young children and their parents, the road to reform became a collaborative endeavor. Judges, lawyers, case managers, and child advocates observed that some parents finally understood what their young children needed from them and, with that understanding, were able to modify their behavior. Teen parents, who learned how to play and respond reciprocally with their babies for the first time, would joyfully talk about their babies' healthy reaction to them by explaining, "My baby finally loves me." Parents came to court and said things such as

- "I have learned that everything I do affects my baby."

- "When I was on drugs I was not there for my baby. I let my son have anything he wanted so I would not have a hassle, and now I see how that has hurt him."

- "I learned to talk to my baby and follow his lead instead of telling him what to do all the time."

- "I learned that being a mother is really hard. I used to think it was easy."

JUDICIAL PERSPECTIVE

For many parents, usually those who come from emotional impoverishment, learning to nurture their child is a Herculean task. No book, no class, no lecture, and no video can teach them what they need to know. The hands-on, individual, intensive work in CPP, effective parent education, and a coordinated system of care is the best way to break through the barrier of ignorance and deprivation and to stop the intergenerational transmission of child maltreatment. In some cases, despite the best efforts of the judge and professionals involved, reunification is not possible. However, if in these instances, a parent understands that it is best for his or her baby to live with someone who is not abusing drugs or parenting three special needs children, that insight and empathy for the child are still signs of success. Even when reunification is not possible, parents can use the nurturing and new skills to meet the needs of the children they have now or may have in the future.

Those involved with this initiative's development and implementation over the past 10 years believe that a successful outcome includes how well the system as a whole responds to the needs of very young children and their parents. Signs of this success can be seen not only in individual cases, but also in the gradual shift in beliefs and practices around babies and toddlers in care. Now, even the parents' lawyers request CPP for their clients, realizing that this intervention offers the *best* hope for a parent of a young child to learn how to bond and to actualize reunification. The child welfare agency has accepted that better outcomes overall can be gained from a parenting program that actually helps to change behaviors, rather than simply hands out certificates. Lawyers are overheard discussing bonding and attachment with therapists and caseworkers. Science is used every day to make more informed decisions. The judge, as a conductor of the process, oversees a caring orchestra of lawyers, providers, professionals, volunteers, and clinicians who are all reading from the same piece of music and take pride in the spirit of hope in the music they are producing.

VIEW FROM THE BENCH
Looking Back on a Decade
of Successes and Lessons Learned

Before the Miami Juvenile Court Project was instituted, parents with young children who appeared in court before me at the first hearing after removal of their children had a chance of getting their children back. Now that chance is greatly enhanced. Before, I had far too many reunified parents return to my courtroom each time a new child was born. As a system, we simply could not offer these families with young children what they needed to heal and break the cycle of continued neglect and maltreatment. It wasn't a matter of lack of money, it was a matter of lack of knowledge and a cohesive system of care.

Even with the new opportunities for growth and change offered by the Miami Juvenile Court Project efforts, a decade of sitting daily on the dependency court bench caused me to doubt the ability of the parents to accept responsibility for what they had done and to modify their behavior. Many times, to my delight, they proved me wrong. Families that would never have been reunified before the Miami Juvenile Court Project was instituted were now going home with their children. Everyone in the courtroom observed families for whom we had little or no hope be reunified and not return back to the child welfare system. And those moments, when I see a woman, unrecognizable as a mother when she first came to court, interacting reciprocally and lovingly with her child, make my spirit soar. Even if other circumstances prevent her from regaining custody of her baby, the relationship has been healed, and we, as a system, have hopefully broken the ugly cycle of intergenerational child maltreatment.

Early Interventionist Perspective

Even the most intelligently designed and well-funded interventions and entitlement programs can have little impact on children's outcomes. Parents must learn how to access the best services, must understand how to negotiate the culture and rules of each system, and must actively participate in the decision making for their child's developmental success, or they cannot succeed. Obstacles such as lack of trust, uncaring and unresponsive providers, ineffective services, cultural and linguistic mismatching of services, compromised literacy, and overall cumulative disadvantage are impediments that child welfare professionals and related system partners must work together to overcome.

Solution-focused, responsive early intervention specialists and early care and education professionals are essential to engaging and supporting very young children and their parents involved with the child welfare system. Success from this perspective is measured by keeping a family engaged and involved with a set of services designed to improve child and family outcomes. In addition, each parent who learns how to access early intervention, child care, and early education services for her baby or toddler develops important advocacy skills on behalf of her child. When a toddler with a hearing impairment resulting from physical abuse is able to hear her older sister's voice for the first time and a whole new world is opened, or when an infant born prenatally drug exposed is warmly greeted each day by nurturing caregivers at her early intervention program, a small success has been achieved for that child. Her course toward healthy development has been corrected, even if only partially.

Success is also achieved when quality child care is secured for a 3-year-old with few developmentally appropriate materials at home. Now, he has access to the world of books, art, and music and is guided in healthy social and emotional development. This success becomes even more important when his positive early childhood education experiences allow him to enter kindergarten "ready to learn."

Clinician Perspective

Success is not always measured by focusing on only optimal outcomes. Success must be seen as decreasing risk for future abuse and neglect and achieving safety and permanency for a young child. Ideally, that will be achieved through intensive intervention with the parent and child together that is built on the parent's motivation to change.

From a mental health perspective, there are complex developmental issues for infants and toddlers who are adjudicated dependent due to abuse and neglect. The effects on a young child's physical, social-emotional, and cognitive growth and development are compounded by a multitude of risk factors. Because young children grow and thrive in positive relationships, it is crucial to look for and focus on the strengths, however few, already present in the parent–infant relationship and to intervene in meaningful ways to change maladaptive patterns. Remarkable transformation is possible if the clinician is able to build a trusting relationship with the parent (often the first such relationship for the parent) and to help her understand how very important she is for her child. At the same time, through relationship-based CPP, the clinician works with the parent or caregiver to keep the child safe and to help support her development.

When the mental health clinician and team see the child and parent relating in a very different, positive way and gaining much pleasure from being together, the intervention has been successful, regardless of whether reunification has been achieved. Clinically speaking, success is measured by the progress toward correcting the harm that had taken place in the relationship, helping the child achieve a more normal developmental course, and supporting the parent in being able to take care of both herself and her child.

FINAL THOUGHTS

There can never be too many advocates working on behalf of young children, and we can never begin too soon. No matter your profession or role in the child's life—teacher, clinician, child care worker, social worker, case manager, lawyer, guardian, foster parent, or kin—you can make a contribution that can change the trajectory of a young child's life in the foster care system. There are resources in every community that can help you find the path. Whether it be calling a helpline or Child-Find to identify early intervention or child care programs, becoming a volunteer guardian ad litem (GAL) or court appointed special advocate (CASA), offering support to a family member in recovery, or simply doing your very best work on behalf of each young child and their parents every day, it will make a difference.

Babies and toddlers, even before they can speak, can show us, through their interactions with others and their emotions, that they are struggling and need help. We have to learn to be better observers and more knowledgeable about ways to identify them and provide them with the services they need. We need to believe unequivocally that no infant or toddler is too young to benefit from help. We need to *know what we know* about child development and *what we don't know* when it comes to helping them. That way, we can connect with community colleagues with the right expertise for the overall good of the child. It is not about our personal self-esteem; it is about getting the job done well. If it means shoring up our courage to speak in the courtroom about a case that is going in the wrong direction, being unpopular with negligent colleagues, or being the one identifying the appropriate services or acting to stop inappropriate services, we need to take the lead together and fight for young children and their families.

There will be significant challenges. System inertia and the comfort of the status quo are enormous obstacles to overcome. New partners who may not have worked with the court before have to be recruited. It is crucial to learn how to work in an adversarial court system in which the focus is on the adjudication of rights. The abandonment of the "one size fits all" service provision philosophy is essential. Data collection and evaluation must be included with a focus on fidelity. Capacity must be developed in the best programs to meet the needs of the community. Sustainability has to be an ongoing part of the work even if, as is so often the case, it seems impossible. The problems seem insurmountable, but they are not.

The majority of parents love their children and want what is best for them. So many just need to know *how* to change and to learn the ways to support the development of their children; often these are new ways of relating to their children which may, at times, be difficult to understand because of the parents' own early experiences. They need professionals and programs that will stand by them and truly help them through the process, giving them the greatest chances of success in their recovery, treatment, and intervention programs. The programs may already exist in our communities or they may need to be built through the types of community and provider collaborations discussed in this book.

We have survived many challenges, and yet many challenges are ongoing. But for this collective, collaborative work, parents who would never have been able to be successfully reunified are now living safely together with their young children and providing nurturing, safe, supportive environments. When reunification is not an option, young children are able to live with permanent caregivers who have been given tools—through early intervention, infant mental health, and early care and education—to support the child's healthy development. New people are working together and with the court for the first time, forming a permanent collaborative team. This integrated, systemic approach is fundamentally improving young children's lives, breaking maladaptive intergenerational patterns, and healing families and communities.

Questions Every Judge and Lawyer Should Ask About Infants and Toddlers in the Child Welfare System

This publication was developed for use by judges, attorneys, child advocates, and other child welfare professionals faced with meeting the wide range of needs of very young children in the child welfare system.

QUESTIONS EVERY JUDGE AND LAWYER SHOULD ASK ABOUT INFANTS AND TODDLERS IN THE CHILD WELFARE SYSTEM

By
Joy Osofsky, Ph.D., Candice Maze, J.D.,
Judge Cindy Lederman,
Justice Martha Grace, and Sheryl Dicker, J.D.

NATIONAL COUNCIL OF
JUVENILE AND FAMILY COURT JUDGES

December 2002

Brief Authored by:

Joy O. Osofsky, Ph.D.
Professor, Department of Psychiatry
Louisiana State University
New Orleans, Louisiana

Candice Maze, J.D.
Director, Dependency Court Intervention Program for Family Violence
Miami, Florida

Judge Cindy S. Lederman
11th Judicial Circuit, Juvenile Division
Miami, Florida

Justice Martha P. Grace
Chief Justice, Juvenile Court
Boston, Massachusetts

Sheryl Dicker, J.D.
Executive Director, Permanent Judicial Commission on Justice for Children
White Plains, New York

Technical Assistance Brief is a publication of the Permanency Planning for Children Department of the National Council of Juvenile and Family Court Judges. The National Council of Juvenile and Family Court Judges wishes to acknowledge that this material is made possible by Grant Nos. 96-CT-NX-0001 and 95-JS-FX-K002 from the Office of Juvenile Justice and Delinquency Prevention, Office of Justice Programs, U.S. Department of Justice. Points of view or opinions in this document are those of the authors and do not necessarily represent the official position or policies of the U.S. Department of Justice or the National Council of Juvenile and Family Court Judges.

Honorable David B. Mitchell
Executive Director
National Council of Juvenile
and Family Court Judges

Mary Mentaberry
Director
Permanency Planning
for Children Department

Office of Juvenile Justice and
Delinquency Prevention

NATIONAL COUNCIL OF
JUVENILE AND FAMILY COURT JUDGES

INTRODUCTION[1]

Increasing numbers of infants and young children with complicated and serious physical, mental health, and developmental problems are being placed in foster care.[2] The following checklists have been developed for use by judges, attorneys, child advocates, and other child welfare professionals in meeting the wide range of health care needs of this growing population.

PHYSICAL HEALTH

Has the child received a comprehensive health assessment since entering foster care?

Because children are likely to enter foster care as a result of abuse, neglect, homelessness, poverty, parental substance abuse, or mental illness, all foster children should receive a comprehensive physical examination shortly after placement that addresses all aspects of the child's health. Under the Early and Periodic Screening, Diagnosis, and Treatment provisions of federal Medicaid law[3], foster children should receive a comprehensive assessment that can establish a baseline for a child's health status, evaluate whether the child has received necessary immunizations, and identify the need for further screening, treatment, and referral to specialists.[4] A pediatrician or family practice physician knowledgeable about the health care problems of foster children should perform the examination.[5]

Ensuring the healthy development of foster children requires that they receive quality medical care. Such care should be comprehensive, coordinated, continuous, and family-supported. One person should be identified who will oversee the child's care across the various agencies and systems, including early childhood services, early intervention services, education, and medical and mental health. Family-supportive care requires sharing the child's health information with the child's caregivers and providing caregivers with education and training programs in order to meet the needs of their foster child.

Are the child's immunizations complete and up-to-date for his or her age?

Complete, up-to-date immunizations provide the best defense against many childhood diseases that can cause devastating effects. Immunization status is an important measure of vulnerability to childhood illness and can reveal whether the child has had access to basic health care. Incomplete or delayed immunization suggests that the child is not receiving adequate medical care and is not regularly followed by a provider familiar with the child's health needs. A child should have a "well-baby" examination by two to four weeks of age. Immunizations are recommended at two, four, six, and 12 months of age. A child should have at least three visits to a pediatrician or family practice physician during the second year of life with basic immunizations completed by two years of age.[6]

Has the child received a hearing and vision screen?

Undetected hearing loss during infancy and early childhood interferes with the development of speech and language skills and can have deleterious effects on overall development, especially learning. Hearing loss during early childhood can result from childhood diseases, significant head trauma, environmental factors such as excessive noise exposure, and insufficient attention paid to health problems that may affect hearing. Studies reveal that 70 percent of children with hearing impairments are initially referred for assessment by their parents.[7] Because foster care children often lack a consistent caregiver who can observe their development and note areas of concern, they should receive ongoing evaluations of hearing, speech, and language development.

Vision screening is an essential part of preventative health care for children. Problems with vision are

---

[1] Several of the questions follow the format of and contain excerpts from the "Checklists for Healthy Development of Foster Children," *Ensuring the Healthy Development of Foster Children: A Guide for Judges, Advocates, and Child Welfare Professionals.* New York State Permanent Judicial Commission on Justice for Children, 1999. Excerpted with permission.
[2] American Academy of Pediatrics, Developmental issues for young children in foster care. *Pediatrics*, Vol.106, No. 5, pp.1145-1150. November 2000. American Academy of Pediatrics, Health care of young children in foster care. *Pediatrics*, Vol.109, No.3 pp. 536-541. March 2002.
[3] 42 U.S.C. Section 1396(a)(10) and (43)(2000); 42 U.S.C. Section 1396d(a)(4)(B)(2000) and 1396(r).
[4] 42 U.S.C. Section 1396(a)(10)(2000); 42 U.S.C. Section 1396d(a)(4)(B)(2000).
[5] *Supra* note 1.
[6] American Academy of Pediatrics, Immunizations and your child. *American Academy of Pediatrics website*, June 27, 2002.
[7] NIH Consensus Statement, Early identification of hearing impairment in infants and young children. Online 1993 March 1-3 [cited October 8, 2002]; 11 (1):1-24.

the fourth most common disability among children in the United States and the leading cause of impaired conditions in childhood.[8] Early detection and treatment increase the likelihood that a child's vision will develop normally, and, if necessary, the child will receive corrective devices.

Has the child been screened for lead exposure?

Children who are young, low-income, and have poor access to health care are vulnerable to the harmful effects of lead.[9] Ingested or inhaled lead can damage a child's brain, kidneys, and blood-forming organs. Children who are lead-poisoned may have behavioral and developmental problems. According to the Centers for Disease Control and Prevention (CDC), however, lead poisoning is one of the most preventable pediatric health problems today. Screening is important to ensure that poisoned children are identified and treated and their environments remediated.

The CDC recommends lead-poisoning screening beginning at nine months of age for children living in communities with high-risk lead levels. The CDC also recommends targeted screening based on risk assessment during pediatric visits for all other children.

Has the child received regular dental services?

Preventative dentistry means more than a beautiful smile for a child. Children with healthy mouths derive more nutrition from the food they eat, learn to speak more easily, and have a better chance of achieving good health. Every year, thousands of children between one to four years old suffer from extensive tooth decay caused by sugary liquids – especially bottles given during the night. Children living below the poverty level have twice the rate of tooth decay as children from higher income levels.[10] Furthermore, poorer children's disease is less likely to be treated.

Early dental care also prevents decay in primary ("baby") teeth which is currently at epidemic proportions in some U.S. populations and is prevalent among foster children.[11] The American Academy of Pediatric Dentistry recommends that before the age of one year, a child's basic dental care be addressed during routine "well-baby" visits with a primary care provider, with referral to a dentist if necessary. For children older than one year, the Academy recommends a check-up at least twice a year with a dental professional.

Has the child been screened for communicable diseases?

The circumstances associated with the necessity for placement in foster care – such as prenatal drug exposure, poverty, parental substance abuse, poor housing conditions, and inadequate access to health care – can increase a child's risk of exposure to communicable diseases such as HIV/AIDS, congenital syphilis, hepatitis, and tuberculosis.

A General Accounting Study found that 78 percent of foster children were at high-risk for HIV, but only nine percent had been tested for the virus.[12] Early identification of HIV is critical to support the lives of infected children and to ensure that they receive modified immunizations. Modified immunizations are necessary to prevent adverse reactions to the vaccines while still providing protection against infectious diseases such as measles and chicken pox. The American Academy of Pediatrics recommends that all prenatally HIV-exposed infants be tested for HIV at birth, at one to two months of age, and again at four months. If the tests are negative, the child should be re-tested at 12 months of age or older to document the disappearance of the HIV antibody.

Does the child have a "medical home" where he or she can receive coordinated, comprehensive, continuous health care?

All children in foster care should have a "medical home," a single-point-of-contact practitioner knowledgeable about children in foster care who oversees their primary care and periodic

---

[8] American Academy of Pediatrics, Developmental surveillance and screening of infants and young children. *Pediatrics* Vol. 108, No. 1, pp.192-196. July 2001.
[9] American Academy of Pediatrics, Screening for elevated blood lead levels (RE9815). *Pediatrics* Vol. 101, No. 6, pp. 1072-1078. June 1998.
[10] Testimony of Ed Martinez, Chief Executive Officer San Ysidro Health Center, San Diego, CA to the Senate Subcommittee on Public Health, in support of Senate Bill 1626. June 25, 2002.
[11] American Academy of Pediatrics, Early childhood caries reaches epidemic proportions (Press Release). February 1997.
[12] General Accounting Office, "Foster Care: Health Needs of Young Children Are Unknown and Unmet." GAO/Health, Education and Human Services Division, pp. 95-114. May 1995.

reassessments of physical, developmental, and emotional health, and who can make this information available as needed.

DEVELOPMENTAL HEALTH

Has the child received a developmental evaluation by a provider with experience in child development?

Young foster children often exhibit substantial delays in cognition, language, and behavior. In fact, one half of the children in foster care show developmental delay that is approximately four to five times the rate of delay found in children in the general population.[13] Early evaluation can identify developmental problems and can help caregivers better understand and address the child's needs.

Developmental evaluations provide young children who have identified delays with access to two federal entitlement programs:
- The Early Intervention Program for children under the age of three years, also known as Part C of the IDEA [20 U.S.C. Section 1431 (2000)], and
- The Preschool Special Education Grants Program for children with disabilities between the ages of three to five [20 U.S.C. Section 1419 (a) (2000)].[14]

Are the child and his or her family receiving the necessary early intervention services, e.g., speech therapy, occupational therapy, educational interventions, family support?

Finding help for young children may prevent further developmental delays and may also improve the quality of family life. Substantial evidence indicates that early intervention is most effective during the first three years of life, when the brain is establishing the foundations for all developmental, social, and cognitive domains. "The course of development can be altered in early childhood by effective interventions that change the balance between risk and protection, thereby shifting the odds in favor of more adaptive outcomes."[15] Children with

developmental delays frequently perform more poorly in school, have difficulty understanding and expressing language, misunderstand social cues, and show poor judgment.

Early intervention provides an array of services including hearing and vision screening, occupational, speech and physical therapy, and special instruction for the child, as well as family support services to enable parents to enhance their child's development. Such services can help children benefit from a more successful and satisfying educational experience, including improved peer relationships.[16] Foster children can be referred for early intervention and special education services by parents, health care workers, or social service workers. Early intervention services are an entitlement for all children from birth to three years and their families as part of Part C, IDEA. Both biological and foster families can receive Early Intervention Family Support Services to enhance a child's development.

MENTAL HEALTH

Has the child received a mental health screening, assessment, or evaluation?

Children enter foster care with adverse life experiences: family violence, neglect, exposure to parental substance abuse or serious mental illness, homelessness, or chronic poverty. Once children are placed in foster care, they must cope with the separation and loss of their family members and the uncertainty of out-of-home care. The cumulative effects of these experiences can create emotional issues that warrant an initial screening, and, sometimes, an assessment or evaluation by a mental health professional. Compared with children from the same socioeconomic background, children in the child welfare system have much higher rates of serious emotional and behavioral problems.[17] It is important to both evaluate them and offer counseling and treatment services when needed so that early difficulties are addressed and later problems are prevented.

---

[13] Dicker, S. and Gordon, E., Connecting healthy development and permanency: A pivotal role for child welfare professionals. *Permanency Planning Today*, Vol. 1, No. 1, pp. 12-15. 2000.

[14] Website: http://www.nectac.org/default.asp.

[15] Shonkoff, J. P. and Phillips, D. A., From Neurons to Neighborhoods: Committee on Integrating the Science of Early Childhood Development. National Academy Press, Washington, D.C. 2000.

[16] American Speech-Language-Hearing Association, Frequently asked questions: Helping children with communication disorders in the schools – speaking, listening, reading, and writing. *American Speech-Language-Hearing Association website*, July 1, 2002.

[17] Halfon, N., Berkowitz, G., and Klee,L., Development of an integrated case management program for vulnerable children. *Child Welfare*, Vol. 72, No. 4, pp. 379-396. 1993.

Children exhibiting certain behaviors may also signal a need for a mental health assessment and neurological and educational evaluations. Many of the symptoms associated with juvenile emotional and behavioral health problems can be alleviated if addressed early. The American Academy of Child and Adolescent Psychiatry recommends assessments for infants who exhibit fussiness, feeding and sleeping problems, and failure to thrive.[18] For toddlers, the Academy recommends assessments for children exhibiting aggressive, defiant, impulsive, and hyperactive behaviors, withdrawal, extreme sadness, and sleep and eating disorders.[19]

Is the child receiving necessary infant mental health services?

The incidence of emotional, behavioral, and developmental problems among children in foster care is three to six times greater than children in the general population.[20] Children with emotional and behavioral problems have a reduced likelihood of reunification or adoption.[21] Children with externalizing disorders, e.g., aggression and acting out, have the lowest probability of exiting foster care.[22] During infancy and early childhood, the foundations are laid for the development of trusting relationships, self-esteem, conscience, empathy, problem solving, focused learning, and impulse control.[23]

To promote and facilitate permanency, children identified with mental health problems should receive care from a mental health professional who can develop a treatment plan to strengthen the child's emotional and behavioral well-being with caregivers. Services may include clinical intervention, home visiting, early care and education, early intervention services, and caregiver support for young children.

EDUCATIONAL/CHILDCARE SETTING

Is the child enrolled in a high-quality early childhood program?

Children cannot learn unless they are healthy and safe. Children learn best in high-quality settings when they have stable relationships with highly skilled teachers.[24] Such programs nurture children, protect their health and safety, and help ensure that they are ready for school. Early childhood programs also provide much-needed support for caregivers. Considerable research has indicated that early education has a positive impact on school and life achievement. Children who participate in early childhood programs have higher rates of high school completion, lower rates of juvenile arrest, fewer violent arrests, and lower rates of dropping out of school.[25] Many foster children are eligible for early childhood programs such as Head Start, Early Head Start, and publicly funded pre-kindergarten programs for four-year-olds.

Is the early childhood program knowledgeable about the needs of children in the child welfare system?

Most children are placed in foster care because of abuse or neglect occurring within the context of parental substance abuse, extreme poverty, mental illness, homelessness, or physical disease, e.g., AIDS. As a result, a disproportionate number of children placed in foster care come from the segment of the population with the fewest psychosocial and financial resources and from families that have few personal and extended sources of support.[26] For all of these reasons, it is very important that these children's child care staff and teachers be well trained and qualified.

---

[18] American Academy of Child and Adolescent Psychiatry, Practice parameters for the psychiatric assessment of infants and toddlers. *Journal of the American Academy of Child and Adolescent Psychiatry,* Vol. 36, (10 suppl.). 1997.
[19] *Ibid.*
[20] Marsenich, L., Evidence-based practices in mental health services for foster youth. California Institute for Mental Health. March 2002.
[21] *Ibid.*
[22] *Ibid.*
[23] Greenough, W., Gunnar, M., Emde, N., Massinga, R., and Shonkoff, J., The impact of the caregiving environment on young children's development: Different ways of knowing. *Zero to Three,* Vol. 21, pp. 16-23. 2001.
[24] National Association for the Education of Young Children. Week of the young child: April 18-24. *Early Years Are Learning Years,* Vol. 99, No. 6. 1999.
[25] Reynolds, A., Temple, J., Robertson, D., and Mann, E., Long-term effects of an early childhood intervention on educational achievement and juvenile arrest: A 15-year follow-up of low-income children in public schools. *Journal of the American Medical Association,* Vol. 285, No. 18, pp. 2339-2346. 2002.
[26] National Commission on Family Foster Care, A Blueprint for Fostering Infants, Children, and Youths in the 1990s. Child Welfare League of America, Washington, D.C. 1991.

PLACEMENT

Is the child placed with caregivers knowledgeable about the social and emotional needs of infants and toddlers in out-of-home placements, especially young children who have been abused, exposed to violence, or neglected?

Do the caregivers have access to information and support related to the child's unique needs?

Are the foster parents able to identify problem behaviors in the child and seek appropriate services?

Childhood abuse increases the odds of future delinquency and adult criminality by 40 percent.[27] Maltreated infants and toddlers are at risk for insecure attachment, poor self-development, and psychopathology.[28] Children in out-of-home placements often exhibit a variety of problems which may be beyond the skills of persons without special knowledge or training. Therefore, foster parents need and should receive information about the child's history and needs as well as appropriate training.[29] Early interventions are key to minimizing the long-term and permanent effects of traumatic events on the developing brain and on behavioral and emotional development. It is imperative that

caregivers seek treatment for their foster children and themselves as soon as possible.[30]

Are all efforts being made to keep the child in one consistent placement?

An adverse prenatal environment, parental depression or stress, drug exposure, malnutrition, neglect, abuse, or physical or emotional trauma can negatively impact a child's subsequent development. Therefore, it is essential that all children, especially young children, are able to live in a nurturing, supportive, and stimulating environment.[31] It is crucial to try to keep children in one, consistent, supportive placement so that they can develop positive, secure attachment relationships.

To develop into a psychologically healthy human being, a child must have a relationship with an adult who is nurturing, protective, and fosters trust and security...Attachment to a primary caregiver is essential to the development of emotional security and social conscience.[32]

What happens during the first months and years of life matters a lot, not because this period of development provides an indelible blueprint for adult well-being, but because it sets either a sturdy or fragile stage for what follows.[33]

---

[27] Widom, C.S., The role of placement experiences in mediating the criminal consequences of early childhood victimization. *American Journal of Orthopsychiatry*, 61 (2), pp. 195-209. 1991.

[28] Widom, C.S., Motivations and mechanisms in the "cycle of violence." In D. Hansen (Ed.), *Motivation and child maltreatment: Nebraska Symposium on Motivation*, Vol. 46, pp.1-37. 2000.

[29] National Foster Parent Association, *Board manual: Goals, objectives, position statements, and by-laws*. Gig Harbor, Washington. 1999.

[30] Carnegie Task Force on Meeting the Needs of Young Children, *Starting Points: Meeting the Needs of our Youngest Children*. New York, NY, Carnegie Corporation. 1994.

[31] *Supra note 2.*

[32] *Ibid.*

[33] *Supra note 15.*

National Council of Juvenile and Family Court Judges
P. O. Box 8970, Reno, NV 89507

B

Sample Court Reports

Dependency Parenting Provider Initiative Court Reports:

- Completion and Submission Guidelines 124
- Initial Report 127
- Status Report 132
- Final Report 137
- Notice of Termination of Services 143

Early Head Start Sample Court Report 148

Infant Mental Health Therapist Court Report 151

Dependency Parenting Provider Initiative Report Completion and Submission Guidelines

These guidelines and the reports they describe were developed collaboratively by child welfare case management agencies and parenting program providers. The development process was facilitated by the Miami-Dade Community-Based Care Alliance and the Miami Administrative Office of the Court.

Note: An asterisk (*) indicates that the report template is included in this appendix.

General Information
- One report per parent
- List all children of the parent who is the subject of the report.
- All reports will be submitted to Judge (via the court case management unit), full care management agency (FCMA) parenting point person, Department of Children and Families (DCF) children's legal services, Guardian ad Litem (GAL) program, and the parent. Contact information is attached.

Referral Form—please see separate instructions

Cover Sheet
Purpose: To serve as a cover sheet for all parenting program reports for a parent and to eliminate the need for the parenting program to retype key identifying information for each report
When completed/submitted: The cover sheet is created after receiving the referral and will serve as the cover page for the Referral Screening, Initial Report, Status Reports, Final Report, and Termination of Services report.

Referral Screening
Purpose: To acknowledge referral from FCMA and to provide information to FCMA regarding anticipated date that parent will start parenting course, if appropriate, and if there is availability
When completed/submitted: Within 10 business days of receipt of the standard referral for a dependency court–involved family for a parenting program. Parenting providers will strive to meet the referred parent during this time frame and complete an intake appointment.

Initial Report*
Purpose: To provide information about the parent's enrollment in the course, the anticipated completion date, initial scores on the preservice behavioral observation (if applicable) and the preservice AAPI-2, areas that will be addressed and additional service/treatment concerns
When completed/submitted: Within 2 days after the preservice behavioral observation (if applicable) and the preservice AAPI-2 (whichever happens last) and before the family begins the parenting program (whenever possible)
Attachments: Pre AAPI-2 Summary and Pre Behavioral Observation (if applicable) score sheets and one-page description of evidence-based parenting program

Status Report*
Purpose: To provide current information on the progress of the parent in the parenting course, to address issues of concern as they arise, and to serve as ongoing communication between the parenting provider and child welfare team

(continued)

When completed/submitted: Within 2 business days after each four-session period the family is in the parenting course. Note that if a parenting course is not evenly divided by four sessions, a status report will be completed and submitted within 2 business days after the final session.

Final Report

Purpose: To summarize the family's progress and to document the current strengths and weaknesses in the family. Also to document change in the parent and parent–child interaction over time and the parent's ability to use the tools and strategies offered

When completed/submitted: Within 10 business days of the completion of the parenting program, the post-service behavioral observation (when applicable) and the post-service AAPI-2

Attachments: Pre and post AAPI-2 Summaries and pre and post Behavioral Observation Score Sheets

Notice of Termination of Services

Purpose: To advise the child welfare team that a parent has been terminated early from services, to document the reasons why, and to capture progress made up to the point of termination

When completed: Within a week of the early termination of a parent from a parenting program

Dependency Parenting Provider Initiative
Initial Report

This report provides the court with the baseline assessment data collected by the assigned parenting provider and outlines the individualized curriculum needs that will follow.

This report is the first completed by the parenting program facilitator prior to the parent beginning the program and after an initial observation and administration of the Adult-Adolescent Parenting Inventory–2 (AAPI-2).

Dependency Parenting Provider Initiative
Initial Report

By: _Parenting Program Inc._
approved parenting provider agency name

This report summarizes the scores of the **pre (baseline) valid and reliable parenting inventory measure** (i.e., the Adult-Adolescent Parenting Inventory–2 (AAPI-2). For a parent with children
ages 0–5, this report also summarizes the **pre (baseline) behavioral observation** between the parent named below and his/her child in the 0–5 age range. Both the behavioral observation and/or the AAPI-2 are completed **before** the parent starts a parenting program. The summaries provided are most useful as baseline information to identify the strengths and challenges of a particular parent so the parenting program can be tailored to meet his/her particular needs. The same measures will be completed upon the parent's completion of the parenting program and will be reported in the Final Report.

INSERT CLIENT INFORMATION SHEET

Dependency case #: _____ Judge: _____

Referring agency: _____ Referral date: _____

Case manager: _____ Telephone/fax: _____

Supervisor: _____ Telephone/fax: _____

Guardian ad Litem program appointed? ___ No ___ Yes (GAL name: _____)

Client Information

Parent's name: _____
                     Last   First
If a foster parent/relative/nonrelative (circle one) is participating in the program rather than the parent, please list that individual's name.

Child(ren)'s name(s): _____ DOB _____ Age (years, months)

_____ _____ _____
     Last   First

_____ _____ _____
     Last   First

_____ _____ _____
     Last   First

Please place an * by all children who participated in a Behavioral Observation.

Parenting Program Information

Parent is enrolled in the following program(s) offered by our agency. Please see attached (or below) for a full program description(s).

___ Nurturing Parenting   ___ Strengthening Families

___ Baby & Me   ___ Other: _____

Parent–child interaction ___ is ___ is not a component of our parenting program at this time.

Parent–child interaction will be focused on _____ who is _____ old.

Languages offered (circle all that apply): English   Spanish   Creole   Other: _____

This program has _____ sessions over _____ weeks.

The service is delivered (circle one): at our agency   at the parent's home

Scheduled start date: _____   Anticipated completion date: _____

Behavioral Observation Information (only for children ages 0–5)

The Behavioral Observation rating scales were developed for children ages birth to 5 years old by Dr. Joy Osofsky, Louisiana State University, and Dr. Anne Hogan, Florida State University Center for Prevention and Early Intervention, as an adaptation of their clinical version. The parenting facilitator who completed this report was trained by experienced clinicians who were trained directly by Dr. Osofsky in the procedural methods. The preservice behavioral observation provides a window into the strengths and weaknesses of the parent–child interactions/communications, and so forth, that will need to be addressed in the parenting classes at the onset.

The preservice behavioral observation of the above-named parent and
_____, who was _____ year(s), _____ month(s) old, took place on _____.
      child's name   date

Preservice Behavioral Observation Summary:

[Behavioral observation information pertaining to other children ages 0–5 who participated in a behavioral observation with this parent should be inserted here.]

(continued)

Adult-Adolescent Parenting Inventory–2 (AAPI-2)[1]

The Adult-Adolescent Parenting Inventory–2 is designed to assess the parenting and child-rearing attitudes of adults and adolescent parents and pre-parent populations. Based on the known parenting and child-rearing behaviors of abusive parents, responses to the inventory provide an index for practicing behaviors known to be attributable to child abuse and neglect. Responses to the AAPI-2 provide an index of risk in five specific parenting and child-rearing behaviors:

Construct A: Inappropriate expectations of children
Construct B: Parental lack of empathy toward children's needs
Construct C: Strong parental belief in the use of corporal punishment
Construct D: Reversing parent–child family roles
Construct E: Oppressing children's power and independence

The preservice AAPI-2 was completed on: _____

Preservice Adult-Adolescent Parenting Inventory-2 Summary:

Construct A: Inappropriate expectations of children

Construct B: Parental lack of empathy toward children's needs

Construct C: Strong parental belief in the use of corporal punishment

Construct D: Reversing parent–child family roles

Construct E: Oppressing children's power and independence

Strengths and Challenges

Strengths:

Challenges:

Areas to focus on during parenting program:

[1]Bavolek, S.J., & Keen, R.G. (1999). *Adult-Adolescent Parenting Inventory, Version 2 (AAPI-2): Administration and development handbook.* Park City, UT: Family Development Resources.

Additional comments:

Completed by: _____   Date completed: _____
parenting facilitator

Approved by: _____   Date approved: _____
parenting program director/coordinator

Submitted (via fax, U.S. mail, and/or hand delivery) on _____ to the following:
date

- Judge
- DCF Children's Legal Services
- Full Case Management Agency Parenting Program Point Person
- GAL Program
- Parent/Client

Attachments:

- Preservice behavioral observation summary score sheet (if applicable)
- AAPI-2 score sheet
- Parenting program description (note that parenting providers may provide a description in the text of the report)

Dependency Parenting Provider Initiative
Status Report

This document is an example of a status report completed by the parenting program facilitator every four sessions.

This report is produced with the frequency required by the court and allows those involved with the case to review what progress the parent has made and/or challenges the parents is facing.

Dependency Parenting Provider Initiative
Status Report

Starting : _____ and ending _____

By: _____

This report provides an update on the status of the progress made by the parent and child(ren) named below who are enrolled in our agency's parenting program. These status reports will be provided to the case manager every four (4) weeks during the parent's enrollment in the parenting program until the parent's successful completion of the program or early termination from the program.

Dependency case #: _____ Judge: _____

Referring agency: _____ Referral date: _____

Case manager: _____ Telephone/fax: _____

Supervisor: _____ Telephone/fax: _____

Guardian ad Litem program appointed? ___ No ___ Yes (GAL name: _____)

Client Information

Parent's name: _____
                 Last   First

If a foster parent / relative / nonrelative (circle one) is participating in the program rather than the parent, please list that individual's name.

Child(ren)'s name(s):		DOB	Age (years, months)
Last	First		
Last	First		
Last	First		
Last	First		

Please place an * by all children who participated in a behavioral observation.

(continued)

Parenting Program Information

Parent is enrolled in the following program(s) offered by our agency. Please see program description(s) attached to/included in the Initial Report for details.

___ Nurturing Parenting   ___ Strengthening Families

___ Baby & Me   ___ Other: _____

Parent–child interaction ___ is ___ is not a component of our parenting program at this time.

Parent–child interaction will be focused on _____ who is _____old.

Languages offered (circle all that apply): English   Spanish   Creole   Other: _____

The service is delivered at the parent's home at our agency (circle one)

Start date: _____   Anticipated completion date: _____

Completion date extended: _____ No _____ Yes (because: _____)

Attendance, Participation, and Progress

Note: *The following information is an overall assessment that pertains to the past _____ weeks of this parent's participation in the parenting program.*

The parent has attended _____ out of _____ sessions offered to date.

Overall, the parent (circle one) has attended / has not attended the sessions on time.

During the parent group sessions, the parent (circle one):

actively participates   participates with prompting   does not participate

As evidenced by: _____

_____

During the parent–child interactive segment (if applicable), the parent demonstrates appropriate parenting (circle one):

most of the time   some of the time   none of the time   not applicable

As evidenced by: _____

_____

Additional Comments

Note: These comments are meant to provide a snapshot of parent/child functioning drawn from weekly facilitator notes, the preservice structured behavioral observation (if applicable), the preservice parenting inventory (AAPI-2), participation levels, and the quality of the parent–child(ren) interactions (if applicable).

Additional Service and/or Treatment Needs

Note: The following are only recommendations and should be evaluated in the context of the case plan and the services already provided/required of the family. *Please be advised that this agency will NOT make referrals for any of the services suggested below.*

Additional treatment or service needs of PARENT (check all that apply):
- Domestic violence counseling for victims
- Batterers intervention program
- Anger management
- Substance abuse screening/treatment
- Mental health counseling
- Life skills
- Vocational skills training
- Economic services
- Developmental services
- Physical health concerns: _____
- Other: _____
- None recommended at this time

Additional treatment or service needs of CHILD(REN) (check all that apply):

Child's name: _____
- Child care
- After-school program
- Mental health counseling
- Play therapy
- Part C evaluation (ages 0–3)
- Kidcare
- Part B evaluation (ages 3–5)
- Medical care for: _____
- Dental care for: _____
- Other: _____
- None recommended at this time

(continued)

Child's name: _____

- Child care
- After-school program
- Mental health counseling
- Play therapy
- Part C evaluation (ages 0–3)
- Kidcare
- Part B evaluation (ages 3–5)
- Medical care for: _____
- Dental care for: _____
- Other: _____
- None recommended at this time

[Cut and paste this section for additional children.]

Completed by: _____   Date completed: _____
parenting facilitator

Approved by: _____   Date approved: _____
parenting program coordinator/director

Parenting provider: _____   Telephone: _____

Submitted (via fax, U.S. mail, and/or hand delivery) on _____ to the following:
date

Judge
DCF Children's Legal Services
Full Case Management Agency Parenting Program Point Person
GAL Program
Parent/Client

Dependency Parenting Provider Initiative
Final Report

This document is an example of a final report completed by the parenting program facilitator. This report details the progress or lack thereof for the parent enrolled in the parenting program. All data collected as part of the pre- and post-assessments and/or weekly progress notes are attached and recommendations as to satisfactory completion are included.

Dependency Parenting Provider Initiative
Final Report

By: _____

approved parenting provider agency name

This report summarizes the progress made by the parent named below at the completion of this agency's parenting program and includes the post-service behavioral observation (with children ages 0–5) (if applicable) and the post-service Adult-Adolescent Parenting Inventory–2 (AAPI-2).

Dependency case #: _____ Judge: _____

Referring agency: _____ Referral date: _____

Case manager: _____ Telephone/fax: _____

Supervisor: _____ Telephone/fax: _____

Guardian ad Litem program appointed? ___ No ___ Yes (GAL name: _____)

Client Information

Parent's name: _____
                         Last   First

If a foster parent/relative/nonrelative (circle one) is participating in the program rather than the parent, please list that individual's name.

Child(ren)'s name(s):   DOB   Age (years, months)

_____ _____   _____   _____
       Last   First

_____ _____   _____   _____
       Last   First

_____ _____   _____   _____
       Last   First

Please place an * by all children who participated in a behavioral observation.

138

Parenting Program Information

Parent is enrolled in the following program(s) offered by our agency. Please see program description(s) attached to the Initial Report for details.

___ Nurturing Parenting   ___ Strengthening Families

___ Baby & Me   ___ Other: _____

☒

Parent–child interaction ___ is ___ is not a component of our parenting program at this time.

Parent–child interaction was focused on _____, who is _____ old.

Languages offered (circle all that apply): English Spanish Creole Other: _____

The service is delivered (circle one) at our agency ☒ at the parent's home ☒

Start date: _____   Completion date: _____

Attendance, Participation, and Progress

Note: The following information is an overall assessment that pertains to the parent's participation throughout the course of the parenting program.

The parent has attended _____ out of _____ sessions provided.

Overall, the parent (circle one) ☒ attended the sessions on time / ☒ did not attend the sessions on time.

During the parent group sessions, the parent (circle one):

actively participated   participated with prompting   did not participate

As evidenced by: _____

_____

During the parent–child interactive segment (if applicable), the parent demonstrated appropriate parenting (circle one):

most of the time   some of the time   none of the time   not applicable

As evidenced by: _____

_____

(continued)

Behavioral Observation Information
(only for children ages 0–5, description attached)

The Behavioral Observation rating scales were developed for children ages birth to 5 years old by Dr. Joy Osofsky, Louisiana State University, and Dr. Anne Hogan, Florida State University Center for Prevention and Early Intervention, as an adaptation of their clinical version. The parenting facilitator who completed this report was trained by experienced clinicians who were trained directly by Dr. Osofsky in the procedural methods. The post-service behavioral observation provides feedback as to the integration of positive parenting skills and positive changes in the parent–child interactions subsequent to the completion of the parenting program.

The post-service behavioral observation of the above-named parent and

_____, who was ___ year(s), _____ month(s) old, took place on _____.

Postservice Behavioral Observation Summary:
Adult-Adolescent Parenting Inventory–2 (AAPI-2)[1]

The AAPI-2 is designed to assess the parenting and child-rearing attitudes of adults and adolescent parents and pre-parent populations. Based on the known parenting and child-rearing behaviors of abusive parents, responses to the inventory provide an index for practicing behaviors known to be attributable to child abuse and neglect. Responses to the AAPI-2 provide an index of risk in five specific parenting and child-rearing behaviors:

Construct A: Inappropriate expectations of children
Construct B: Parental lack of empathy toward children's needs
Construct C: Strong parental belief in the use of corporal punishment
Construct D: Reversing parent–child family roles
Construct E: Oppressing children's power and independence

The post-service AAPI-2 was completed on: _____

Postservice Adult–Adolescent Parenting Inventory-2 Summary:

Construct A: Inappropriate expectations of children
Construct B: Parental lack of empathy toward children's needs
Construct C: Strong parental belief in the use of corporal punishment
Construct D: Reversing parent–child family roles
Construct E: Oppressing children's power and independence

Changes in Parenting Behavior and Beliefs

Summary of changes observed from pre to post during the behavioral observation process (if applicable):
Summary of changes noted on the AAPI-2 from pre to post:
Construct A: Inappropriate expectations of children
Construct B: Parental lack of empathy toward children's needs
Construct C: Strong parental belief in the use of corporal punishment

[1]Bavolek, S.J., & Keen, R.G. (1999). *Adult-Adolescent Parenting Inventory, Version 2 (AAPI-2): Administration and development handbook.* Park City, UT: Family Development Resources.

Construct D: Reversing parent–child family roles
Construct E: Oppressing children's power and independence
Other Comments:

Summary of parent–child current functioning from weekly facilitator notes as well as the structured behavioral observations, the parenting inventories, participation levels, and the quality of the parent–child(ren) interactions:

Additional Service and/or Treatment Needs

Note: The following are only recommendations and should be evaluated in the context of the case plan and the services already provided/required of the family. Please be advised that this agency will NOT make referrals for any of the services suggested below.

Additional treatment or service needs of PARENT (check all that apply):
- Domestic violence counseling for victims
- Batterers intervention program
- Anger management
- Life skills
- Vocational skills training
- Economic services
- Developmental services
- Substance abuse screening/treatment
- Mental health counseling
- Parenting support group
- Physical health concerns: _____
- Other: _____
- None recommended at this time

Additional treatment or service needs of CHILD(REN) (check all that apply):

Child's name: _____
- Child care
- Afterschool program
- Mental health counseling
- Play therapy
- Part C evaluation (ages 0–3)
- Kidcare
- Part B evaluation (ages 3–5)
- Medical care for: _____
- Dental care for: _____
- Other: _____
- None recommended at this time

(continued)

Child's name: _____

- Child care
- Afterschool program
- Mental health counseling
- Play therapy
- Part C evaluation (ages 0–3)
- Kidcare
- Part B evaluation (ages 3–5)
- Medical care for: _____
- Dental care for: _____
- Other: _____
- None recommended at this time

[Cut and paste for additional children.]

Completed by: _____　　　Date completed: _____
　　　　　　　　　　parenting facilitator

Approved by: _____　　　Date approved: _____
　　　　　　　　parenting program coordinator/director

Parenting provider: _____　　Telephone: _____

Submitted (via fax, U.S. mail, and/or hand delivery) on _____ to the following:
　　　　　　　　　　　　　　　　　　　　　　　　　　date

Judge
DCF Children's Legal Services
Full Case Management Agency Parenting Program Point Person
GAL Program
Parent/Client: hand delivery

Attachments:
- Preservice *and* postservice behavioral observation summary sheets (if applicable)
- Preservice and postservice AAPI-2 score sheets

Dependency Parenting Provider Initiative
Notice of Termination of Services

This is an example of a notification of early termination of parenting services. This report is completed when a parent either drops out of the parenting program or is required to leave the program. It details the reason why the parenting program's services have been terminated and reports progress or lack thereof for the client enrolled in the parenting program up until the date of termination of services. Any data collected as part of the assessment and/or weekly progress notes are attached and recommendations (if applicable) are included.

Dependency Parenting Provider Initiative
Notice of Termination of Services

This form is being sent to inform you that the parent below named has been terminated early from our agency's parenting program. Our termination policy is as follows:

Dependency case #: _____ Judge: _____

Referring agency: _____ Referral date: _____

Case manager: _____ Telephone/fax: _____

Supervisor: _____ Telephone/fax: _____

Guardian ad Litem program appointed? ___ No ___ Yes (GAL name: _____)

Client Information
Parent's name

_____
               Last   First

Child(ren)'s name(s):   DOB   Age (years, months)

_____   _____   _____
     Last   First

_____   _____   _____
     Last   First

_____   _____   _____
     Last   First

_____
     Last   First

Please place an * by all children who participated in a behavioral observation.

Parenting Program Information

Parent was enrolled in the following program(s) offered by our agency. Please see program description(s) attached to/included in the Initial Report for details.

___ Nurturing Parenting   ___ Strengthening Families

___ Baby & Me   ___ Other: _____

Began parenting program on: _____

Was expected to complete program on: _____

Preservice behavioral observation completed on (if applicable): _____

Preservice AAPI-2 completed on: _____

Termination Information

Parent was terminated from services on: _____

Parent was terminated from services because he/she did not comply with the following terms of the participant contract and/or (check all that apply):

- Had _____ unexcused absences

- Had _____ excused absences

- Engaged in inappropriate behavior with other participants

- Parent no longer wishes to participate and did not respond to efforts to reengage in the parenting program

- Did not complete the preservice Behavioral Observation despite efforts to engage the parent

- Did not complete the preservice AAPI-2 despite efforts to engage the parent

- Parent became incarcerated

- Parent was deported

- Was not appropriate for this parenting program due to _____

- Was unable to complete the program due to _____

- Other: _____

(continued)

Attendance, Participation, and Progress

The parent attended _____ out of _____ sessions prior to termination.

Overall, the parent (circle one) ☒ has attended / has not attended the sessions on time. During the parent group sessions, the parent (circle one):

actively participated   participated with prompting   did not participate

As evidenced by: _____

_____

During the parent–child interactive segment, the parent demonstrated appropriate parenting (circle one):

most of the time   some of the time   none of the time   not applicable

As evidenced by: _____

_____

Additional Comments

Note: These comments should provide a snapshot of parent/child functioning at the time of termination of services drawn from weekly facilitator notes, the preservice structured behavioral observation (if applicable), the preservice parenting inventory (AAPI-2), participation levels, and the quality of the parent–child(ren) interactions.

Additional Service and/or Treatment Needs

Note: The following are only recommendations and should be evaluated in the context of the case plan and the services already provided/required of the family. *Please be advised that this agency will NOT make referrals for any of the services suggested below.*

Additional treatment or service needs of PARENT (check all that apply):
- Domestic violence counseling for victims
- Batterers intervention program
- Anger management
- Life skills
- Vocational skills training
- Economic services
- Developmental services
- Physical health concerns: _____
- Other: _____
- None recommended at this time

Additional treatment or service needs of CHILD(REN) (check all that apply):

Child's name: _____

- Child care
- Afterschool program
- Part C evaluation (ages 0–3)
- Kidcare
- Part B evaluation (ages 3–5)
- Medical care for: _____
- Dental care for: _____
- Other: _____
- None recommended at this time

[Cut and paste for additional children.]

Completed by: _____   Date completed: _____
parenting facilitator

Approved by: _____   Date approved: _____
parenting program director

Submitted (via fax/U.S. mail/hand delivery) on _____ to the following:
date

Judge
DCF Children's Legal Services
Full Case Management Agency Parenting Program Point Person
GAL Program
Parent/Client

Early Head Start Sample Court Report

This sample report illustrates important information that the EHS teacher and/or social worker can provide to the court and other parties/participants in the case.

This report template was developed through the Miami EHSCWS collaborative (2006) with funding from a U.S. Department of Health and Human Services grant (Award # 06CH0119).

Early Head Start / Child Welfare Services Initiative
Teacher/Social Worker Court Report

Child's name: _____ Dependency case: _____

              Last   First

Hearing date/type:_____ Judge: _____

Teacher: _____ Social worker: _____

              name   name

Phone: _____

Early Head Start Information

Enrollment date: _____ EHS Center: _____

Number of unexcused absences (from beginning of school year to report date): _____

Concerns/comments (if any) about attendance:_____

_____

Parent/Caregiver and Case Worker Involvement
Level of parent participation:

❑ High ❑ Moderate ❑ Minimal ❑ None ❑ N/A (parent not allowed contact with child)

Explanation/concerns: _____

_____

Level of foster parent/relative or nonrelative caregiver participation:

❑ High ❑ Moderate ❑ Minimal ❑ None ❑ N/A (child placed with parent[s] or other
permanent caregiver)

Explanation/concerns:_____

_____

Last contact with CWS partners:

❑ Case manager:_____ ❑ GAL/child's attorney:_____

                        date   date

❑ LRIC/IMH therapist: _____ ❑ Other: _____

                        date   agency/name

(continued)

Child's Progress and Service Provision Needs

Developmental progress of child:

❑ Age appropriate ❑ Minimal delays ❑ Significant delays

*If minimal or significant delays, please describe status of early intervention referrals/services: _____

_____

Overall impressions of child's well-being: _____

_____

Concerns about child's well-being: _____

_____

Additional comments or child needs:_____

_____

Respectfully submitted,

_____ _____ Will attend hearing? ❑ Yes ❑ No
teacher's signature   date

_____ _____ Will attend hearing? ❑ Yes ❑ No
teacher's signature   date

Reviewed by: _____
EHS Infant Toddler Coordinator

cc: CWS Case Manager
       IMH Therapist
       DCF Attorney
       Attorney for parent(s)
       Attorney for child

Infant Mental Health Therapist Court Report

The infant mental health therapist provides a report to the court at the beginning of the case (baseline) and at regular intervals thereafter. The report contains information about the child–parent attachment, the strengths of the relationship, and areas of concern that need to be addressed through the clinical treatment plan. Through clinical observations and by collecting additional data from the parent using questionnaires, screening tools, and assessment measures, the therapist is able to capture the status of the child–parent relationship over the course of treatment and present it to the court.

Infant Mental Health (IMH)
Therapist Report

Child's name: _Gloria Noorman_   Date of birth: _09/15/2004_

Chronological age: _29 months_   Corrected age: _N/A_

Race/ethnicity: _White/Hispanic_   Gender: _Female_

Mother's name: _Juliana Noorman_   Father's name: _Thomas Russen_

Age: _16_   Age: _26_

Race/ethnicity: _White/Hispanic_   Age/ethnicity: _White/Hispanic_

Referral source: _Judge Arlington_   Primary caregiver: _Stephanie Tampelli_

Observation/interview dates: _February 2, 2007, February 8, 2007, February 27, 2007, March 6, 2007_

Observation/Interviews/Assessment Instruments

Face-to-face contact with biological mother (home visit)

Clinical observations of parent–child interaction with biological mother

Ages & Stages Questionnaires, 2nd Edition (ASQ-2)

Ages & Stages Questionnaires: Social-Emotional (ASQ:SE)

Pediatric intake

Background information form

Collateral Information obtained from Meredith Gorson, case worker; Ben Kirkman, case worker; and Bridgette Emerson, Guardian Ad Litem Assistant Supervisor.

Reason for Referral

The referral was initiated by Judge Arlington for the purpose of evaluating the child, Gloria Noorman, with her mother and providing Child–Parent Psychotherapy (CPP) if appropriate. In October 2006, a Petition for Court Ordered Services and Protective Services was filed and accepted by the court. According to the Verified Petition for Dependency, the Department of Children and Families received a report regarding allegations that "the mother had been diagnosed with bipolar disorder and the maternal grandparents suffer from depression with psychotic features." The Petition also reports that Thomas Russen, the father of the mother's youngest child, Christina, was arrested on August 6, 2006, due to physically abusing the mother. Allegations also include a history of domestic violence between the mother and Mr. Russen. It is reported that the children were present during the domestic violence incidents, and that Gloria was struck during the altercation that led to Mr. Russen's arrest.

Background Information

Family History

Juliana Noorman, 16 years old, is the biological mother of 29-month-old Gloria Noorman. Juliana Noorman also has a 10-month-old daughter, Christina, and is currently approximately 8 months pregnant. Ms. Noorman reports that she is currently living with her fiancé and his family. Ms. Noorman reports to have attended school through the tenth grade, during which she dropped out. She reports having difficulty reading and spelling. She is currently not working. She reports to have only worked for about a month when she was about 13 years old, helping with hurricane damage home inspections. Ms. Noorman reports to have been diagnosed with bipolar disorder when she was six years old. She further reports that she had been taking medication since she was diagnosed but is currently not taking any medication because she is pregnant. Ms. Noorman could not recall the names of her medications.

Ms. Noorman reports that she was removed from her mother's care at a very young age due to her mother's substance abuse. She reports the she was placed in her father's care for a short period of time and then placed with her grandmother because her father could not care for her at that time. She reports that her parents got back together when she was about 6 years old and she lived with them at that time. Ms. Noorman reports that her mother was in and out of the house and was heavily involved with drugs and alcohol. She reports that her mother would physically abuse her and allow her boyfriends to physically and sexually abuse her, even when Ms. Noorman was as young as six years of age. Ms. Noorman reports that since her father allowed her mother to reside in the home, Ms. Noorman was then removed from her father's custody and placed in a foster home when she was about 13 years old. She was in a foster home when she gave birth to Gloria. Ms. Noorman was reunified with her father when Gloria was about 7 months old, and Ms. Noorman has been in her father's custody since then.

Thomas Russen, 26 years old, is named as the father on the birth certificate. According to the mother, the father attends court hearings and reports that he wants visitation with Gloria. According to the Verified Petition for Dependency, Mr. Russen is incarcerated and waiting trial for beating the minor mother. The mother reports that Gloria and Christina were present when Mr. Russen was beating her and that Mr. Russen also hit Gloria. The mother reports that Mr. Russen threatened to kill her and her children. She reports Mr. Russen was violent and that she was scared of him. According to the petition, Mr. Russen has an extensive criminal record including robbery, burglary, making obscene phone calls, loitering, trespassing, petit theft, grand theft, battery, aggravated battery on a pregnant woman, using a false name, and cocaine possession.

Placement History of Child

Gloria Noorman, a Hispanic female, was born when her mother had been removed from her parents and was residing in a foster home. Upon Gloria's birth, a petition for protective supervision was filed and subsequently dismissed. Due to allegations of domestic violence and the mother's mental health concerns, a second petition was filed and Gloria was placed under protective supervision when she was about 25 months old.

Gloria has been in her mother's care since birth. She spent the first 2 weeks of life with her mother in her mother's foster home. The mother reports that Gloria was repeatedly

(continued)

hospitalized from age two weeks until age 4 months of her life for acid reflux and observation. Once released from the hospital, Gloria was placed again with her mother in her foster home. Ms. Noorman was reunified with her father when Gloria was about 7 months old. Gloria has been living with her mother and maternal grandfather since she was about 7 months old until about the beginning of January 2007. At this time, the mother and maternal grandfather, along with Gloria and her sibling, moved in with the great maternal grandfather and great maternal step-mother and maternal aunt. The mother reports that Gloria has been living with her at the maternal grandfather's home during the week and at her fiancé's home on the weekends.

Collateral Reports of Gloria's Functioning

The mother is highly concerned about Gloria's behavior. She reports that Gloria has tantrums on a daily basis and exhibits aggression by hitting adults and other children, including her younger sister. The mother reports that Gloria pulls her own hair and hits herself. The mother is also concerned about Gloria's speech and language, as the mother reports that Gloria is only saying one-word sentences and her speech is difficult for others to understand. The mother is also concerned about Gloria's eating habits and explains that it is difficult for her to have Gloria sit down to eat a meal. The mother describes Gloria as very active and that "she only eats when she wants to eat." The mother also reports that she is concerned that Gloria may be "depressed," as she has observed her several times appearing sad, withdrawn, and disinterested in playing. Another concern that the mother reports is that Gloria appears to be overly friendly with strangers. The mother reports that Gloria sleeps well at night.

The caseworker, Lisa Barnes, also reports concerns regarding Gloria's speech and language and her overall development. Gloria is not attending child care.

Developmental and Medical History

The mother reports that she received regular prenatal care during her pregnancy with Gloria. The mother reported that she was pregnant with twins, but that Gloria's twin died at birth due to the umbilical cord being wrapped around the neck. The mother stated that she delivered Gloria at Overlook Hospital at 43 weeks' gestation. At birth, Gloria's weight was 8 pounds and length was 22 inches.

The mother reports that Gloria was hospitalized for a week when she was 2 years old due to a dog bite to the face. The mother reported that she had left Gloria under supervision of Thomas Russen. The mother reported that they took Gloria to the emergency room at about 3:00 a.m. but since the hospital could not see her immediately, they went back to sleep and took Gloria to the hospital the next day.

The mother could not recall the exact date of Gloria's last physical exam but reports that it was about five months ago. She reports that there were no concerns and that Gloria is up-to-date on her immunizations.

Observations/Assessments

Ages & Stages Questionnaires, Second Edition (ASQ-2): The ASQ-2 is administered to children between the ages of 2 months and 60 months. The instrument is a caregiver-monitoring screening instrument based on a caregiver interview with an early education specialist. This screening does not predict the child's long-term performance but rather provides guidance regarding necessary interventions.

Gloria's ASQ-2 was completed in English with her mother at 27 months old. Following are her scores:

	Score	Cutoff
Communication	20	35.0
Gross motor	55	25.0
Fine motor	60	25.0
Problem solving	40	25.0
Personal-social	60	25.0

Gloria appears to be functioning at age level in gross motor, fine motor, problem solving, and personal-social functioning. Gloria appears to have a significant delay in the area of Communication.

Ages & Stages Questionnaires: Social-Emotional (ASQ:SE)
The ASQ:SE is administered to children between the ages of 6 months and 60 months. The ASQ:SE is a caregiver-monitoring screening instrument based on the caregiver and child interview with an early childhood specialist. Like the ASQ-2 developmental question-naire, this screening tool is only to be interpreted as a guideline for practitioners to indicate a need for further assessment and for possible referrals for interventions.

Gloria's ASQ:SE was completed in English with her mother at 30 months old. Following is her score:

Score	Cutoff
130	57

The scores above the cutoff, as with Gloria's scores, indicate a significant delay in social-emotional functioning.

Clinical Observation of Parent–Child and/or Caregiver–Child Interaction:
The following observations and interpretations are of a clinical nature and are not derived as a result of standardized psychological measures.

The Crowell is a semistructured assessment that consists of a 10-minute free play period, clean up, one transition activity, three structured tasks, and a separation and reunion period. The assessment takes place in a playroom setting in which a variety of toys are provided to the primary caregiver and child. The instructions are given to the parent prior to the start of the assessment, and each task is demonstrated. When it is time to transition to the next activity, the clinician signals to the caregiver without interrupting the assessment. The interactions are video recorded with the consent of the primary caregiver.

Clinical Observation Between Gloria and Her Mother:
Ms. Noorman arrived early for the evaluation. She came with her father, Albert Noorman, and her two daughters, Gloria and Christina. The mother's appearance was disheveled. The child's hygiene was appropriate but she was wearing an oversized sweater and oversized pants. The mother was cooperative and polite. After discussing the purpose of

(continued)

the evaluation and the instructions of the evaluation, the mother was able to confirm that she comprehended what was expected of her.

Gloria was hesitant to leave her maternal grandfather. She screamed and cried when she had to separate from him to go into the play observation room with her mother. Once Gloria saw the toys in the room, she ceased crying and engaged in play with the toys. Despite the mother's reports of being Gloria's primary caregiver, it appears from this separation, that the maternal grandfather is Gloria's primary caregiver. The mother verbally minimized the child's distress as evidenced by asking her to stop crying.

During the clinical observation with the mother, the therapist observed neutral affect as to the mother. The mother's responsiveness toward Gloria was primarily one of disinterest. When the mother interacted with Gloria, its appeared forced or with a sense of obligation. Juliana did not exhibit any overt signs of irritability, anger, or hostility toward Gloria. The majority of the free play portion of the evaluation consisted of parallel play in which the mother and daughter played separately and did not interact with each other. When the mother would interact with Gloria, the mother would structure the play in a way that was inappropriate for Gloria's developmental level and Gloria's interests. The mother had difficulty responding to Gloria's emotional needs.

The mother's participation improved during the structured play, during which the mother was given specific instructions of how to complete the activity with Gloria. The mother used some modeling and praise to encourage Gloria to complete the task. Even though the mother attempted to engage Gloria in the tasks, Gloria did not respond to her mother's efforts.

Gloria exhibited an overall neutral affect and her responsiveness to her mother was one of indifference. Gloria was interested in the toys but was not enthusiastic about the play with her mother. She had her back turned to her mother and was playing on her own throughout most of the free play portion of the evaluation. She maintained physical distance from her mother and rejected her mother's few attempts to engage her in play. Gloria was noncompliant with her mother's directives. She was aggressive toward her mother during a tantrum and attempted to bite her mother's arm.

Concerns regarding Gloria's development were observed during the observation. Gloria's speech and language was observed to be significantly delayed. Gloria was also observed to be awkward in her walking, which may suggest concerns regarding her gross motor skills. Gloria would also often lie on her side or tilt her head while she was playing, and it is unclear whether this was in reference to visual, auditory, or sensory difficulties.

During the separation and reunion portion of the observation, Gloria kept her back turned to her mother when the mother returned to the room. Gloria did not acknowledge when her mother returned and did not seek interaction with her. Gloria continued to play with her toys and did not reference her mother. The mother went directly to Gloria when she returned and talked to Gloria, but Gloria ignored her.

Conclusion

Gloria is a 29-month-old white Hispanic female. She has been under her mother's care since birth. The referral was initiated by Judge Arlington for the purpose of evaluating the child, Gloria Noorman, with her mother, Juliana Noorman, and providing CPP if appropriate. According to the court records, Gloria and her sister, Christina, were brought under court supervision due to allegations that "the mother is diagnosed with bipolar disorder and the maternal grandparents suffer from depression with psychotic features." Thomas Russen, the father of Gloria, was arrested for beating the mother.

Ms. Noorman did not exhibit overt signs of irritability, anger, or hostility toward Gloria. However, there is a great concern regarding the relationship between Ms. Noorman and her daughter. The mother's responsiveness toward Gloria is primarily one of disinterest. When the mother interacts with Gloria, the interaction appears forced or with a sense of obligation. Ms. Noorman lacks warmth and nurturing and is not responsive to Gloria's emotional needs. The mother is observed to display inconsistent responses to her child's cues. The mother lacks the skills necessary to comfort her child when she is in distress. It appears that Ms. Noorman's disengagement with her daughter may be the result of Ms. Noorman's feeling that she does not have any influence or impact over her child's behavior or emotional state. In addition, Ms. Noorman is young, immature, and egocentric, all of which may explain the lack of emotional connection between Ms. Noorman and her daughter. It appears that the mother's emotional unavailability has had a negative impact on the parent–child relationship and has had a serious impact on Gloria's ability to develop a sense of security and trust with her mother, which is needed if Gloria is to develop a secure attachment and the ability to manage her emotions.

Ms. Noorman is a very young parent, who has experienced a childhood of neglect, physical abuse, and sexual abuse. Ms. Noorman's limited parenting abilities appear to be the result of the abusive and neglectful parenting she received. She is overwhelmed with all the responsibilities that come along with being a mother of two and pregnant, at age 16, and with being in economic hardship. If Ms. Noorman is to be successful, she needs a great deal of support services. Without intensive services for the mother, the children will be at risk for future neglect and risk of harm.

There is concern that the mother reported that she carried Gloria for 43 weeks' gestation. This may suggest that the mother is uninformed regarding the fact that a full-term pregnancy is 36 weeks and provided an incorrect gestation length. Another possibility may be that the mother was either not receiving prenatal care or not following up on her prenatal care in a timely manner.

There are serious concerns regarding Gloria's developmental, emotional, and behavioral functioning. Based on observations made thus far and the results of the ASQ-2, Gloria is significantly delayed in communication and social-emotional functioning. In addition, Gloria has difficulty regulating her emotions and is distressed most of the time. When Gloria becomes distressed, her behaviors become infant-like, which may be due to her inability to communicate her needs. Gloria was also observed to be awkward in her walking, which may suggest a delay in her gross motor skills. Gloria would also often lie on her side or tilt her head while she was playing, and it is unclear whether this is in reference to visual, auditory, or sensory difficulties. It has been reported by mother and observed by this therapist that Gloria has frequent temper tantrums, is defiant and oppositional at times, more than what is age appropriate, and exhibits aggression. The

(continued)

mother also reports that Gloria has a depressed affect most of the time. Gloria's significant delays in communication, social-emotional development, and behavior appear to be connected to poor-quality parenting.

Diagnostic Impression
DC: 0-3R

Axis I: R/O Posttraumatic Stress Disorder
            R/O 800 Other Disorders (299.81 Pervasive Developmental Disorder-NOS)
            R/O Regulation Disorders of Sensory Processing, 430: Sensory Stimulation-Seeking/Impulsive

Axis II: PIR-GAS: 30 Severely Disordered (with mother) Underinvolved

Axis III: Speech and Language Delay
            Social-Emotional Delay

Axis IV: Psychological Stress: Severe
            Source of stress: hospitalization (2 weeks to 3 months); disruption from home (8 months and 28 months); witness of domestic violence (18 months to 23 months); victim of domestic violence (23 months); dog bite and hospitalization (24 months); parental illiteracy; parental mental illness (birth to present)

Axis V: Emotional and Social Functioning
            Functions immaturely with mother. Additional assessment of the capacity for forming relationships and mutual engagement is necessary.

Recommendations

1. It is recommended that Ms. Noorman and her daughter Gloria participate in CPP (dyadic therapy) in order to address serious concerns in the relationship.

2. It is extremely important that Gloria and her sister be placed in a quality child care center immediately.

3. There are serious concerns regarding Gloria's speech and language and social-emotional development. In addition, there is concern regarding her sensory processing difficulties. A full developmental evaluation, including sensory integration assessment, through the Early Steps program, is strongly recommended.

4. In order to ensure that the children are receiving regular medical care, it is recommended that the mother provide documentation of up-to-date medical records, including immunization and physical forms. If not already completed, Gloria should receive a hearing test due to Gloria's speech and language delay and a vision screening due to the close proximity in which she held the toys.

5. It is recommended that the mother be referred to an agency specializing in sexual abuse cases.

(continued)

6. It is unclear where the mother is residing with her children at this time, and there is concern regarding the stability and level of safety of the children's home environment. It is recommended that a home study be completed on the mother's residence immediately.

7. The mother reported that she has difficulty reading, writing, and spelling. It is recommended that the mother receive help enrolling in classes that will address these issues.

8. There are concerns regarding the mother's fiancé's criminal record. The mother's fiancé, Thomas Russen, should be included in the case plan. Recommended case plan tasks for Mr. Russen should include psychological evaluation, substance abuse evaluation, and parenting classes.

9. It is recommended that the mother and her fiancé participate in random drug testing due to the reported drug history with Gloria's father, mother's previous boyfriend, and the reported drug history of the mother's current fiancé, Thomas Russen.

Thank you for the opportunity to be of assistance. This report has been produced incorporating clinical observations and developmental assessments of the referred parties and is intended only as a summary.

_____

Licensed Mental Health Counselor

(continued)

Sample Memorandum of Understanding for Cross-Agency (Child Welfare/University) Collaboration

Memorandum of Understanding for the Haitian Parenting Initiative

This is a sample of an agreement to collaborate for services. It includes the program description, referral process, report-back procedures, and a detailed explanation of what is expected from both parties.

The language for this Memorandum of Understanding was developed to allow for cross-agency work on behalf of Haitian parents in Miami-Dade County, Florida.

The Haitian Parenting Program is a specialized interactive parenting program for Creole-speaking families which was adapted for parents of young children who either have a dependency petition or who are seeking early intervention/prevention services to prevent their children's removal from the home. The University collaborates on an ongoing basis with the dependency system and has contractual agreements for federal, state, and locally funded projects that provide research-based services to families at high risk of entering the dependency system and to those who are already part of the system.

Program Description

The conceptual framework for the program was developed through years of practice in the multicultural context of Little Haiti in Miami-Dade County. It is a culturally sensitive curriculum that addresses the needs of Haitian and other immigrant parents to adjust to their new culture. The program is designed to assist parents in reflecting on traditional parenting values and practices of their culture, honoring and reinforcing the positive, and rejecting the ineffective. It helps them build new parenting concepts and strategies that are consistent with the practice of a democratic approach to family systems interactions.

Parenting groups meet once a week for 12 weeks. The sessions last for 90 minutes and include two components. In the first component, parents and their children engage in play activities for 30–45 minutes. The second component is a 60-minute parent-only session. The group facilitators observe the interactions and monitor the parents' compliance and participation level at each session. The entire family attends the weekly session, dinner is served, and attendance and participation are supervised and monitored.

This interactive parenting program adaptation is focused on families who have at least one target child between 6 months and 5 years of age. The older children in the family attend the program and are involved in age-appropriate activities with supervision and receive homework assistance while their parent(s) participate interactively with the younger, target child.

Incentives for participation include a $20 food voucher (at the beginning [pre] and end [post] of the intervention); age-appropriate toys for the target child (weekly); and at the end of the program, those parents with perfect attendance participate in a raffle for a grand prize. Pre and post data are collected. Informed consent is obtained.

Referral Process and Turnaround Time

Once the referral is accepted, an appointment for a preassessment intake will be scheduled before the classes begin. The protective investigator (PI) or case worker, depending on the referral source, will be notified on the same day via fax and/or phone if the client does not come for the initial appointment.

If something troublesome is observed at the time of intake, a call will be made immediately after the intake to the PI and/or supervisor and the case worker as assigned.

162

Report-Back Mechanism

Progress reports will be faxed to the appropriate point person every 4–5 weeks during the parenting group. However, if something is observed during the group or if the parent was absent, a call will be made immediately.

What You May Expect from Us

A completed referral form to start the process will be acknowledged the same business day received or on Monday if sent over the weekend.

A start date for the next program group will be provided.

Once the referral is accepted, an appointment for a preassessment intake will be scheduled before the classes begin. You will be notified if the client does not come for the appointment the same business day it was scheduled. If we observe anything worrisome at the time of intake that should be brought to your attention, a call will be made immediately after the intake to you (or to your supervisor if we cannot reach you).

Once the client starts the program, reports will be faxed and/or emailed to the appropriate person every 4–5 weeks during the parenting group and will include the following: attendance/punctuality, degree of participation in the session, and recommendations for additional referrals if warranted. If there are concerns that need immediate attention, a call will be made to you in addition to the faxed report either right after the session, if warranted, or within 24 hours.

What We Will Expect from the Referring
PI/Crisis Intervention or Case Worker Referral Contact

Multiple contact numbers and contact information must be supplied for the referred family so immediate contact can be made.

Multiple contact numbers of the referring PI, crisis intervention/case worker contact person (including office phone, cell phone, supervisor contact information, and fax numbers) must be supplied.

We will expect call backs within the same business day when we contact you or your supervisor; we will do the same in return.

_____   _____
Referring protective investigator/crisis intervention/case worker contact   (date)

_____   _____
Parenting Coordinator   (date)

_____   _____
Program Director   (date)

Sample Court Orders

Miami Juvenile Court Order for Early Intervention Services
Evaluation Through Part C of the Individuals with Disabilities
Education Act (IDEA) 166

Miami Juvenile Court Order of Referral to Healthy Start 168

Miami Juvenile Court Order for Early Intervention Services Evaluation Through Part C of IDEA

This is a sample order that would be signed by the judge for a referral for a Part C evaluation to determine whether early intervention services are needed for a given child.

IN THE CIRCUIT COURT OF THE ELEVENTH JUDICIAL CIRCUIT IN AND FOR DADE COUNTY, FLORIDA

Juvenile Division

IN THE INTEREST OF:

Case No. _____

Child/Children

_____/

Order for Part C Evaluation Pursuant to IDEA

IT IS HEREBY ORDERED that _____, D/O/B _____ , a child under the jurisdiction of the dependency court as a result of an ongoing dependency proceeding and in the custody of (circle one: DCF, relative, nonrelative, or parent) be immediately provided with a Part C evaluation at Miami Children's Hospital or the Mailman Center for Child Development, Early Intervention Program. The Department of Children and Families is ordered to contact the appropriate Part C Provider within 5 days and schedule an appointment for the Part C Evaluation.

The written report or EIP (early intervention plan) is to be provided to this Court within 60 days of the order.

DONE AND ORDERED, in Miami-Dade County, Florida on this the _____ day of _____, 2010.

_____
Circuit Court Judge

Please submit referrals to:
Child Protection Team

Child Protection Team will forward to:

MIAMI CHILDREN'S HOSPITAL
Early Intervention Program, South

MAILMAN CENTER FOR CHILD DEVELOPMENT
Early Intervention Program, North

Miami Juvenile Court Order of Referral to Healthy Start

This is a sample order signed by a judge when he or she requires a parent to participate in the Healthy Start Services Home Visitation Program.

IN THE CIRCUIT COURT OF THE ELEVENTH JUDICIAL CIRCUIT IN AND FOR DADE COUNTY, FLORIDA

Juvenile Division

IN THE INTEREST OF:

Case No. _____

Child/Children

_____/

Order of Referral to Healthy Start Services Home Visitation Program

THIS CAUSE came before the Court and the Court hereby orders:

(1) That _____, DOB _____, Residing at _____, is pregnant and under the Jurisdiction of the juvenile dependency court.

(2) Said person is ordered to actively participate in the Healthy Start Services Home Visitation Program.

(3) Failure to cooperate with and fully participate in Healthy Start Services Home Visitation Program will constitute a violation of this court order and may result in contempt of court.

(4) Regular progress reports are to be filed by the Healthy Start Services Home Visitation Program and mailed to the Judge's chambers.

DONE AND ORDERED, at Miami-Dade County Florida, on this the _____ day of _____, 2010.

_____
Circuit Court Judge

Contact Person:

Miami-Dade County Health Department/School Healthy & Healthy Start

E

Sample Protocol for Identifying Accredited Early Care and Education Program Placement for Children Involved with the Dependency Court

This sample protocol shows the background information that an accredited child care center must provide. The protocol developed for a case worker provides criteria for deciding when and how a child should be moved into an accredited child care setting upon removal from his or her parents or placement in a new home.

Our Kids Resources and Utilization
Management Accredited Child Care Center Protocol

1. Purpose: The purpose of this protocol is to ensure that children age birth through five who are both dependent and eligible for child care services through Miami-Dade County and the Early Learning Coalition are referred and registered to attend accredited programs. The Rilya Wilson Act, (Florida Statute 39.604), requires that any child age three to school entry and under court ordered supervision or in the custody of the Family Safety Program Office of a community-based agency must be enrolled to participate 5 days weekly in a licensed early education or child care program.

2. Notice to the Protective Service Investigators and Full Case Management Agencies (FCMA): Dependent children who are eligible for child care services require the following action be taken immediately following their removal:

    A. Obtain a list of accredited centers online at http://Myflorida.com/childcare/provider or from the Miami-Dade County Child Development Services local office and provide with the referral to Child Development Services.

    B. Review the list of accredited child care providers with the caregiver and indicate that an accredited site must be selected. Along with accreditation, the caregiver may consider proximity to home or work, and the availability of openings for enrollment.

3. Exclusionary Criteria: Under the following circumstances, children may be excused from enrollment in an accredited child care center:

    A. Child is enrolled in or requires a special needs program.

    B. Child is enrolled in Early Head Start / Head Start.

    C. Nearest accredited child care provider with an opening is 10 miles or more from the caregiver's residence and place of work.

    D. In the event that transportation logistics or expenses are presenting a barrier to the child's enrollment in an accredited child care program, the Early Care and Education Liaison from the FCMA will contact Project Safety Net through Miami-Dade County Child Development Services to seek assistance through the Transportation for the Disadvantaged program.

BY DIRECTION OF THE EXECUTIVE DIRECTOR OF OUR KIDS:
(Signed original copy on file)

_____

Executive Director

Note: An asterisk (*) indicates that the report template is included in this appendix.

Individualized Family Support Plan (IFSP) for Early Intervention Services and Evaluation Report (Florida)[1]

The individualized family service plan (IFSP) documents and guides the early intervention process for children with disabilities and their families. The IFSP is the mechanism through which effective early intervention is implemented in accordance with Part C of the Individuals with Disabilities Education Act (IDEA). It contains information about the services necessary to facilitate a child's development and support the family's capacity to support that development. Through the IFSP process, family members and service providers work as a team to plan, implement, and evaluate services that correspond with the family's priorities for their young child.

[1]Bruder, M. Educational Resources Information Center (U.S. Department of Education). Washington, D.C. www.eric.ed.gov

early steps
Children's Medical Services

Individualized Family Support Plan and Evaluation Report

Form A: Your Family's Information   Page _____ of Form A

Child's Name: _____ _____ _____ **A.K.A:** _____
　　　　　　　　　　　　　　Last　　　　　　　　　　First　　　　　　MI

DOB: _____ **Child's ID#:** _____ **Gender:** ☐ Male ☐ Female

Child's Race (Check all that Apply): ☐ American Indian or Alaska Native ☐ Asian ☐ Black or African American ☐ Hispanic/Latino ☐ Native Hawaiian or Other Pacific Islander ☐ White

Child's Primary Language/Mode of Communication: ☐ English ☐ Spanish ☐ Creole ☐ Other:_____

Check One: ☐ Parent ☐ Guardian ☐ Foster Parent ☐ Surrogate Parent ☐ Other: _____

Name(s):_____

Address: _____

City: _____ Zip Code: _____ County: _____

Phone: (_____) _____ Work Phone: (_____) _____ Cell Phone: (_____) _____

Best time to call: _____ E-mail: _____

Primary language used in home/mode of communication: ☐ English ☐ Spanish ☐ Creole ☐ Other: _____

Check One: ☐ Parent ☐ Guardian ☐ Foster Parent ☐ Surrogate Parent ☐ Other: _____

Name(s):_____

Address: _____

City: _____ Zip Code: _____ County: _____

Phone: (_____) _____ Work Phone: (_____) _____ Cell Phone: (_____) _____

Best time to call: _____ E-mail: _____

Primary language used in home/mode of communication: ☐ English ☐ Spanish ☐ Creole ☐ Other:_____

Is an interpreter needed for the family? ☐ Yes ☐ No   If so, what kind of interpreter? _____

The following people can help you with your questions and concerns:

Service Coordinator:_____ Agency: _____

Phone: (_____) _____ Fax: (_____) _____ E-mail: _____

Address: _____ City: _____ Zip Code: _____

Family Resource Specialist: _____

Phone: (_____) _____ Fax: (_____) _____ E-mail: _____

Address: _____ City: _____ Zip Code: _____

Referral Date:_____   IFSP Periodic Review Due Date: _____

Interim IFSP Date: _____   IFSP Periodic Actual Review Date: _____

Initial IFSP Date:_____   Annual IFSP Due Date: _____

Current IFSP Date:_____   Transition Conference Due Date: _____

Rev. 7/09/2010

Name: _____ DOB: _____ IFSP Date: _____

ID#: _____ Service Coordinator: _____

Form B: Planning for Your Child's Evaluation/Assessment   Page ____ of Form B

Date(s) this Information Gathered: _____   Chronological Age: _____

Tell us about your child's health:

Was your child born full term? ☐ Yes ☐ No

How many weeks? _____ Birth weight: _____

Date of your child's last well-child check-up: _____

Are immunizations current? ☐ Yes ☐ No

Is your child currently on any medication(s)? ☐ Yes ☐ No
If so, what types and why:

Does your child have allergies? ☐ Yes ☐ No Describe:

Does your child have a medical diagnosis? ☐ Yes ☐ No
If so, what is it?

Does your child see any medical specialists?
☐ Yes ☐ No If so, who and what type:

Has your child been hospitalized? ☐ Yes ☐ No
Please tell us when and why:

Tell us about your child's vision and hearing:

Has your child's hearing been previously screened or tested?
☐ Yes ☐ No When? _____

Do you have concerns about your child's hearing?
☐ Yes ☐ No Describe:

Has your child's vision been previously screened or tested?
☐ Yes ☐ No When? _____

Do you have concerns about your child's vision?
☐ Yes ☐ No Describe:

Tell us about your child's sleep patterns/nutrition:

Describe your child's sleep patterns (bedtime, naps, hours of sleep):

Describe your child's nutritional habits/preferences:

Your Insurance Information:

Medicaid (Title XIX)

    Medicaid HMO/PSN ☐ Yes ☐ No ☐ Pending

    Group: _____

    CMS ☐ Yes ☐ No ☐ Pending

    CMS Nurse Case Manager: _____

    Medicaid Medipass ☐ Yes ☐ No ☐ Pending

    SSI ☐ Yes ☐ No ☐ Pending

    Medicaid #: _____

Comments/Changes: _____

KidCare/MediKids ☐ Yes ☐ No ☐ Pending

CMS (Title XXI) ☐ Yes ☐ No ☐ Pending

Private Insurance: ☐ Yes ☐ No

    Type: ☐ HMO ☐ PPO

Company Name: _____

Phone Number: _____

Policy/Individual #: _____ Group #: _____

Primary Health Care Provider: _____

Your Child's Developmental Screening:

A developmental screening was conducted ☐ Yes ☐ No   If yes, please check which tools/methods used:

☐ Developmental Checklists (specify) ☐ Parent Report ☐ Observation ☐ Record Review ☐ Ages & Stages

☐ Other: _____   Language used: _____

Does the collected information from above indicate a possible developmental delay/concern in any of the following areas:

☐ Fine motor ☐ Gross motor ☐ Communication ☐ Cognitive ☐ Social-emotional ☐ Adaptive-self-help skills

Comments: _____

Describe any other information about child's health, development, and/or family medical history that may be important for the team to know:

_____

_____

_____

Rev. 7/09/2010

Name: _____ DOB: _____ IFSP Date: _____

ID#: _____ Service Coordinator: _____

Form C: Your Family's Routines/Concerns/Priorities/Resources   Page ____ of Form C

Date(s) this Information Gathered: _____

Family: Who are the people living in your home? Please include names and relationships. Include ages and gender of children.

Daily Routines: What are your child's and your family's daily activities? Where does your child spend the day? With whom does your child regularly interact? (Include your child's activities, routines and favorite toys.) What activities, routines, and places are challenging to your child and family?

Family's Areas of Concern: What concerns do you have about your child's development and/or any other family challenges? Questions and concerns about your child may include issues such as feeding/nutrition (*such as weight gain or loss, difficulties with eating, special diets or feeding equipment, elimination habits*), sleeping, playing, communicating, behavior, health, transportation, food/shelter, etc.

Priorities: Which concerns above would you like to focus on first? What do you hope Early Steps can help you with?

Friends/Supports/Resources: When you need help, who do you call and how do they help you? What types of resources do you have to meet your family's needs? These may include family strengths, childcare, transportation and financial resources.

Recommendations for Evaluation and Assessment/Team Updates: _____

_____

_____

Rev. 7/09/2010

Name: _____   DOB: _____   IFSP Date: _____

ID#: _____   Service Coordinator: _____

Form D: Your Child's Eligibility Evaluation Information

(Complete Form D for the initial IFSP only)

Page ____ of Form D

For your child's first IFSP, an evaluation may be completed with your child to determine eligibility, prior to or during assessment. The eligibility information is recorded on this page.

Date of Evaluation (if performed): _____ Chronological Age: _____ Language Used: _____

Method(s) of Evaluation: ☐ Test Instrument(s) Administered: _____

☐ Parent Report ☐ Professional Observation ☐ Collateral Information/Source: _____

Eligibility Evaluation Results	Results
Using Hands and Body (Gross/Fine Motor Skills) Comments:	
Eating, Dressing, and Toileting (Self-Help/Adaptive Skills) Comments:	
Expressing and Responding to Feelings and Interacting with Others (Social/Emotional) Comments:	
Playing, Thinking, Exploring (Academic/Cognitive including pre-literacy skills) Comments:	
Understanding and Communicating (Receptive and Expressive Communication) Comments:	

Evaluation Team Signatures

☐ The eligibility evaluation team is the same as the assessment team. Please see Form E for signatures.

☐ The eligibility evaluation team is different from the assessment team. Please sign below.

Evaluator: _____   Discipline: _____   Signature: _____

Evaluator: _____   Discipline: _____   Signature: _____

Evaluator: _____   Discipline: _____   Signature: _____

Eligibility Determination

☐ Eligible for Early Steps (Part C: Early Intervention) based on the following:

☐ Established Condition of: _____

☐ Developmental Delay in the area(s) of: _____

☐ Not eligible for Early Steps (Part C: Early Intervention) based on evaluations completed this day and the IFSP does not need to be completed. The evaluation team makes the following recommendations to the family: _____

_____

_____ Rev. 7/09/2010

Name: _____ DOB: _____ IFSP Date: _____

ID#: _____ Service Coordinator: _____

Form E: Your Child's Assessment Information

Page ____ of Form E

A developmental assessment is completed with your child and/or ongoing assessment information is gathered. This information helps us understand your child's developmental strengths, as well as some of the things that are challenging for your child and may be affecting how he/she is able to participate in family and community activities.

Date of Assessment: _____ Chronological Age: _____ Language Used: _____

Method(s) of Assessment: ☐ Test Instrument(s) Administered: _____

☐ Parent Report/Interview Tool: _____ ☐ Professional Observation ☐ Collateral Information/Source: _____

Summary of Present Status: Abilities, Strengths, and Needs

Using Hands and Body (Gross/Fine Motor Skills)

Things we like and things we do well:	Things that we need help with:

Eating, Dressing, and Toileting (Self-Help/Adaptive Skills)

Things we like and things we do well:	Things that we need help with:

Expressing and Responding to Feelings and Interacting with Others (Social/Emotional)

Things we like and things we do well:	Things that we need help with:

Playing, Thinking, Exploring (Academic/Cognitive including pre-literacy skills)

Things we like and things we do well:	Things that we need help with:

Understanding and Communicating (Receptive and Expressive Communication)

Things we like and things we do well:	Things that we need help with:

Vision and Hearing Status: _____

_____

Observations/Comments: _____

_____

_____

Assessor: _____ Discipline: _____ Signature: _____

Assessor: _____ Discipline: _____ Signature: _____

Assessor: _____ Discipline: _____ Signature: _____

Rev. 7/09/2010

Name: _____   DOB: _____   IFSP Date: _____

ID#: _____   Service Coordinator: _____

Form F: Your Family's Outcomes

OUTCOME #: _____ What would you like to see happen for your child and family as a result of Early Steps supports and services?

GOALS, TIMELINES AND CRITERIA FOR PROGRESS: When will we review progress toward this outcome and what will progress look like?

STRATEGIES: Who will do what within your child's everyday routines, activities, and places to achieve this outcome?

Rev. 7/09/2010

Name: _____ DOB: _____ IFSP Date: _____

ID#: _____ Service Coordinator: _____

Form G: Your Family's Supports and Services

Services authorized by the IFSP team to address identified family/child outcomes.

Page____ of Form G

Date	Service	Outcome #	Units	Frequency, Intensity, Group (G) or Individual (I)	Provider Information (Name/Discipline/Agency) *Indicates the Primary Service Provider (PSP)	Location Code	Natural Environment Y / N	Start Date End Date Authorization Period	Payer of Service

Location Codes: 1=Home 3=Hospital 4=School 5=Childcare Center 6=Other 7=Clinic 8=Residential Facility 9=Early Intervention Classroom A=Community Agency F=Family Daycare Home P=Public Place **Service Codes** (optional): See IFSP Guidance Document

Natural Environment Justification: Supports and services must be provided to your child in settings that are natural or typical for children of the same age (natural environments). If, as a team, we decide that we cannot provide a service in a natural environment, we need to explain how we made that decision:

Complete only for Early Intervention Sessions:

Addresses the following domain(s): ☐ Fine motor ☐ Gross motor ☐ Communication ☐ Cognitive ☐ Social-emotional ☐ Adaptive-self-help skills

Early Intervention Sessions are: ☐ Individual (Medicaid procedure code T1027SC or T1027HM)
                                   ☐ Group (Medicaid procedure code T1027TTSC or T1027TTHM)

ICD9 Code(s) _____ ICD9 Description(s) _____

Modifications to Services

☐ I understand that Form G serves as prior notice of proposed new, changed, or terminated services as written above and I understand the reason(s) for taking the action(s).

☐ I have received a copy and explanation of my procedural safeguards (*Summary of Family Rights*).

(Parent/Guardian Signature) _____ Date: _____

OTHER SERVICES: In addition to the Early Steps services listed above, you have identified that your child and family receive, or may like help arranging to receive, the following services such as specialized medical services or those activities or services that you choose independent of those authorized by the IFSP team.

Service/Activity	Activities/Steps Needed	Timeline	Provider/Agency Name

Rev. 7/09/2010

Name: _____ DOB: _____ IFSP Date: _____

ID#: _____ Service Coordinator: _____

Form H: Your Individualized Family Support Plan Team

My family and the following individuals participated in the development of this IFSP and/or will help to implement it.

Printed Name / Credential *Indicates a LHCP providing direction and support to ITDS, if applicable	Signature	Position/ Role	Address	Telephone	Receive Copy of IFSP (Family Initial)
		Parent			
		Service Coordinator			
		Primary Service Provider			
		Primary Health Care Provider			

I/We received the following:

☐ Copy of procedural safeguards (*Summary of Family Rights*) for Part C or Part B of IDEA, as appropriate, and these rights and safeguards have been explained to me
☐ Copy of Early Steps brochure with Central Directory phone number (initial IFSP only)

☐ Explanation of procedure for requesting new service coordinator
☐ Copy of Individualized Family Support Plan or understand it will be mailed to me within 15 days

Informed Consent by Parents/Guardians:

☐ I participated fully in the development of this plan.
☐ I give consent for all of the services described in this Individualized Family Support Plan (IFSP) to be provided as written.
☐ I do not provide consent for the following service(s) as described in this IFSP to be provided, however, I do give consent for all other services described in this IFSP to be provided: _____
_____

☐ I give permission for copies of this plan to be released to the individuals(s) noted above as indicated by my initials beside each name.

_____   _____   _____
Parent/Guardian Signature   Relationship   Date

_____   _____   _____
Parent/Guardian Signature   Relationship   Date

Rev. 7/09/2010

Name: _____ DOB: _____ IFSP Date: _____

ID#: _____ Service Coordinator: _____

Form I: Your Family's Transition Plan

Page ____ of Form I

Transition Planning Steps (Check all boxes that apply)

1. **Notification:**
   a. ☐ The *Understanding Notification* brochure was provided. Date Provided: _____
   b. ☐ The family opted out of notification. Date: _____
   c. ☐ Notification to the school district was provided. Date Provided: _____

2. **Program Options:**
   a. ☐ Program options available within the community (e.g., local school district, Head Start, Agency for Persons with Disabilities, other early care and education programs, etc.) were discussed.
   b. ☐ At this time, the family is interested in the following options:

3. **Referral:**
   ☐ With family consent, a referral packet was provided to the school district and/or other agencies and community providers as follows:
   a. Agency/Program to which child is referred: _____ Referral Date: _____
   b. Agency/Program to which child is referred: _____ Referral Date: _____

4. **Transition Conference:** Date of Conference: _____
   a. ☐ Concerns of the family related to transition were discussed. Those concerns are listed below. If there are no concerns, please indicate "none."

   b. ☐ List activities to address the above concerns, if applicable.

   c. ☐ School district information was provided regarding services to prekindergarten children with disabilities. This information should include the district's evaluation/eligibility process and how the Individual Educational Plan (IEP) is developed. Comment:

   d. ☐ Services/activities to support our child's transition into a new setting/environment: (Agency/program visitations, parent training, transportation issues, assistive technology needs, immunizations, additional evaluations needed, etc.)

Services/Activities	Person(s) Involved	Timeframe(s)

We attended the transition conference and participated in the development of this transition plan. We provide consent to the steps and services related to transition.

_____ _____ _____
Parent/Guardian Parent/Guardian Date

We attended the transition conference and participated in the development of this transition plan.

_____ _____ _____
Service Coordinator IFSP Team Member/Title Local School District Representative/Title

_____ _____ _____
Community Representative/Agency/Title IFSP Team Member/Title Other/Title

Rev. 7/09/2010

Name: _____   DOB: _____   IFSP Date: _____

ID#: _____   Service Coordinator: _____

Form J: Your Family's Individualized Family Support Plan Periodic Review   Page ____ of Form J

Outcome #	Date Reviewed	Describe Progress / Modification (If these modifications result in a change of service, please complete the *Modifications of Services* section on Form G)	Status (Check One)
			☐Outcome reached ☐New outcome developed (# ____) ☐Outcome continued ☐Outcome modified
			☐Outcome reached ☐New outcome developed (# ____) ☐Outcome continued ☐Outcome modified
			☐Outcome reached ☐New outcome developed (# ____) ☐Outcome continued ☐Outcome modified
			☐Outcome reached ☐New outcome developed (# ____) ☐Outcome continued ☐Outcome modified
			☐Outcome reached ☐New outcome developed (# ____) ☐Outcome continued ☐Outcome modified
			☐Outcome reached ☐New outcome developed (# ____) ☐Outcome continued ☐Outcome modified

Team Member Signatures

Print Name / Credentials *Indicates a LHCP providing direction and support to ITDS, if applicable	Signature	Date

G

Infant Mental Health–Related Documents and Tools

Sample Referral Eligibility Checklist 186

Early Childhood Relationship Observation Coding Scales (EC-ROCS) 188

Examples of Developmentally Appropriate Toys 193

Sample Child–Caregiver Relationship Assessment 195

Sample Referral Eligibility Checklist for Child–Parent Psychotherapy

This sample shows the information a case worker is expected to provide with a referral to participate in Child–Parent Psychotherapy. This form must be completed in order for a client to begin therapy or to be placed on a wait list for therapy.

The eligibility checklist is sent back to the case worker by the clinician in response to the referral sent for treatment. The form identifies compliance and services that must be established for the client before the initial baseline assessment is scheduled.

Referral Eligibility Checklist for Child–Parent Psychotherapy

To _____   _____   _____   _____
         Agency   Case worker   Supervisor   Date

A referral has been made for: _____   on   _____
                                         Child's name   Date of referral received

In order to be eligible to participate in Child–Parent Psychotherapy, the following items must be in place for this client:
(CW, please circle Yes/No and initial)

1. **Parent is compliant with all services mandated by case plan (e.g., mental health services, substance abuse treatment, anger control, domestic violence).**
   Yes / No _____ CW   Confirmation at time of follow-up   Yes / No _____ (date and initials)

2. **Visitation is in place and parent is in compliance.**
   Yes / No / NA child resides with parent _____ CW   Confirmation at time of follow-up   Yes / No _____ (date and initials)

3. **Case Worker confirms that transportation for child to participate is in place.**
   Yes / No _____ CW   Confirmation at time of follow-up   Yes / No _____ (date and initials)

4. **Child is between the ages of 6 and 48 months.**
   Yes / No _____ CW   Confirmation at time of follow-up   Yes / No _____ (date and initials)

Please be advised that your client will not be placed on our waitlist or given a start date until this form has been returned to our case manager and all items are confirmed.

_____   _____
Case worker's signature   Supervisor's signature   Date

Follow-up:
Agency CW/Supervisor must respond via phone/email/fax/mail with updated information by _____; otherwise client will be removed from waitlist and a new referral will be required.

Availability:
- Slot ready assuming all necessary documents have been received _____
- Waitlist with anticipated start date: _____
- No slots available; send referral to another agency _____

Early Childhood Relationship Observation Coding Scales (EC-ROCS)

This is a sample coding form that an infant mental health clinician completes when observing interactions between a young child and his or her caregiver.

Free Play/Bubbles

Relationship: Mutual Positive Engagement   *Area of concern?*

Behavioral Indicators:

Child references caregiver (e.g., looks for approval, shows toys)	Yes No N/A	__
Child seeks physical closeness with caregiver	Yes No N/A	
Caregiver responds positively to child's attempts at engaging (child-friendly tone of voice, physical/verbal demonstration of affection)	Yes No N/A	__
Mutual positive affect (e.g., laugh together)	Yes No N/A	__
Interaction during play (versus parallel play)	Yes No N/A	__

Other/comments_____

Overall rating of **Relationship: Mutual Positive Engagement:**

Outstanding/ No problem	Good enough/ Not focus of Tx	Needs improvement	Primary focus of Tx

Caregiver's Awareness of Child's Developmental Needs   *Area of concern?*

Behavioral Indicators:

Caregiver allows the child to choose toys and ways to play w/toys	Yes No N/A	__
Caregiver expands child's play themes (e.g., imaginary play)	Yes No N/A	__
Physical intrusiveness (e.g., physically in child's face, unwanted kisses)	Yes No N/A	__
Verbal intrusiveness (e.g., repeats directions)	Yes No N/A	__
Intrusiveness in play (e.g., directive, ignores child's preferences)	Yes No N/A	__
Caregiver directs play below/above child's developmental level	Yes No N/A	__

Other/comments_____

Overall rating of **Caregiver's Awareness of Child's Developmental Needs:**

Outstanding/ No problem	Good enough/ Not focus of Tx	Needs improvement	Primary focus of Tx

Caregiver Rejection   *Area of concern?*

Behavioral Indicators:

Caregiver ignores the child	Yes No N/A	__
Caregiver teases child (frightens w/toys, mocks distress)	Yes No N/A	__
Caregiver speaks to child in harsh tone	Yes No N/A	__
Caregiver handles child harshly	Yes No N/A	__

Other/comments_____

Overall rating of **Caregiver Rejection:**

No problem	Not focus of Tx	Needs improvement	Primary focus of Tx

Child's Negativity Toward Caregiver   *Area of concern?*

Behavioral Indicators:

Child maintains physical distance from caregiver	Yes No N/A	__
Rejects caregiver's attempts to engage child	Yes No N/A	__

(continued)

189

Overly compliant (mechanical compliance, lack of age-appropriate assertiveness)		Yes No N/A	__
Noncompliance		Yes No N/A	__
Aggression		Yes No N/A	__
Other/comments_____			

Overall rating of **Child Negativity Toward Caregiver:**

No problem	Not focus of Tx	Needs Improvement	Primary focus of Tx

Clean Up

Caregiver's Limit Setting

Behavioral Indicators: *Area of concern?*

Demonstrates skill in helping with this transition between tasks (e.g., explains clean up as preparation for next task)	Yes No N/A	__
Caregiver sets limits (ensures child completes clean-up task)	Yes No N/A	__
Caregiver makes clean up fun (e.g., sings songs, throw toys in bucket)	Yes No N/A	__
Use of praise	Yes No N/A	__
Ability to give clear directives	Yes No N/A	__
Negative discipline (speaking harshly, physical harshness)	Yes No N/A	__
Other/comments_____		

Overall rating of **Caregiver Limit Setting:**

Outstanding/ No problem	Good enough/ Not focus of Tx	Needs improvement	Primary focus of Tx

Child's Response to Clean Up

Behavioral Indicators: *Area of concern?*

Overly compliant (mechanical compliance, lack of age-appropriate assertiveness)	Yes No N/A	__
Noncompliance	Yes No N/A	__
Completes task with minimal difficulty	Yes No N/A	__
Other/comments: _____		

Overall rating of **Child's Response to Clean-Up:**

Outstanding/ No problem	Not focus of Tx	Needs improvement	Primary focus of Tx

Structured Tasks *Area of Concern?*

Relationship: Mutual Positive Engagement

Child references caregiver (e.g., looks for approval, shows toys)	Yes No N/A	__
Child seeks physical closeness with caregiver	Yes No N/A	__
Caregiver responds positively to child's attempts at engaging (child-friendly tone of voice, physical/verbal demonstration of affection)	Yes No N/A	__
Mutual positive affect (e.g., laugh together)	Yes No N/A	__
Interaction during play	Yes No N/A	__
Other/comments_____		

Overall rating of **Relationship: Mutual Positive Engagement:**

Outstanding/ No problem	Good enough/ Not focus of Tx	Needs improvement	Primary focus of Tx

Caregiver Teaching/Helpfulness with Tasks and Awareness of Child's Developmental Needs

Area of Concern?

Behavioral Indicators:

Use of praise	Yes	No	N/A	__
Modeling	Yes	No	N/A	__
Scaffolding	Yes	No	N/A	__
Age-appropriate assistance	Yes	No	N/A	__
Allows child to work independently according to child's ability	Yes	No	N/A	__
Caregiver is rigid in how child must complete tasks	Yes	No	N/A	__
Caregiver allows child to explore toys	Yes	No	N/A	__
Physical intrusiveness (e.g., physically in child's face, unwanted kisses)	Yes	No	N/A	__
Verbal intrusiveness (e.g., repeats directions in a nonhelpful manner)	Yes	No	N/A	__

Other/comments_____

Overall rating of **Caregiver's Teaching, Helpfulness and Awareness of Child's Needs:**

Outstanding/ No problem	Good enough Not focus of Tx	Needs improvement	Primary focus of Tx

Caregiver Rejection

Area of Concern?

Behavioral Indicators:

Caregiver ignores child	Yes	No	N/A	__
Caregiver teases child (e.g., mocks distress or inability)	Yes	No	N/A	__
Caregiver speaks to child in harsh tone	Yes	No	N/A	__
Caregiver handles child harshly	Yes	No	N/A	__

Other/comments_____

Overall rating of **Caregiver Rejection:**

No problem	Not focus of Tx	Needs improvement	Primary focus of Tx

Child's Negativity Toward Caregiver

Area of Concern?

Behavioral Indicators:

Child maintains physical distance from caregiver	Yes	No	N/A	__
Rejects caregiver's attempts to engage child	Yes	No	N/A	__
Overly compliant	Yes	No	N/A	__
Noncompliance	Yes	No	N/A	__
Aggression	Yes	No	N/A	__

Other/comments_____

Overall rating of **Child Negativity Toward Caregiver:**

No problem	Not focus of Tx	Needs improvement	Primary focus of Tx

Separation and Reunion

Caregiver

Area of concern?

Behavioral Indicators:

Prepares child for separation	Yes	No	N/A	__

Parent's response to separation (if observed)_____ *(continued)*

Upon Return

Approaches child: comments _____	Yes No N/A	__
Smiles at child: comments _____	Yes No N/A	__
Explains absence and/or comforts child verbally _____	Yes No N/A	__
Picks child up (if child wants to be picked up): comments _____	Yes No N/A	__
Picks child up (if doesn't want to be picked up): comments _____	Yes No N/A	__
Returns to play (if child wants to play): comments _____	Yes No N/A	__
Returns to play (if child doesn't want to play): comments _____	Yes No N/A	__
Mocks child's distress (if distressed): comments _____	Yes No N/A	__

Other/comments_____

Overall rating of **Caregiver:**

Outstanding/	Good enough/	Needs	Primary focus
No problem	Not focus of Tx	improvement	of Tx

Child

Behavioral Indicators:

Level of distress during separation: comments_____None / Moderate / High

What child does during separation: _____

Upon Return

Area of concern?

Looks toward caregiver: comments_____	Yes No N/A	__
Approaches caregiver: comments _____	Yes No N/A	__
Smiles at caregiver: comments _____	Yes No N/A	__
Reaches for caregiver: comments _____	Yes No N/A	__
Calms when held (if distressed): comments_____	Yes No N/A	__
Shows caregiver what has been doing: comments_____	Yes No N/A	__
Invites caregiver to play: comments_____	Yes No N/A	__
Returns to play alone: comments_____	Yes No N/A	__
Turns away from caregiver: comments _____	Yes No N/A	__
Expresses anger toward caregiver (verbal or non) comments _____	Yes No N/A	__
Resists caregiver's approach: comments _____	Yes No N/A	__

Other/comments_____

Overall rating of **Child:**

Outstanding/	Not focus of Tx	Needs	Primary focus
No problem		improvement	of Tx

Mutual positive affect: comments_____ Yes No

Examples of Developmentally Appropriate Toys

This document provides a list of developmentally ordered play situation toys. It can help the clinician to prepare the assessment environment for the child.

Possible Play Materials for Relationship Assessment Organized by Age

	0–12 months	12–18 months	19–28 months	28–36 months
Free play with examiner and with parent	Rattles Blocks Cheerios Mirror Soft ball	Doll and bottle Hair brush Telephones (2) Pretend food/dishes Soft ball Cars/trucks	Same as 12–18 months *plus* Emergency vehicles Doctor kit Toy animals (wild/domestic)	Same as 19–28 months *plus* Dolls/accessories Puppets (good/bad)
Structured task for parent and child		Stacking cups (2–3) Blocks Stacking rings Books	Stacking cups (4–6) Blocks Windup toy Puzzle (shapes)	Shape sorter Crayons/paper Stacking rings (order/color) Puzzle

Prepared by LSUHSC Harris Center for Infant Mental Health, New Orleans.

Relationship-Based Assessment Instructions

This describes the step-by-step procedures for a relationship-based observation that is incorporated into the infant mental health (IMH) therapist report (see Appendix B).

Relationship-Based Assessment
(based on work of Judith Crowell)

General instructions to share at the start of the session:
Between each task, I will remind you what to do; however, I will review everything with you now so you will have an idea of what is going to happen. First, I want you to play with the child, and then I will ask you to have him/her clean up all of the toys. You can help the child if you think he/she needs it. I will then ask you to do each of the following tasks with the child. Some of these tasks will be easy for the child and some will be more difficult; you may help if you think the child needs it. (Review the three to four tasks.) After the last task, I will ask you to leave the room. You can come back into the monitoring room and watch the child. After a few minutes I will ask you to return to the child and the two of you will play for a few more minutes.

Individual episodes	Instruction given over the phone/during transitions
Free play (10 minutes)	Play with the child as you would at home.
Cleanup (no more than 5 minutes)	Have the child clean up, helping if you feel the child needs help.
Bubbles (3–5 minutes)	
Task 1 (2–4 minutes)	Specific task instructions
Task 2 (2–4 minutes)	Specific task instructions
Task 3 (3–5 minutes)	Specific task instructions
Task 4 (3–5 minutes, if used)	Specific task instructions
Separation (no more than 3 minutes; have parent take bubbles)	Open the cabinet doors so that the child can see the task toys, and then leave the room as you would at home.
Reunion (3 minutes)	Knock on the door, call the child's name, and step all the way into the room.

- The parent is given basic instructions prior to the session and each task is demonstrated. During the session, the clinician calls the parent into the monitoring room to give specific instructions between each transition.
- Tasks 1 and 2 should be somewhat below the child's developmental level; ideally, the child should be able to do the task with little or no assistance. Tasks 3 and 4 (if used) should be above the child's developmental level so that the child needs the parent's assistance to complete the task.
- The length of time allowed for each task varies. If the child finishes the task quickly, allow time for the task to be done one or two more times. If time is up but the dyad is close to completing the task, allow time for completion and sharing. If the child is getting frustrated and/or the task is far from complete and the time is up, end the task.

LSUHSC Harris Center for Infant Mental Health, New Orleans (Description developed by Amy Dickson, Psy.D.)

Index

Throughout this index, *f* indicates a figure, *t* indicates a table, *n* indicates a note, and *b* indicates a box.

Abuse
  attachment difficulties from, 39
  child development and, 2–3, 3*b*, 4*b*
  Child–Parent Psychotherapy (CPP) effectiveness in, 39
  Nurturing Parenting Programs and, 19*b*
  rates of, xx, 2
  sample report, 152–159
  see also Intergenerational cycle of abuse; Maltreatment
Administration for Children and Families, 47
Administration on Children, Youth and Families (ACYF), 64*b*
Adoption and Safe Families Act (ASFA) of 1997 (PL 105-89), 20*n*1, 56, 101*b*
Adult criminality, 88, 120
Adult-Adolescent Parenting Inventory–2 (AAPI-2), 19*b*, 28, 30*b*, 130, 140
Ages & Stages Questionnaires®, Third Edition (ASQ-3), 54*b*, 56, 60
Ages & Stages Questionnaires®, Second Edition (ASQ-2), 154–155
Ages & Stages Questionnaires®: Social-Emotional (ASQ:SE), 155
Aggressive behavior, 5, 10, 39, 41, 119
Alcohol abuse
  domestic abuse and, 11
  early, 8
  mental illness and, 6
  during pregnancy, 7–8
  to self-medicate, 101, 102*b*
Alcohol-related birth defects (ARBD), 7
Alcohol-related neurodevelopmental disorder (ARND), 7
American Academy of Child and Adolescent Psychiatry, 119
American Academy of Pediatric Dentistry, 117
American Academy of Pediatrics, 117
"Angels in the nursery," 12
Appeals, 95–96
Assessment
  accuracy of, 30
  developmental delays, 54*b*
  for early intervention services, 56
  in the Miami-Dade model, 28–29
  of the parent–child relationship, 19, 19*b*, 44, 45*t*, 193–194
  of physical health, 116
  samples, 128–131, 152–159
  see also Evaluation
Attachment disorders, 5, 10, 39, 69–70, 120
Attachment theory, 4–5
Attendance, intervention program
  assisting parents with, 32
  reunification based on, 21*b*–22*b*, 30*b*
  sample progress report on, 134, 139, 146
  see also Participation

Behavior
  assessing parental, 19, 19*b*, 45, 45*t*, 193–194
  cultural diversity and, 60
  early intervention and, 119
  modifying, xxiv, xxvi, 92–93, 109
  normal child, xx, 42, 44
  regulation of, 5, 38
  resilient, 12
Behavior problems
  aggressiveness, 4, 5, 10, 39, 119
  alcohol abuse and, 7–8
  depression, 3*b*, 5, 9, 9*b*, 11
  maltreatment and, xxii–xxiii*b*, 2–3, 39–41, 69–70
  withdrawal, 5, 39, 119
Bipolar personality disorder, 10, 152–159
Bureaucracies, 102–103

CAPTA, *see* Child Abuse and Prevention Treatment Act
Care management, 41
Caregivers, 4–5, 9*b*, 34, 58
  see also Foster care; Parents
Caring for Children in Child Welfare (CCCW), 24*b*
CASA, *see* Court Appointed Special Advocate
CB, *see* Children's Bureau
Center for Prevention and Early Intervention Policy (CPEIP), 29, 129, 140
Centers for Disease Control and Prevention (CDC), 10, 117

Child Abuse and Prevention Treatment Act (CAPTA; PL 93-247), 55, 56
Child care programs
  checklist for, 70, 71
  choosing quality, xxiii, 64, 172–173
  early intervention and, 55
  environment of, 67–71
  foster children and, 65, 119
  requirements of, 69
Child development
  communication, 59b
  early child care and, 64
  hearing and vision and, 116
  maltreatment and, xxii–xxiiib, 2–3, 3b, 4b
  parental understanding of, xx, 42, 43
  system change considerations of, 65, 81, 86
  using the science of, 77
Child welfare system
  bureaucracy of, 102–103
  developmental delay incidence in, 54
  diversity within, 22, 23b
  fathers in, 33–34
  importance of effective services in, 20–21
  service integration in, xxiv–xxvi, 74–75, 85–86
  young children in, xx
  see also Early Head Start/Child Welfare Services Initiative (EHS/CWS)
Child–Parent Psychotherapy (CPP)
  core components of, 40–41
  culturally diversity and, 39b
  intervention strategies used in, 41–44
  Miami-Dade model, 46–47
  observation coding scales for, 186–190
  overview of, xxii, 38–39
  Pam case study, 38
  samples of, 155–158, 184–185
  see also Intervention programs
Children and Families Program, RTI International, xxv
Children's Bureau (CB), 64b, 66
Clinician
  observation example by, 155–158
  personal reactions of, 48, 49, 103
  perspective of, 111
  relationship with parents, 31–34, 48–50
Cognitive development, xxii–xxiiib
Collaboration
  to change the system, xxv, 77–78
  in a child care program, 71
  in creating the IFSP, 58
  necessity of, 13
  promoting, 85–86
Collaborative
  challenges and solutions, 84–89
  convening, 77–78
  goals of, 78
  sample memorandum on, 162–163
  see also Early Head Start/Child Welfare

Services Initiative (EHS/CWS); Miami-Dade model
Common Sense Parenting (Burke & Herron, 2006), 24b
Communicable disease screening, 117
Communities
  changing systems in, 25–27, 30, 77
  interventions and practices chosen by, xxi
  resources of, 67
Compassion fatigue, xxvi, 100–105
Confidentiality, 32, 104
Conscious Discipline (Bailey, 2000), 104
Co-occurring conditions, 11
Court appointed special advocate (CASA), 111
Court system
  appearing in, 94
  appellate process, 95–96
  changing the role of, 92–93
  decision-making process in, 97–98
  process of, 94–95
  as protectors of children, xxiv
  sample reports for, 148–150, 151–159
  service integration in, 74–75
  testifying in, 96–97
CPEIP, see Center for Prevention and Early Intervention Policy
Cross-examination, 95
Culturally diverse families
  Child–Parent Psychotherapy (CPP) and, 39b
  developmental delays and, 60
  early childhood environments in, 72b
  evidence-based programs and, 22, 23b
  Haitian Parenting Initiative, 23b, 162–163
  service delivery and, 89b
  view of fathering, 34
Custody
  loss of, 7, 10, 65
  permanent, 20n1
  jregaining, 31, 48, 50, 96
  see also Reunification

Decision making, 81, 93, 97–98, 101b
Delinquency, 2, 10, 88
Dental services, 117
Department of Children and Families, 27, 47
Department of Justice, 11
Dependency drug court, 93b
Dependency Parenting Provider Initiative
  EHS sample report, 148–150
  final report, 137–142
  implementation of, 27–29
  infant mental health therapist court report, 151–159
  initial report, 127–131
  status report, 132–136
  submission guidelines, 125–126
  termination of services, 143–147

Depression, 3b, 5, 9, 9b, 11
Development of child, see Child development
Developmental delays
    foster children and, 118
    incidence of, 54
    maltreatment and, xxiii, 2, 3b
    screening for, 54b
Developmental domains, 56, 59b
Direct examination, 95
Discipline, parental, 8, 41
Domestic violence, 2–3, 11
Dropping out, see Participation
Dysregulated behavior, 40

Early and Periodic Screening, Diagnosis, and
    Treatment, 116
Early Care and Education Workgroup, 60
Early Childhood Relationship Observation
    Coding Scales (EC-ROCS), 28, 186–190
Early Head Start (EHS), 69, 119
Early Head Start/Child Welfare Services
    Initiative (EHS/CWS), 47, 64b–65b, 65–67,
    148–150
    see also Child welfare system
Early intervention
    age for, 13–14, 111–112
    assessment for, 56
    federal programs for, 55–56
    foster children and, 118
    home visitation, 59–60
    Miami-Dade model, 60–61
    perspective of, 110–111
    to reduce traumatic events, 120
    services in, 57–59, 58b–59b
    using genograms in, 61b
Early Learning Coalition, 70
Early Steps program, 56, 60
EC-ROCS, see Early Childhood Relationship
    Observation Coding Scales
Education for All Handicapped Children Act
    of 1975 (PL 94-142), 55b
Emotionally absent parents, 8, 9, 9b
Emotions
    assessing parental, 45
    regulation of, 5, 9, 39, 103
    sensitizing, 42
Empowerment, 49–50, 104
Engaging Moms Program (EMP), 8b
Environment, 3, 57b, 67–71
Evaluation, 26, 44–46, 118
    see also Assessment
Evidence-based programs
    availability of, 88–89
    defined, 22
    engaging parents into, 31–34, 31b, 47–50
    evidentiary support of, 21–22, 24b
    funding and, 87
    identifying, 24–26
    implementing, 29–30, 30b

initiating, 26–27
Miami-Dade model, 27–29
professional knowledge about, 23–24
researchers in, 82n2
rewards of, 108–109
service integration in, 74–75
success through, 21b, 30b–31b
"Ex parte" communications, 76b
Experimental evaluation design, 22

Family, 31–32, 31b, 61b
Fatalities, child, 2, 87
Fathers, 33–34
Federal programs, 54–56
Fetal alcohol effects (FAE), 7
Fetal alcohol spectrum disorder (FASD), 7
Fetal alcohol syndrome (FAS), 7
Florida Infant and Young Child Mental
    Health Pilot Program, 46
Florida State University Center for
    Prevention and Early Intervention Policy
    (CPEIP), 29, 129, 140
Foster care
    child care programs while in, 65, 119
    developmental screening for children in,
        54b
    early intervention in, 118
    health checks and, 116
    rates of children in, xx
    tools for, 120
    see also Caregivers
Funding, 71, 87, 89

Genograms, 61b
"Ghosts in the nursery," 6, 12
"Good enough" parent, xx, xxi
Guardian ad Litem (GAL), 111

Haitian Parenting Initiative, 23b, 162–163
Harris Center for Infant Mental Health
    (LSUHSC), 45t, 46
    see also Louisiana State University Health
    Sciences Center
Head Start, 47, 68b–69b, 69, 119
Healthy Start Services, 168–169
Hearing impairments, 116
HighScope (Schweinhart, 2000), 104
HIV risk, 117
Home visitation, 59–60
Honesty, 49

ICMS, see Intensive case management
    services
IDEA, see Individuals with Disabilities
    Education Act of 2004 (PL 108-446)
Immunizations, 116

Incredible Years, The (Webster-Stratton, 1992), 24*b*
Individual resilience, 12
Individualized family service plan (IFSP), 58, 176–182
Individuals with Disabilities Act of 1990 (PL 101-476), 55*b*
Individuals with Disabilities Education Act (IDEA) of 2004 (PL 108-446)
　entitlements under, 55, 55*b*, 118
　home visitation under, 59–60
　sample court order in, 166–167
　Infant and Young Child Mental Health Pilot Project, 46
Infants
　ability to be comforted, 5, 74
　attachment to mother, 4, 4*b*, 69–70
　in the courtroom, 10*b*
　mental health of, 3–6, 119
　needs of from a system of care, 83*b*
　Nurse-Family Partnership model for, 59
　parental depression and, 9*b*
　parental substance abuse and, 6–9
　vulnerability of, xx
Intensive case management services (ICMS), 8*b*
Intergenerational cycle of abuse
　breaking, xxiii–xxiv, 75, 112
　fathers and the, 34
　judicial views on, 93, 109, 110
　Miami-Dade model and, 47
　Nurturing Parenting Programs and, 19*b*
　Pam case study, xxviii, 20
　reasons for, 5, 6
　therapeutic jurisprudence and, xxv
Intervention programs
　barriers to, 110
　engaging parents into, 31–34, 31*b*, 47–50
　model programs, 26
　selection of, 24–25, 30
　substance abuse, 8, 8*b*
　see also Child–Parent Psychotherapy (CPP)

Judges
　approaching for assistance, 76*b*
　in dependency drug court, 93*b*
　determining witness credibility, 96, 97
　in juvenile and family court, 93–94
　leading a system of change, xxv, 75–76, 76*b*, 83
　partnering with, 85–86
　perspective of, 109–110
　role of, xxv, 76*b*, 94*b*, 109
　stress felt by, 101*b*
Judicial views
　Child–Parent Psychotherapy (CPP) and reunification, 44*b*
　infants in court, 10*b*
　measuring change, 30*b*–31*b*

Miami Juvenile Court Project, 110*b*
　necessity of quality child care, 70*b*
　observing the child, 57*b*
　role of the judge, 76*b*
　value of evidence-based parenting programs, 21*b*–22*b*
　vicarious traumatization, 101*b*
Juvenile dependency court, xxiv

Keeping Children and Families Safe Act of 2003 (PL 108-36), 54

Labeling, 14, 32
Lead exposure screening, 117
Level of care (LOC) assessment, 56
Licensing, child care center, 69, 71
Linda Ray Intervention Center, 27, 46, 66–67
Linguistically diverse families, 22, 23*b*, 162–163
Listening, empathetic, 48
Louisiana State University Health Sciences Center, 27, 44, 45*t*, 46, 129, 140
　see also Harris Center for Infant Mental Health (LSUHSC)

Maltreatment
　adult criminality and, 120
　child development and, xxiii, 2, 3*b*, 4*b*
　early alcohol abuse and, 8
　incidence of mortality from, 87
　infants and, xxii–xxiii*b*
　parental behaviors indicating, 19*b*
　see also Abuse
Medicaid, 116
Medical care, 5, 116, 117–118
Memoranda of understanding, 81, 161–163
Mental health
　compassion fatigue, xxvi, 100–105
　Head Start performance standards in, 68*b*–69*b*
　of infants, 3–6, 119
　judicial, 94, 101*b*
　need for early intervention in, 13–14
　screening of, 118
　services for, 87–88
　supporting teacher, 68
　vicarious traumatization, xxvi, 100–105
Mental illness, 6–11
Miami Juvenile Court, 27, 46, 66, 83, 110*b*
Miami-Dade Community Action Agency, 23*b*, 47, 66, 162–163
Miami-Dade Community Based Care Alliance, 27
Miami-Dade model
　challenges and solutions, 84–89

Child–Parent Psychotherapy (CPP) in, 46–47
culturally appropriate programs in, 23b
Dependency Parenting Provider Initiative, 125–131
Early Head Start/Child Welfare Services Initiative (EHS/CWS), 66–67
evidence-based program survey in, 23–24
evidence-based programs in, 27–29
linking early intervention and the child welfare system, 60–61
system changes in, 83–84
see also Collaborative; System of care
Monitoring program compliance, 27, 30

National Association for the Education of Young Children (NAEYC), 67–68
National Child Traumatic Stress Network (NCTSN), 26, 39
National Coalition Against Domestic Violence (NCADV), 11
National Criminal Justice Reference Service (NCJRS), 26
National Implementation Research Center, 29
National Institute of Child Health and Human Development (NICHD), 64, 69
National Institute of Mental Health, 19b
National Registry of Evidence-Based Programs and Practices (NREPP), 23b, 25
National Survey of Child and Adolescent Well-Being (NSCAW), xxiii, 24b
Natural environment, 57b
Normed, 22n2
Nurse–Family Partnership model, 59–60
Nurturing Parenting Programs, 18, 18b–19b, 21b

Objections, 95, 97
Occupational therapy, 58b–59b
Office of Head Start, 64b, 66
Office of Juvenile Justice and Delinquency Prevention (OJJDP), 10, 26, 47
Our Kids, Inc., 27, 29, 172–173
Outcomes
child care programs and, 69
for children with depressed parents, 9
in evidence-based programs, xx, 29
intended in child welfare, 25
measuring by reunification, 108
monitoring, 82
Overrule, 95

Pam case study
background information, xviii–xix
child care programs in, 64, 68, 70

Child–Parent Psychotherapy (CPP) and, 38, 43–44
conclusions, 108
in court, 92
development of Victor, 54, 56, 57–58
example of a system disconnect, 74
parent–child relationship in, 2
parenting programs in, 18–20
teacher empathy to Victor, 100
Paper implementation, 29
Parent management training (Kazdin, 2005), 24b
Parent–Child Early Relational Assessment, 44, 45t
Parent–child interaction therapy (Eyberg, 1988), 24b
Parent–child relationship
alcohol abuse and, 8
assessment of, 19, 19b, 44, 45t, 193–194
healing, xx, xxii, 20, 25, 50
infant attachment in, 4, 4b, 69–70
shifting focus to, 14, 108, 109
training in, 21b
see also Relationships
Parenting
difficulty with basic skills of, 5–6
impact of mental illness on, 5–6, 9, 9b, 10
repeating history of, 3, 5, 43
themes for success in, 21b
training in, xx, 21b
Parenting program providers
engaging the family, 31–34, 31b, 47–50
getting feedback from, 82
maintaining open communication between, 50
Miami-Dade model, 28
monitoring compliance of, 27, 85
requesting changes from, 84–85, 87
service integration within, 74–75
system changes through, 26–27
Parenting programs, traditional, xxi, 18, 20, 21b–22b, 24b
Parents
engaging into programs, 31–34, 31b, 47–50
fathers, 33–34
finding strengths of, 13, 45–46
"good enough," xx, xxi
high risk, 6–11
learning to access services, 110
mental illness in, 5–6, 9, 9b, 10
treatment of in evidence-based program, 31–33
unresolved childhood issues of, 43
young, 5b
Part B of IDEA, 58
Part C of IDEA
entitlements under, 55, 57b, 118
home visitation, 59–60
sample court order in, 166–167

Participation
  incentives for, 32, 33
  overcoming barriers for, 47b–48b
  sample progress report on, 134, 139, 146
  see also Attendance, intervention program
Patience, 48–49
Physical health, xxiii, 116–117
Physical therapists, 59b
PL 101-476, see Individuals with Disabilities
  Act of 1990
PL 105-89, see Adoption and Safe Families
  Act (ASFA) of 1997
PL 108-36, see Keeping Children and
  Families Safe Act of 2003
PL 108-446, see Individuals with Disabilities
  Education Act (IDEA) of 2004
PL 93-247, see Child Abuse and Prevention
  Treatment Act
PL 94-142, see Education for All
  Handicapped Children Act of 1975
Play, 4, 40–42
Point of entry, 39, 55
Posttraumatic stress disorder, 5
Preschool Special Education Grants
  Program, 118
Problem solving, 48
Problem-solving courts, xxiv–xxv, 92–93
Process implementation, 29
Programs, see Intervention programs
Project 12-Ways (Wesch & Lutzker, 1991), 24b
Promoting Safe and Stable Families (PSSF),
  64b
Protective factors, 12–13
Psychoeducation, 42–43

Quasi-experimental evaluation design, 22

Referrals
  appropriate, 75
  by the court, 168–169
  dealing with high volume of, 60–61, 86
  for early intervention, 55–56
  mental health services, 88
  monitoring, 30
  sample request for, 158
Reflective supervision, 103
Regulation of child care programs, 69, 71
Relationship-Based Assessment Instructions,
  193–194
Relationships
  child–father, 34
  genograms, 61b
  healing, xx, xxii, 20, 25, 50
  importance of, 111
  infant–mother, 4, 4b, 69–70
  parent–clinician, 31–34, 47–50, 111
  as a protective factor, 12
  teacher–child, 68, 104
  see also Parent–child relationship

Research and Reform for the Children in
  Court, Inc., 23
Resilience, 10, 12–13, 12b–13b
Resources, 102, 111
Responsibility, parental acceptance of, 50
Reunification
  focus on, 82
  impossible, 109, 112
  measuring outcomes by, 108
  Miami-Dade model, 110b
  see also Custody
Risk-taking behaviors, 2

Safe Start Promising Approaches, 47
Scaffolding, 33
Schizophrenia, 10
Screening, see Assessment
Secondary traumatization, 100–101, 102b
Self-regulation, 5, 7, 9, 38
Service delivery, 14, 47, 87, 89b
Sexual abuse, 11
Sidebar, 95
Social risks, 7–9
"Speaking for the infant," 42
Speech therapy, 59b
Speech-language pathologists (SLPs), 59b
Stakeholders, 77
Starlight Pediatrics, 54b
Strengths-based approach, 13, 31, 33,
  45–46, 111
Stress
  child development and, 4b
  depression and, 9b
  infant response to, 5
  judicial, 101b
  maltreatment, 3b
  NCTSN information on, 26
  over inadequate resources, 102–103
  secondary traumatization and, 100–101,
    102b, 103
  training in, 68
  see also Trauma
Substance abuse
  co-occurring conditions and, 11
  dependency drug court, 93b
  in foster care, 7
  parental, 6–9
vicarious traumatization and, 101
Substance Abuse and Mental Health
  Services Administration (SAMHSA), 25
Sustain, 95
System of care
  assessing progress of, 82
  challenges and solutions, 84–89
  implementing, 81–82
  mapping current, 78–79, 79b
  meeting infant and toddler needs, 83b
  planning new, 79–81
  rewards of, 112
  service integration in, xxiii–xxiv, 74–75

signs of success, 109
see also Miami-Dade model

Teachers, 68, 104
The International Resilience Project, 12*b*
Therapeutic jurisprudence, xxv, 92
Therapy, 58, 58*b*–59*b*
Toys, 40, 191–192
Training
    about evidence-based programs, 24
    about vicarious traumatization, 104
    in a child care program, 71
    for a collaborative, 77–78, 83–84
    cross, 67
    to develop competent work force, 88–89
    in Miami-Dade model, 28, 29
    in stress and trauma consequences, 68,
        87–88
Trauma, 3*b*, 5, 40, 68, 87
    see also Stress
Treatment programs, *see* Intervention
    programs

Trust
    parent–child, 38, 41
    parent–clinician, 47–50, 111
    teacher–child, 68, 104

United Way, 23*b*
University of Miami's Linda Ray
    Intervention Center, 27, 46, 66–67
Unpredictability, 8

Vicarious traumatization, xxvi,
    100–105
Views from the bench, *see* Judicial views
Violence, 3, 10–11, 40, 68
Visual impairments, 116–117
Volunteer Guardian ad Litem (GAL), 111

Web sites, 25–26
Withdrawal, 5, 39, 119
Witnesses, 94, 95, 96–97, 98